21ST C

BABIES NAMES

In the same series

Asian Babies' Names
The Expectant Father

Uniform with this book

Where to find *Right Way*

Elliot *Right Way* take pride in our editorial quality, accuracy and value-for-money. Booksellers everywhere can rapidly obtain any *Right Way* book for you. If you have been particularly pleased with any one title, do please mention this to your bookseller as personal recommendation helps us enormously.

Please send to the address on the back of the title page opposite, a stamped, self-addressed envelope if you would like a copy of our *free catalogue*. Alternatively, you may wish to browse through our extensive range of informative titles arranged by subject on the Internet at **www.right-way.co.uk**

We welcome views and suggestions from readers as well as from prospective authors; do please write to us or e-mail: **info@right-way.co.uk**

21ST CENTURY BABIES' NAMES

Jacqueline Harrod

RIGHT WAY

Copyright notice

© Elliot Right Way Books MMVI

Some of the material in this book was originally published as *The New A-Z Of Babies' Names* MCMXCV

All rights reserved. No part of this book may be reproduced, stored in a retrieval system, or transmitted, in any form or by any means, electronic, photocopying, mechanical, recording or otherwise, without the prior permission of the copyright owner.

Conditions of sale

This book shall only be sold, lent, or hired, for profit, trade, or otherwise, in its original binding, except where special permission has been granted by the Publisher.

Whilst care is taken in selecting Authors who are authoritative in their subjects, it is emphasised that their books can reflect their knowledge only up to the time of writing. Information can be superseded and printers' errors can creep in. This book is sold, therefore, on the condition that neither Publisher nor Author can be held legally responsible for the consequences of any error or omission there may be.

Typeset in Times 10/11pt by Letterpart Ltd., Reigate, Surrey.

Printed and bound in Great Britain by Cox & Wyman Ltd., Reading, Berkshire.

The *Right Way* series is published by Elliot Right Way Books, Brighton Road, Lower Kingswood, Tadworth, Surrey, KT20 6TD, U.K. For information about our company and the other books we publish, visit our website at www.right-way.co.uk

DEDICATION

For my mother and father, who chose the perfect names for
their children.

CONTENTS

INTRODUCTION

The very first gift that we receive on being born is our name. Few of us have to answer to 'it' or the apocryphal 'mother's little helper' when asked.

Sadly, a few children will have just cause to loathe the misplaced sense of 'fun' which will make their life difficult from the beginning, however loving their family.

You do not believe me? The records show such horrors as Larry Harry Barry, Periwinkle Porker and Everest Mountain; River Jordan, Misty Miller, Rilla Cotton, Ima Hogg and Windsor Castle; Mineral Water and Born Free – but I will not go on. Enough to say that it takes very little imagination to envisage the misery of their first introduction to school life or the business world. It would be clearly impossible for a Fifi Trixiebell or a Scout La Rue to be held in high esteem as a High Court Judge or Speaker of the House of Commons; laughter would keep breaking in.

Germany has a law which dismisses the right of parents to give children names which would prove a burden. And the standards are very strict; even Lafayette and Hemingway have been rejected.

Of course, this is not a totally new problem. An eighteenth century Scottish supporter of the Young Pretender named all his ten sons 'Charles Edward' in his honour. The mind boggles at how they would organise their mail and bills if this happened today.

A more modern sufferer retaliated by inserting the following in the Personal column of a daily newspaper: 'Percival Montgomery Plantagenet de Brassey Ronald Basil Irvine Graham Marmaduke Alexander Montague has decided, if he ever has a son, to call him John.'

Some Anglo-Saxon names were speedily jettisoned by the conquered population at the arrival of the Normans in 1066. Looking back through the mists of time to Aelgifu, Aelfheah and Sidroc, one can be nothing but thankful.

The Middle Ages had a refreshingly simple approach. Barely four dozen names served for most boys and girls: John, Richard,

Thomas and William were the first choice for the boys; while Joan, Alice, Agnes, Cicely and Matilda were top of the popularity stakes for the girls. (I cannot think that we would now care to be quite so restricted.)

The Puritans of the seventeenth century, abandoning the names of the saints with a fanatical zeal, scoured the Bible to pile obscure names on their defenceless infants; although they introduced as first names the abstract virtues of Faith, Hope and Patience still liked today, and rightly.

Poets and playwrights of the sixteenth and seventeenth centuries coined many names favoured by modern parents. Marina, Vanessa, Amanda and Araminta spring to mind.

And through it all, as now, royal names were consistently adopted; while aristocratic surnames began to be used as Christian names by those who had no family connection.

Victorians, for some unknown reason, began the craze for botanical names – Poppy, Heather, Lily, Daisy – and extended this to the names of minerals and precious stones.

But it was the twentieth century which unleashed a vast number of beautiful names (and those not so mellifluous).

Russia, Germany, Italy, Ireland, France and Spain all had an influence. Film stars, popular singers and characters in television series made acceptable names which would have seemed outlandish to our great-grandparents.

Now, having entered the twenty-first century, we find the floodgates are open wide. There is *no* name too unusual for consideration.

Fish, flowers, birds, Sumerian goddesses, abstract concepts, colours, names spelt backwards or in complex combinations . . . all have their supporters. Mythological characters appear freshly minted. The revival of Anglo-Saxon and Norman names grows apace. The American use of surnames is popular. (No numerals so far.)

So, all I venture to say, is *do* look at initials (**P**olly **I**sobel **G**rant, for example). And please remember that the delightful baby will have to live with your choice for a very long time.

Glossary

b. = born	d. = died
c. = circa (about)	q.v. = quod vide (which see)

BOYS' NAMES

AARON
From the Hebrew, meaning 'high mountain'. In the Bible, the name of Moses' older brother (by three years) and the first High Priest of Israel. Aaron had a rod which transformed into a snake, devouring the rods of Pharaoh's sorcerers, proving his divine calling.

Two notable possessors of the name are Aaron Hill, the poet (1685–1750), and the American composer Aaron Copland, most famous for his orchestral suite *Appalachian Spring*.

ABEL
From the Hebrew, meaning 'breath', or the Assyrian, meaning 'son'. The second son of Adam and Eve, a shepherd, murdered in a fit of jealousy by his brother, Cain.

The Puritans made the name popular as they scrutinised the Bible for names to replace those of non-Biblical saints.

Abel was King of Denmark 1250–1252.

ABRAHAM
From the Hebrew, meaning 'father of a multitude'. The Old Testament Abraham was father of the Hebrew nation: his son, Isaac, was born when the patriarch was 100 years old. (In the Koran Abraham is entitled El Khalil, 'the friend of God'.)

Although borne by several early Christian saints, and mentioned in the Domesday Book, the name was only made popular in Britain by the Puritans of the seventeenth century.

ADAM

From the Hebrew, meaning 'red'. Perhaps this denotes the colour of the earth used by the Almighty to form the Biblical first man.

The name was most popular in the north of England in the thirteenth century because of an outlaw, Adam Bell, a Robin Hood type hero.

Adam de la Hale was the author of the first known opera *The Play of Robin and Marion*, performed in Naples in 1275.

ADRIAN

From the Latin, meaning 'man from the Adriatic'. The only Englishman to become Pope, Nicholas Brakespear, took the name Adrian IV and was head of the church from 1154–1159.

AIDAN

Gaelic diminutive, meaning 'little fiery one'. St Aidan was a seventh century Irish monk who founded a monastery on Lindisfarne, where English boys were educated. He was known as the Apostle of Northumberland. He died at Bamburgh in 651. His emblem in art is a stag.

AINSLEY (Ainslie)

Originally a surname, meaning 'my meadow', which has become a popular first name.

AIRLIE

An aristocratic Scottish title, now used as a first name. The motto of the earls Airlie is '*A fin*' or 'To the end'.

ALAN (Allan, Allen, Alun)

A Celtic name, meaning 'harmony'. It was introduced into England at the time of the Norman Conquest. Two companions of William the Conqueror, Alain, Count of Brittany and Alain le Roux, 1st Earl of Richmond, popularised the name but not the spelling, which was speedily altered by the English.

ALARIC
From the Old German, meaning 'ruler of all'. The Visigoth King, Alaric I, was responsible for the sacking of Rome in AD 410.

The Victorians revived the name in the mid-nineteenth century.

ALASDAIR (Alastair, Alistair)
The Gaelic form of Alexander (q.v.), Alastair and Alistair are popular phonetic spellings of this name.

ALBAN
From the Latin, meaning 'white'. St Alban was the first British martyr. A Romano-Briton, he lived in Verulamium, now the city of St Albans. During Diocletian's persecution, he gave shelter to a fleeing Christian and was beheaded for this act of charity in AD 209. St Alban's Abbey stands on the site.

ALBANY
A royal dukedom and most desirable London address, now used as a first name.

The actor David Garrick was very upset at the drowning of his friend's teenage son, Albany Wallis, in 1776. He arranged for a memorial to be erected in the cloisters of Westminster Abbey, writing the inscription himself.

And Albany is the capital of the state of New York.

ALBERT (Bert, Bertie)
From the Old German, meaning 'noble knight'. St Albert the Great (1206–1280) is called 'The Universal Teacher' because he wrote on many topics from theology to physics and botany.

Prince Albert of Saxe-Coburg-Gotha married Queen Victoria in 1840 and made the name very popular.

ALEXANDER (Alasdair, Alastair, Alec, Alex, Alick, Alistair)
From the Greek, meaning 'defending man'. Bestowed upon many saints, martyrs and kings, it has been a popular name for over 3,000 years.

Alexander the Great (356–323 BC), conqueror of most of the known world, was admired for his courage and acts of humanity and became the hero of numerous English and French medieval romances.

The inventor Alexander Graham Bell (1847–1922) and Sir Alexander Fleming (1881–1955), discoverer of penicillin, are worthy of note.

ALFRED (Alf, Alfie, Freddie)
From the Old English, meaning 'elf counsel'. King Alfred the Great (849–899) was responsible for England's first navy and was the first English king to have his face on a coin.

Other famous men to bear the name include the poet Alfred, Lord Tennyson (1809–1892), and the Swedish inventor Alfred Nobel (1833–1896), founder of the annual Nobel prizes.

ALGERNON (Algie)
From the French, meaning 'with whiskers'. Supposedly a nickname given to an eleventh century Count of Boulogne named Eustace, to avoid confusion with his father who had the same name.

Algernon Moncrieff is the debonair friend of Jack Worthing, hero of Oscar Wilde's masterpiece *The Importance of Being Earnest*.

AMBROSE
From the Greek, meaning 'pertaining to the Immortals'. Ambrosia was the food of the gods, as nectar was their drink.

St Ambrose (c.334–397), Bishop of Milan, is numbered among the four great Latin Doctors of the Church and was the first to make extensive use of hymns for both teaching and divine praise.

ANDREW (André, Andy, Drew)
From the Greek, meaning 'manly'. The first apostle called by Jesus, brother to St Peter and patron saint of both Scotland and Russia. Over 600 churches are dedicated to St Andrew in England alone.

An enduringly popular name borne by Prince Andrew, Duke of York (b. 1960).

ANEURIN (Nye)
From the Welsh, meaning 'gold'. The Welsh Labour politician Aneurin Bevan (1897–1960) made this name famous in modern times. He introduced the National Health Service in 1948.

ANGELO
From the Greek, meaning 'messenger', now generally used. Henry Angelo (d. 1854), the famous swordsman, tutored fashionable gentlemen (including Lord Byron) at his fencing academy off Piccadilly.

ANGUS
From the Gaelic, meaning 'one choice'. The legendary Aonghus Turimleach was one of three Irish brothers who invaded Scotland. They brought with them the 'Stone of Scone', which later resided beneath the Coronation Chair in Westminster Abbey until it was returned to Scotland.

The Clan MacDonell have used the name Angus since the fifteenth century.

ANTHONY (Anton, Antony, Tony)
The name of an ancient Roman family, the most famous of whom was Mark Antony (83–30 BC), the lover of Queen Cleopatra.

Many saints have this name, including St Anthony of Egypt (251–356), the founder of monasticism, and St Anthony of Padua (1195–1231), a famous preacher and patron of lost property.

The abbreviation Tony first appeared in the seventeenth century.

ARCHIBALD (Archie)
From the Old German, meaning 'very bold'. Another of the names brought to England at the Norman Conquest. The clans Campbell and Douglas particularly favour this name.

Archie Armstrong was court jester to James I of England. Archie Rice is the anti-hero of John Osborne's play *The Entertainer*. And an Archibald of renown was the teddy bear loved by Sir John Betjeman, mentioned in his poetic autobiography *Summoned by Bells*.

ARNOLD
From the Old German, meaning 'eagle power'. This name evolved from the Norman version, Arnaud. It was rare until the 1870s; revived in honour of Thomas Arnold, reforming headmaster of Rugby, and his poet son, Matthew Arnold, perhaps?

ARTHUR
From the Gaelic, meaning 'stone', or the Celtic, meaning 'a bear'. King Arthur, who supposedly flourished in the fifth to sixth centuries, is the most famous bearer of the name.

Prince Arthur (1486–1502) was the eldest son of Henry VII. The name became popular in the nineteenth century due to Arthur Wellesley, Duke of Wellington (1769–1852), the conqueror of Napoleon.

Tennyson's poem *In Memoriam* was written to commemorate his friend, Arthur Hallam.

ARUNDEL
A place name, and surname, now generally used. St Philip Howard, Earl of Arundel (1557–1595) died in the Tower of London, a prisoner of conscience. He is now enshrined in Arundel Cathedral.

ASHER
From the Hebrew, meaning 'happy'. In the Old Testament, Asher was the eighth son of Jacob, and founder of one of the twelve tribes of Israel.

ASHLEY
From the Old English, meaning 'ash wood'. Originally a place and surname, it may have been used as a first name in honour of Anthony Ashley Cooper, Earl of Shaftesbury (1802–1885), the social reformer. The statue of Eros at Piccadilly Circus in London was erected in his honour.

ASSISI
The name of a hilltop Italian town in Umbria, Assisi is forever linked to St Francis, real name Giovanni Bernardone, born there in 1182.

And Assisi is also the birthplace of the Roman poet Propertius in 54 BC; or so says an inscription on the Temple of Minerva, still standing in the piazza.

ASTLEY
From the Old English, meaning 'eastern wood'. Originally a place name and the family name of the barons Hastings.

ASTON
A place name, meaning 'eastern place', and surname. Now used as a first name.

ATTICUS
An increasingly popular name. Harper Lee won the Pulitzer Prize in 1961 for the novel *To Kill a Mockingbird*. Atticus Finch is the noble lawyer hero, played so well by Gregory Peck in the film of the same name.

AUBERON (Bron)
From the Old German, meaning 'noble bear'.

AUBREY
From the Old German, meaning 'elf counsel'. It was brought from Normandy to England by the de Veres, who became Earls of Oxford.

The artist Aubrey Beardsley (1872–1898) is well-known for his art-nouveau book illustrations, particularly for *The Yellow Book*.

AUDLEY
A place name, and barony created in 1313, now used as a first name.

Audley End in Essex was built by the Earl of Suffolk so that he might entertain James I. (Alas, the royal visit was never made.) The park was laid out by Capability Brown in the eighteenth century.

AUGUSTINE
A Latin diminutive, meaning 'venerable'. The African St Augustine of Hippo (354–430) wrote two books which are still in print: his autobiography, *The Confessions of St Augustine*, and the *City of God*.

Another St Augustine arrived in Kent in 597 and became the first Archbishop of Canterbury.

AUGUSTUS (Gus)
From the Latin, meaning 'venerable'. This was taken as a title by Roman emperors, beginning with Octavian, the adopted son of Julius Caesar. The month of August is named after him.

The German royal family, the Hanoverians, brought the name to Britain in the eighteenth century and it has been the name of two Polish kings.

AUSTIN
The medieval form of Augustine.

AYLMER
A name pre-dating the Norman Conquest, meaning 'noble famous'. A surname, now used again as a first name.

John Aylmer, master mason of Westminster Abbey, worked on the breathtaking Chapel of Henry VII in the early 1500s.

Aylmer (d. 1260), also known as Aymer, son of Isabella of Angoulême, was a bishop of Winchester.

BAILEY
The medieval occupational surname indicated a 'beadle' or 'bailiff'. It has been used as a first name since the nineteenth century. A bailey is also a fortification.

The Old Bailey, on which street the Central Criminal Court towers in the City of London, has borne the name since 1241.

BALDWIN
From the Old German, meaning 'brave friend'. The name was made popular in England at the coming of William the Conqueror. His father-in-law was Baldwin, Count of Flanders.

The Norman crusader elected first King of Jerusalem in 1100 was Baldwin of Boulogne.

BARNABAS
From the Aramaic, meaning 'son of consolation'. In the New Testament, Barnabas was a companion to St Paul and is believed to have urged St Mark to write his gospel.

Later, St Barnabas went as a missionary to Cyprus, being martyred there at the Port of Salamis.

BARNABY (Barney)
This is the anglicised version of Barnabas. The unfortunate Barnaby Fitzpatrick was whipping boy to the Tudor king, Edward VI.

Dickens' novel about the Gordon Riots, *Barnaby Rudge*, first published in 1841, must always spring to mind.

BARRA
A modern first name, taken from the Hebridean Isle of Barra. This was reputedly bestowed on the place in honour of St Finbar.

BARRINGTON
A common English place name and aristocratic surname, now often used as a first name.

The Barrington family motto – '*Honesta quam splendida*' – translates as 'Honourable acquisitions rather than splendid'.

BARRY
From the Celtic, meaning 'spear'. Barry is a place name in both Scotland and Wales, while Barry Island is named after an early Irish hermit.

W. M. Thackeray wrote a novel entitled *The Memoirs of Barry Lyndon*, which first appeared in 1844.

BARTHOLOMEW (Bart)
From the Aramaic, meaning 'son of Talmai'. He was one of the twelve apostles, but little is known about him. Tradition states that he spread the Gospel in India and Armenia, where he was martyred by being flayed alive.

Ben Jonson's comedy *Bartholomew Fair*, first performed in 1614, commemorates an annual fair begun on St Bartholomew's Day, 24th August 1133. This raised funds for St Bartholomew's Hospital in London.

The fair took place every year until 1855, by which time the rowdiness and nuisance caused had become intolerable.

BARUCH
From the Hebrew, meaning 'blessed'. The Old Testament Baruch was a devoted disciple and scribe to the prophet Jeremiah. Both fled to Egypt at the fall of Jerusalem to the Babylonians in 587 BC.

BASIL

From the Greek, meaning 'kingly'. Always a very popular name in Eastern Europe, the Crusaders brought it back with them to England.

St Basil the Great, Doctor of the Church (c.330–379), had a remarkable family: his grandmother, father and mother, his elder sister and two younger brothers are *all* canonised saints! Surely unique.

Basilica originally meant a royal palace before it acquired its modern meaning of church.

BAXTER

An occupational surname, meaning a *female* baker, now used as a first name.

Richard Baxter (1615–1691), clergyman, was a Parliamentarian during the English Civil War, but opposed the execution of Charles I. This did not save him from imprisonment at the Restoration. His *Saints' Everlasting Rest* is a classic of religious writing.

BEAU

From the French, meaning 'handsome'. A bestselling novel by P. C. Wren about life in the French Foreign Legion, first published in 1924, has a hero named 'Beau Geste' (which is also the title of the book).

Earlier than this, a 'beau' was a man obsessed with fashion: 'Beau' Nash of Bath and George 'Beau' Brummell, friend of George IV, are two examples.

BEDE

Old English for 'prayer'. An English historian, the Venerable Bede (c.673–735) was a monk in a monastery at Jarrow.

His most famous work is the *Ecclesiastical History of the English People*, written to cover the period of the Roman Invasion to AD 731. He was the first English Doctor of the Church and the only Englishman named in Dante's *Paradiso*.

BENEDICT

From the Latin, meaning 'blessed'. There are at least five canonised saints named Benedict; the most famous of whom was the founder of the Benedictine Order, dying at the first Benedictine Monastery on Monte Cassino in 547.

Another, St Benedict Labré, is the patron saint of tramps.
Bennett is a medieval diminutive of the name.

BENJAMIN (Ben, Benjie, Benny)
From the Hebrew, meaning 'son of my right hand'. In the Old
Testament, Benjamin was the youngest and favourite son of
Jacob and Rachel.

Benjamin Disraeli, Earl of Beaconsfield (1804–1881), novelist
and Prime Minister, was the most famous bearer of the name in
Victorian times.

'Big Ben', nickname of the bell in the clock-tower of the
Houses of Parliament, was reputedly named after Big Ben
Caunt, the 17-stone, bare-knuckle boxing champion of England
in the 1840s and 1850s. Another, more dignified, theory pro-
posed that it was named in honour of a portly Welshman, Sir
Benjamin Hall. He was First Commissioner of Public Works
from 1855 to 1858, when the bell was ordered.

BENSON
A surname, meaning 'son of Benedict', now used as a first name.
A Benson family of note included Arthur (1862–1925), who
wrote *Land of Hope and Glory*; brother Edward (1867–1940),
who wrote many popular novels, including *Mapp and Lucia*; and
little brother Robert Hugh (1871–1914), a Roman Catholic
priest, who wrote *Come Rack! Come Rope!* and many ghost
stories. Their father was the Archbishop of Canterbury.

BERKELEY
An English place name and surname, meaning 'birch wood',
now used as a first name.

BERNARD (Bernie)
From the Old German, meaning 'brave as a bear'. As with many
names, this was brought to England at the Norman Conquest
and is mentioned several times in the Domesday Book.

St Bernard of Clairvaux (1090–1153) founded the very austere
Cistercian Order.

St Bernard of Montjoux (c.996–1081) had built two rest
houses for travellers at the top of two Alpine passes, now known
as the Great and Little St Bernard. He is the patron saint of
mountaineers.

BERNERS

An aristocratic surname, the barons Berners being created in 1455, now used as a first name.

BERTIE

A pet-form of the names Albert and Bertram, now used independently. The most famous Bertie in Britain is Bertie Wooster, the delightful, upper-class hero of a series of books by P. G. Wodehouse.

BERTRAM

From the Old German, meaning 'bright raven'. The name became popular in the mid-nineteenth century.

Bertram, Count of Rousillon, initially spurns the lovely Helena in Shakespeare's *All's Well That Ends Well*. Well, she *is* a commoner!

BLAIR

From the Gaelic, meaning 'battleground'. A Scottish surname, now used as a first name.

BLAISE

From the Latin, meaning 'stuttering'. Little is known about St Blaise, a bishop martyred in the fourth century, whose feast day is 3rd February. He is the patron saint of diseases of the throat. The *Pensées* of Blaise Pascal (1623–1662), a French philosopher, scientist and writer, are still read.

BLAKE

From the Old Norse, meaning 'pale' or 'shining'. A place name and surname, now used as a first name. It was originally given as a nickname to someone with extremely fair hair or complexion.

BLUE

From the colour, a modern first name. A painting manual *Il Libro dell'Arte*, written in Florence by Cennino Cennini in 1437, describes blue as 'a colour illustrious, beautiful and most perfect, beyond all other colours'.

BOAZ

From the Hebrew, meaning 'in him is strength'. The Old Testament Ruth married the wealthy Boaz. The name was popular with Puritans in the seventeenth century.

BORIS
From the Slavonic, meaning 'to fight'. This popular Russian name came into use in Britain in the twentieth century. Saints Boris (d. 1015) and his brother Gleb, the sons of Russia's first Christian prince, are venerated in the Orthodox calendar on 24th July.

Boris Leonidovich Pasternak (1890–1960), Russian poet and author of the famous novel *Dr Zhivago*, was awarded the Nobel Prize for Literature in 1958. (The Ashmolean Museum, Oxford, possesses a fine portrait of the young Boris and his brother Alexander, painted by their father, Leonid.)

BOYD
From the Celtic, meaning 'yellow haired'.

BRADLEY (Brad)
An Old English place name, meaning 'broad clearing', and surname, now used as a first name.

Bradley Headstone is a character in the Dickens novel *Our Mutual Friend*, first published in 1865.

BRAMWELL
An Old English place name, meaning 'bramble well', and surname, now used as a first name.

William Bramwell Booth (1856–1929), the son of the founder of the Salvation Army, appears to have popularised the name.

BRANDON
An English place name, meaning 'hill covered with broom', and surname, now used as a first name.

Duke of Brandon is one of the many titles of the Duke of Hamilton.

BRANWELL
A variant of Bramwell. The unfortunate (Patrick) Branwell Brontë (1817–1848), brother to the writers Charlotte, Emily and Anne, is the most famous bearer of the name.

BREE
This is a most unusual modern name, seemingly taken from J. R. R. Tolkien's book, *The Lord of the Rings*. The village of

Bree, under Bree-Hill, was the chief village of Bree-land. The men of Bree had brown hair and were short and stocky with a cheerful disposition.

BRENDAN
From the Old Irish, meaning 'stinking hair'. St Brendan (c.486–578) founded the monastery of Clonfert in Galway, which existed until the sixteenth century. A tenth century tale, *Brendan's Voyage*, in which he sailed to the beautiful land of Promise in the Atlantic, spread his fame far and wide.

BRETT
From the Old French, meaning 'man from Brittany'. Brett is the surname of the Viscounts Esher.

BRIAN (Bryan)
From the Irish, meaning 'hill'. The name was popular in both Brittany and Ireland. Brian Boru (941–1014) drove the Danish armies out of Ireland in 1014 at the decisive battle of Clontarf. He was murdered in his tent after the battle.

The Normans brought the name to England at the Norman Conquest and it is mentioned in the Domesday Book.

BROCK
From the Old English, meaning 'badger'. Sir Thomas Brock (1847–1922) was responsible for the sculptures on the Queen Victoria Memorial, outside Buckingham Palace. He was made Knight Commander of the Bath on the platform during the unveiling ceremony.

And in Japanese folklore, badgers are celebrated as lovable characters, although often drunk!

BRODERICK
From the Norse, meaning 'brother'. It was traditionally given to a second son.

BROMLEY
A place name, meaning 'wood with broom shrubs', now used as a first name.

BRUCE
Originally a French place name, which became a Scottish surname. Many boys were named after the Scottish king Robert the

Bruce (1274–1329), who was inspired by a spider to persevere after his defeat at Methven. He went on to defeat the English at the Battle of Bannockburn in 1314: 20,000 English soldiers, led by Edward II, were defeated by 6,000 Scots headed by Robert the Bruce.

BRUNO
From the German, meaning 'brown'. St Bruno (1033–1101), a nobleman from Cologne, founded the Carthusian Order at the Grande Chartreuse, near Grenoble, in 1084.

Lewis Carroll wrote a book for children entitled *Sylvie and Bruno*, first published in 1889.

BRYCE (Brice)
A name of unknown origin, used since medieval times. St Brice of Tours, a bishop of the fifth century, inspired great devotion in England.

James Bryce (1838–1922), English statesman and historian, was one of the founders of the League of Nations.

BRYN
A Welsh place name, meaning 'hill', now used as a first name. The opera singer Bryn Terfel is well known.

BUCHAN
A Scottish place name, meaning 'little hut', and surname, now used as a first name. It is the surname of the barons Tweedsmuir.

BURNEY
From the Old English, meaning 'stream'. A surname, now used as a first name.

Charles Burney (1726–1814), organist, writer and composer, is famous for his massive *General History of Music*, in four volumes.

BYRON
From the Old English, meaning 'at the cattlesheds'. The poet Lord Byron (George Gordon, 6th Baron Byron, 1788–1824) became the most famous Englishman of his time after the publication of *Childe Harold's Pilgrimage* in 1812. He died of fever at Missolonghi while leading the fight for Greek independence.

CALEB (Cal)
From the Hebrew, meaning 'bold'. The Old Testament Caleb set out with Moses from Egypt and was, with Joshua, one of the two original migrants to enter the Promised Land. A popular name with seventeenth century Puritans.

CALLUM (Calum)
The Gaelic form of the name Columba, meaning 'dove'. St Columba (c.521–597) left Ireland with twelve companions to found a monastery on the island of Iona, off the west coast of Scotland.

CALVERT
From the Old English, meaning 'calf herder'. An English surname, now used as a first name. It was very popular in Victorian times.

CALVIN
From the Latin, meaning 'bald'. It was first used as a Christian name to honour John Calvin (1509–1564), the French Protestant theologian and reformer.

Calvin Coolidge was the President of the USA from 1923 to 1929.

CAMERON
From the Gaelic, meaning 'crooked nose'. A Scottish clan name and surname, now used as a first name.

The Clan Cameron were among the first supporters of Charles Stuart, the Young Pretender, better known as 'Bonnie Prince Charlie', crushed so decisively at the Battle of Culloden in 1746.

CAMPBELL
From the Gaelic, meaning 'crooked mouth'. A Scottish clan name and surname, now used as a first name.

The Clan Campbell became infamous in Scottish history for their part in the Massacre at Glencoe on 13th February 1692 when thirty-eight members of the Clan MacDonald were treacherously murdered.

CARADOC
From the Welsh for 'beloved', a variant of Caradog. After years of resistance to Roman invasion, Caradog was captured, betrayed by the Queen of the Brigantes, and taken prisoner to Rome in AD 51. The Emperor Claudius, impressed by his bravery, sent him home laden with gifts.

It is reputedly one of the earliest British names on record.

CARL
The very popular German version of Charles, q.v.

CARLTON
A place name, meaning 'place of the free peasants', and surname. It has been used as a first name since the late nineteenth century.

Richard Carlton published a book of madrigals in 1601. And the mid-eighteenth century Carlton Hall, Carlton-on-Trent is well worth visiting!

CARMICHAEL
A place name, meaning 'fort of Michael', and surname, now used as a first name.

CARSON
A surname, now a first name bestowed on both boys and girls.

Kit Carson (1809–1868), American trapper and guide, crossed the Mohave Desert in 1830. During an action-packed life, he also took part in the conquest of California in the Mexican War, rising to the rank of brigadier general. Even his wedding day was memorable: he had to rescue his bride from a prairie fire!

CARTER
An occupational surname, now given as a first name. Howard Carter was the archaeologist who, in 1922, discovered the tomb of the Egyptian boy-king Tutankhamun in the Valley of the Kings. (Removing all romance, the tomb is classified as KV62.)

CASEY
An Irish surname, now given as a first name to both boys and girls. The American engine driver folk-hero from Kentucky, 'Casey' Jones (1864–1900), saved the lives of his passengers on the 'Cannonball Express' by sacrificing his own.

CASIMIR
The anglicised version of a Polish name, now generally used. This was the name traditionally used by the medieval kings of Poland. Prince Casimir (1458–1484) was named patron saint of Poland in 1602.

CASPER
From the German, meaning 'imperial'. According to tradition, Casper was one of the three kings or wise men who came to Bethlehem to worship the Infant Jesus, bringing gifts of gold, frankincense and myrrh.

CASPIAN
A place name, now used as a first name. The Caspian Sea was so named because the Romans, finding it salty, dubbed it Mare Caspium. (However, many geographers consider it a lake as it is landlocked.)

The Chronicles of Narnia by C. S. Lewis include a volume entitled *Prince Caspian* (1951).

CASSIUS
An ancient Roman family name, now regaining popularity as a first name.

In Shakespeare's *Julius Caesar*, Cassius instigates the murder plot. Caesar wisely says:

> Yon Cassius has a lean and hungry look:
> He thinks too much: such men are dangerous.

The real Cassius, full name Gaius Cassius Longinus, Roman general and politician, committed suicide in 42 BC.

CAXTON

A surname, now used as a first name. William Caxton (c.1422–1491) was the first English printer. He set up business near the Westminster Abbey Chapter House 'at the sign of the Red Pale', translating and publishing nearly eighty titles. His *History of Troy* (1473) was the first book ever printed in English.

CECIL

From the Latin, meaning 'blind'. The surname of a great English family, favoured by Elizabeth I, now used as a first name.

Cecil Rhodes (1853–1902), the British statesman, gave his name to Rhodesia, now Zimbabwe.

CEDRIC

This seems to have been coined by Sir Walter Scott for a character in his novel, *Ivanhoe* (1819). Cedric is the father of the hero, Wilfred of Ivanhoe.

The name became hugely fashionable in the late nineteenth century after the publication of *Little Lord Fauntleroy* (1886) by Frances Hodgson Burnett. The young American hero Cedric Errol won all hearts, despite wearing black velvet suits with lace collars and sporting long yellow curls!

CHAKA

An unusual first name, now used in Britain. Chaka, a member of the Amazulus of South Africa, killed the chief, his uncle, and took his place. He organised the men of the tribe into a formidable army. By the time he was murdered in 1828, Chaka occupied the whole of what is now Zululand, and Natal.

CHANDLER

An occupational surname for someone who made and sold candles, now used as a first name.

London possessed more candlemakers than any other trade in medieval times, indicating their importance.

CHARLES (Carl, Charlie)

From the Old High German, meaning 'man'. This is the most regal of names, beginning with Charles the Great or Charlemagne (742–814). He was crowned Emperor of the Holy Roman Empire on Christmas Day 800.

Ten French kings were named Charles, including Charles the Fat and Charles the Bald; as were sixteen Swedish sovereigns and four Spanish kings.

England had Charles I (1600–1649), executed for treason, and his son, Charles II, nicknamed 'The Merry Monarch'.

The classic writer Charles Dickens and the film star Charlie Chaplin are known worldwide.

CHARLTON

Originally an English place name, meaning 'settlement of peasants', and a surname. Its use as a first name seems to have begun in the 1870s.

The actor Charlton Heston is a well-known bearer of the name.

CHASE

An occupational surname, meaning 'hunter', now used as a first name.

James Hadley Chase, crime writer, is best known for his novel *No Orchids for Miss Blandish* (1939).

CHESTER

A place name, meaning 'fortress' or 'walled town', and surname, now used as a first name.

The Chester Cycle is the name given to 24 medieval mystery plays, performed at Whitsuntide by the guilds of Chester for over 300 years.

CHRISTIAN (Kristian)

From the Greek, meaning 'anointed'. The first use of the name to indicate a 'follower of Christ' occurred at Antioch (Acts 2: 26).

John Bunyan's allegory, *Pilgrim's Progress*, first published in 1684, charts the adventures of Christian as he travels from the City of Destruction to the Celestial City. Ten Danish kings have borne the name.

CHRISTOPHER (Chris)

From the Greek, meaning 'one who carries Christ'. The legendary St Christopher carried the Infant Jesus across a ford. A church was built in his honour as early as 450. He is the patron saint of all travellers.

Sir Christopher Wren (1632–1723), the great British architect and Professor of Astronomy, designed St Paul's Cathedral and many other London churches to replace those destroyed in the Great Fire of London in 1666.

CLARENCE
From the Latin, meaning 'of Clare'. Edward III created the title Duke of Clarence for his son Lionel on his marriage to a young lady of the de Clare family in 1362.

Clarence Harvey was the hero of a Maria Edgeworth novel entitled *Helen*, published in 1834.

CLARK
From the surname, meaning a person who was able to read and write. Clark Gable (1902–1960), the American actor who played Rhett Butler in the film *Gone with the Wind*, popularised the name in modern times.

CLAUDE
From the Latin, meaning 'lame'. It came into use in Britain in the nineteenth century.

Claude Lorraine (1600–1682), the French landscape painter, and Claude Debussy (1862–1918), the French composer notable for the opera *Pelléas and Mélisande* (1902) and the sea symphony *La Mer* (1905), are just two of those who add lustre to the name.

CLAYTON
A British place name, meaning 'settlement on a clay-bed', and surname. It has been used as a first name for over 200 years.

CLEMENT
From the Latin, meaning 'merciful'. A name popular with the early Christians and used by fourteen Popes.

St Clement Slovensky (d. 916) is honoured in Bulgaria as one of the evangelisers of the country.

Clement Attlee (1883–1967), the British Labour politician, became Prime Minister in 1945.

CLIFFORD (Cliff)
An English place name, meaning 'ford near a cliff' and aristocratic surname, now used as a first name.

The Clifford family motto is *'Semper paratus'*, meaning 'Always ready'. The shortened version of the name has been popularised by the singer Cliff Richard.

CLIFTON
A place name, meaning 'settlement on a cliff', and surname, now used as a first name.

CLINTON (Clint)
A place name, meaning 'settlement near a hill', and surname, now used as a first name.

Sir Henry Clinton (1738?–1795) was commander-in-chief of all British forces in America during the American Revolution.

Clint Eastwood (b. 1930), the American actor, has made popular the shortened version of the name.

CLIVE
A place name, meaning 'cliff' and surname, now used as a first name.

Robert Clive (1725–1774), known as 'Clive of India', founded the empire of British India and was governor of Bengal. Employees of the East India Company gave the name to their sons in his honour.

CLOVIS
From the Old German, meaning 'famous warrior'. Clovis (466–511), King of the Franks, set up his capital in Paris. He introduced Salic Law, married a Christian princess and had all his subjects baptised.

Clovis Sangrail is the hero of many of the sardonic short stories by 'Saki' (1870–1916), the pen name of Hector Munro.

CLYDE
From the river, reputedly named in honour of a goddess, and surname. It is now used as a first name.

The River Clyde runs through Glasgow and empties into the Firth of Clyde.

Field Marshal Lord Clyde (1792–1863) is best remembered for suppressing the Indian Mutiny and for the Relief of Lucknow.

CODY
An Irish surname, now a popular first name. The American William Frederick Cody (1846–1917), better known as Buffalo

Bill, had a hectic life. A rider for the Pony Express, frontier scout and buffalo hunter, he became famous for his Wild West Show. He toured Europe with it to tremendous acclaim.

COLIN
A medieval pet-form of Nicholas and enduringly popular. Edmund Spenser (1552?–1599) wrote a long allegorical poem about a shepherd, *Colin Clouts Come Home Againe*.

Colin Craven was a main character in the children's classic *The Secret Garden*, first published in 1911.

COMPTON
A place name and surname, now used as a first name. It is the surname of the marquesses Northampton.

The writer Sir Compton Mackenzie is remembered for his volumes of autobiography, and novels including *Sinister Street* (1914) and *Whisky Galore* (1947).

Compton Castle, a fourteenth century fortified manor house in Devon, was once home to Sir Humphrey Gilbert (d. 1583). Half-brother to Sir Walter Raleigh, he colonised Newfoundland.

CONNOR (Conor)
From the Old Irish, meaning 'lofty desires'. An Irish name now popular all over Great Britain.

CONRAD
From the German, 'brave counsel'. Conrad was the romantic and mysterious hero of Lord Byron's poem *The Corsair*, published in 1814.

CONSTANTINE
From the Latin, meaning 'constant'. Constantine the Great (280?–337) was the first Christian Emperor of Rome. He built the city of Constantinople on the site of ancient Byzantium, now called Istanbul.

There are three early Scottish kings named Constantine, the first of whom was killed in battle by the Vikings in 877.

COREY
An Irish surname, now used as a first name.

CORMAC (Cormick)
From the Gaelic, meaning 'son of the chariot'.

CORNELIUS

From the Latin, meaning 'a hero'. It was the name of a great Roman family and a martyred pope of the third century.

Shakespeare gave the name to a courtier in his tragedy, *Hamlet*.

COSMO

From the Greek, meaning 'order'. Two early saints, the brothers Cosmas and Damian were martyred in Syria.

The name was introduced to Scotland by the Duke of Gordon in the eighteenth century, bestowed on his son in honour of the Grand Duke of Tuscany, Cosimo III.

Cosmo Lang, Archbishop of Canterbury 1928–1942, made the name known.

COURTENAY (Courtney)

An aristocratic surname, now used as a first name for both boys and girls. The family of de Courtenay, Earls of Devon, came originally from Courtenay in France.

CRAIG

A surname, from the Gaelic meaning 'rock', now used as a first name.

It is the surname of the Viscounts Craigavon. *Craig's Wife*, a play by George Kelly, was awarded a Pulitzer Prize in 1926.

CRAWFORD

A Scottish place name, meaning 'ford where the crows gather', and a surname, now used as a first name.

Mary and Henry Crawford play a vital part in Jane Austen's novel *Mansfield Park*.

CRISPIN

From the Latin, meaning 'curly'. Saints Crispin and Crispinian were brother shoemakers of Soissons, martyred c.285. It was a very popular name in the Middle Ages.

Henry V defeated the French at the Battle of Agincourt on St Crispin's Day, 25th October 1415.

CUAN

A Gaelic pet-form of Conan, meaning 'hound', increasing in popularity.

CURTIS
From the Old French, meaning 'courteous'. A surname, now used as a first name. This was given as a nickname to Robert, Duke of Normandy, the eldest son of William the Conqueror.

CUTHMAN
A ninth century saint, St Cuthman was a shepherd. On the death of his father he migrated to Steyning in Sussex. (His mother being too frail to walk, Cuthman pushed her there in a hand-cart.) He built a small church, and remained in Steyning for the rest of his life. Christopher Fry wrote about him in his one-act play, *The Boy with a Cart* (1938).

CYRIL
From the Greek, meaning 'lordly'. St Cyril (c.827–869) and his brother St Methodius are revered as the 'Apostles to the Slavs'. He invented the Cyrillic alphabet now used by the Russians and Bulgarians.

The name came into use in Britain in the nineteenth century, revived by the Tractarians.

DACRE
A Cumberland place name, meaning 'trickling stream', and an aristocratic surname, now used as a first name. The first Baron Dacre was created in 1321 by Edward II.

DAI
The Welsh pet-form of David, q.v.

DALE
A surname, meaning 'dweller in the valley', now used as a first name. In Victorian times this was given to both girls and boys, but now seems to be restricted to the male sex.

DALLAS
A Scottish place name, meaning 'resting-place', now used as a first name.
  George Dallas, the American Vice-President from 1845 to 1849, gave his name to the Texan city.

DAMIAN (Damien)
From the Greek, meaning 'to tame'. Damian and Cosmas were twin brothers who practised medicine and charged no fees to the poor. They were martyred for their Christian faith at Cyrrhus in Syria; the year is unknown, but their feast day is now 26th September. They are the patron saints of physicians. Damian was first used in England in 1205.

DAMON
From the Greek, meaning 'divine power'. Damon and Pythias of Syracuse were close friends. Pythias was sentenced to death, but begged to be allowed to go home to order his affairs. Damon took his place, prepared to die for his friend if he was late in returning. Pythias returned in good time, so impressing the King, Dionysius I, that he both freed and befriended the pair.

DANE
A surname, now used as a first name. The church of St Clement Danes, the first church west of Temple Bar in London, was so called because Harold, a Danish king, and many of his country-men were buried there.

DANIEL (Dan, Danny)
From the Hebrew, meaning 'God has judged', Daniel is found in England before the Norman Conquest, but only as a name for monks and bishops. It became most popular for the ordinary people in the Middle Ages; perhaps to honour the Old Testament Daniel, who stepped unscathed from the lions' den. Daniel Defoe (1660–1731) wrote *Robinson Crusoe* and *A Journal of the Plague Year*.

DARCY

A French place name and surname, now used as a first name. A companion to William the Conqueror, Norman D'Arcy, was granted much land in Lincolnshire.

The arrogant Darcy, beloved by Elizabeth Bennet in Jane Austen's novel *Pride and Prejudice*, must be the archetypal romantic hero.

DARIUS

The name of the great Persian kings, meaning 'he who upholds the good'.

An Old Testament king of Babylon, Darius condemned Daniel to be thrown into the lions' den.

DARREN

The origin of this name is uncertain, perhaps taken from an Irish surname or from Darius. Its popularity seems to date from the early 1950s.

DARRYL (Darrell)

A French place name and surname, carried to England at the time of the Norman Conquest by a family who came from Airelle.

The most prominent bearer of the name in modern times was Darryl F. Zanuck, the American film producer and founder of Twentieth Century Fox.

DAVID (Dave, Davie, Davy)

From the Hebrew, meaning 'darling'. The shepherd-boy David slew the giant Goliath with his slingshot; he became King of Judah and, eventually, of all Israel. He was a poet; many of the psalms are attributed to him. (Strangely, though David was one of the greatest Biblical heroes, no-one else in the Bible is named after him.)

Two Scottish kings have been called David. David I (1084–1153) established a form of central government and issued the first royal coinage. David II (1324–1371) invaded England, suffered defeat and was imprisoned for eleven years.

DAWSON

A surname, meaning 'son of David', now used as a first name.

DEACON
From the Greek, meaning 'servant'. The deacon ranks just below the priest in the Christian church.

DEAN
An Old English place name, meaning 'valley', and surname, now used as a first name.

James Dean (1931–1955), the American actor whose early and tragic death turned him into an enduring cult figure, has done much to popularise the name.

DECLAN
An ancient Gaelic name. Declan was an associate of St Colman of Lindisfarne in the seventh century. Little else is known about him. This name has become hugely popular in recent years.

DEMETRIUS
From the Greek, meaning 'follower of the goddess Demeter'. St Demetrius of Rostov (1651–1709) was the son of a Cossack. A monk, bishop and scholar, he wrote many biographies, dramas and devotional works.

And Demetrius is the character betrothed to Hermia, and loved by Helena, in Shakespeare's *A Midsummer Night's Dream*.

DENNIS (Denis)
A medieval form of the Greek name, Dionysos, the god of wine. St Denis, the patron saint of France, was a missionary sent into Gaul in the year 250. He was beheaded in 258 at a place in Paris called Montmartre ('Martyr's Hill'). The Normans introduced the name into England.

DENZIL
From the Cornish place name, meaning 'stronghold', and surname. It has been used as a first name since the sixteenth century.

In 1629, the Speaker of the House of Commons refused to put forward for consideration by the MPs a proposition opposed by Charles I. Denzil Holles responded to this by holding Speaker Finch down in his chair until he changed his mind. After floods of tears, he did!

DEREK (Derrick)
A shortened version of Theodoric, meaning 'people's ruler'. It was brought to England from Holland in the fifteenth century and became popular in the 1890s.

Sir Derek Jacobi (b. 1938), the actor, is a famous modern bearer of the name.

DERMOT
From the Irish, meaning 'free from envy'. Dermot was the lover of Grainne, the wife of Finn MacCool of Irish legend.

DESMOND
Originally an Irish surname, meaning 'man from South Munster', it has been popular as a first name all over Great Britain from the early 1900s.

DEXTER
An occupational surname, originally denoting a *female* dyer, later both male and female.

In heraldic terms, the right-hand side of a shield (as viewed by the bearer *not* from the front) is the 'dexter' (from the Latin for 'right') and the left-hand side is the 'sinister' (from the Latin for 'left').

DICKON
A pet-name for Richard (q.v.), dating back to the thirteenth century. Dickon was the animal-loving boy in the children's classic *The Secret Garden*, first published in 1911.

DIETER
From the Old German, meaning 'warrior race', now used in Britain.

DIGBY
An English place name, meaning 'a settlement by a ditch', and surname, used as a first name since the late 1800s.

The naval commander and writer Sir Kenelm Digby (1603–1665) was the first to discover how vital oxygen is for plant life.

DIRK
The Dutch version of Derek, now generally used. The actor and writer Dirk Bogarde (1921–1999, born Derek van den Bogaerde) did much to popularise the name.

And no Scottish highlander in full ceremonial dress would be without his dirk, or fighting knife.

DISMAS
The name, in the apocryphal gospels, given to the penitent thief crucified with Jesus. He was considered the patron saint of thieves, hopefully helping them to change their ways.

DOMINIC
From the Latin, meaning 'of the Lord'. It was popular with the early Christians and often given to children born on a Sunday.

St Dominic (1170–1221), a Spaniard, founded the Order of Preachers or 'Dominicans' in 1216. One of his last undertakings was to send thirteen friars to Oxford.

DONALD (Don, Donny)
From the Gaelic, meaning 'proud ruler'. A Scottish clan name and surname, now used as a first name.

Three Scottish kings have borne the name. Donald III (c.1031–1097) was twice deposed, and blinded. He was the last king to be buried on Iona.

DONOVAN
From an Irish surname, meaning 'dark brown', now popular as a first name.

DORAN
There are two meanings possible for this name: from the Greek, meaning 'gift' or from an Irish surname, meaning 'descendant of the exile'.

DORIAN
From the Greek, meaning 'a man from Doris', which is a place in central Greece.

Oscar Wilde appears to have invented this name for the hero of his moral novel, *The Picture of Dorian Gray*, first published in 1891.

DOUGAL
From the Gaelic, meaning 'dark stranger'. This was originally the name given by the Irish to Danish settlers. It later became a nickname given by the Lowland Scots to Highlanders.

DOUGLAS (Doug, Dougie)
A Scottish place name, meaning 'dark water', and a surname, now used as a first name.

The Douglases were the greatest noble family of medieval Scotland. Their founder James Douglas (1286–1330), called 'Black Douglas', invaded England and plundered many towns and villages in the North. He died fighting the Moors in Spain, having stopped off there for a battle on his way to the Crusades.

The Douglases also acquired the French Dukedom of Touraine, when a Scots army led by the Earl of Douglas defeated the English at Beauge in 1421.

The botanist David Douglas (1798–1834) gave his name to the Douglas Fir, bringing the seeds from America to Scotland.

DRAKE
From the surname, meaning 'standard bearer', now given as a first name.

Sir Francis Drake (1540–1596), considered a pirate by the Spanish as he preyed on their vessels in the West Indies, set off to circumnavigate the globe in December 1577.

Returning in 1580, he was knighted by Elizabeth I, and later fought against the Spanish Armada. He died during an expedition to the West Indies. (A full-scale replica of his ship, the *Golden Hinde*, is moored in Southwark.)

DREW
Now considered the diminutive form of Andrew (q.v.), it has a long history. The German name Drogo, meaning 'to carry', was brought to England by followers of William the Conqueror in its French form, Dru. It became popular and was anglicised into Drew.

DRUMMOND
A place name, meaning 'ridge' and surname. Now used as a first name. It is the surname of the earls Perth, their motto 'Gang warily'.

DRYSTAN
A Welsh variant of Tristram, q.v.

DUANE
From an Irish surname, meaning 'little dark one'. It was made popular by the American singer and guitarist Duane Eddy in the 1950s.

DUDLEY

A place name, meaning 'Dudda's clearing', and aristocratic surname, now used as a first name.

Robert Dudley, Earl of Leicester (1532–1588), was the favourite of Elizabeth I and the main character in Sir Walter Scott's novel *Kenilworth*.

The pianist and actor Dudley Moore (1935–2002) made the name popular.

DUFF

From the Gaelic, meaning 'dark' or 'black'. It is the surname of the Dukes of Fife.

DUNCAN

From the Gaelic, meaning 'dark-skinned warrior'. The Scottish king Duncan I (1010–1040) was murdered by his cousin, Macbeth (who is immortalised in the Shakespeare play of the same name). Duncan II (1060–1094) ruled for approximately six months and was murdered by his uncle, Donald III. (Perhaps this explains why no other Scottish rulers have chosen to bear the name.)

DUNSTAN

From the Old English, meaning 'stony hill'.

St Dunstan (c.909–988) revived monasticism in England after the ravages wrought by Scandinavian invasions. He became Archbishop of Canterbury in 959. The present Coronation rite is derived from the one compiled and used by Dunstan in crowning Edgar I King of all England in Bath Abbey in 973. Dunstan also loved playing the harp, working in metal and calligraphy!

Dunstan Cass is a character in *Silas Marner*, the novel by George Eliot.

DYLAN

From the Welsh, meaning 'flood'. In Celtic myth, Dylan was the son of a sea god. As soon as he was born, he plunged into the sea and swam like a fish.

The Welsh poet Dylan Thomas (1914–1953) and the American singer Bob Dylan (b. 1941), real name Robert Zimmerman, have made the name popular.

EAMON/EAMONN
The Irish version of Edmund (q.v.), used generally in Britain since the mid-twentieth century.

Eamon de Valera (1882–1975) was twice President of the Republic of Ireland, only retiring from politics at the age of 90.

EARLE (Earl)
From the Old English, meaning 'warrior' or 'nobleman'. One of the five ranks of the peerage and a surname, now used as a first name.

John Earle (1602–1665) wrote *Microcosmography* (1628), considered one of the finest prose works of the seventeenth century.

EBBE (Ebby)
The pet-form of the German name Eberhard, meaning 'brave wild boar'.

EDEN
From the Hebrew, meaning 'delight'. The name of the Biblical Paradise, the country and garden in which Adam and Eve dwelt.

EDGAR
From the Anglo-Saxon, meaning 'fortunate spear'. This is one of the royal Anglo-Saxon names to survive the Norman Conquest.

King Edgar (944–975) was the first King of all England. The American writer Edgar Allan Poe (1809–1849) wrote haunting poems and horror stories, including *The Pit and the Pendulum*.

EDMUND

From the Old English, meaning 'happy protection'. St Edmund, king and martyr (841–869), the ruler of East Anglia, was murdered by the Danes. His body was enshrined at Bury St Edmunds.

The Astronomer Royal, Edmund Halley (1656–1742), predicted the return of the comet which bears his name.

Edmund was a favourite name of Jane Austen. She wrote, 'There is a nobleness in the name of Edmund. It is a name of heroism and renown.'

EDRIC

From the Old English, meaning 'happy ruler'. A baptismal name of the Anglo-Saxons, revived by the Victorians.

EDWARD (Ed, Eddie, Ned, Ted, Teddie)

From the Anglo-Saxon, meaning 'prosperous protector'. A very popular name, used since Anglo-Saxon times. King Edward the Elder (870–924) had three sons who became kings, and six daughters who married kings or dukes in England, France and Germany

King Edward the Confessor (1003–1066) founded Westminster Abbey and was canonised in 1161.

Eight post-Conquest rulers have borne this name: Edward V (1470–1483) was one of the two tragic Princes in the Tower, supposedly murdered on the orders of their uncle Richard III.

EDWIN

From the Anglo-Saxon, meaning 'fortunate friend'. King Edwin (d. 633) was the first Christian King of Northumberland. The name was revived by the Victorians.

The Mystery of Edwin Drood was the last, unfinished novel of Charles Dickens (1812–1870).

ELDRED

From the Old English, meaning 'old counsel'. An Anglo-Saxon Christian name, one of many revived by the Victorians.

ELFORD

A place name, meaning 'Ella's ford', and surname, now used as a first name.

ELIAS

The Greek form of Elijah, q.v. This has been used in England since the seventeenth century.

The antiquarian Elias Ashmole gave his collection of curiosities to Oxford University in 1677. The museum which bears his name (the Ashmolean) was opened in 1683 and is the oldest public museum in England.

ELIJAH

From the Hebrew, meaning 'My lord is Jehovah'. Elijah, a prophet, was fed miraculously by ravens, and raised the dead son of a widow to life, among many other happenings. He did not die himself, being carried up to heaven in a whirlwind. His life is one of the most fascinating in the Old Testament.

The Puritans of the seventeenth century reintroduced the name.

ELLERY (Ellerie)

A surname, now used as a first name by both girls and boys. Frederic Dannay and Manfred Lee were American cousins who invented the fictional detective, Ellery Queen, hero of many magazine stories and novels.

ELLIOT (Eliot, Elliott)

A medieval diminutive of Elias, meaning 'The Lord is my God'. A surname, now used as a first name.

Thomas Stearns Eliot (1888–1965), the American-born poet, became a British subject in 1927. He is recognised as one of the major influences in the twentieth century. Elliot is the surname of the Earls of Minto.

ELLIS

A popular medieval name, derived from Elias, and surname.

William Webb Ellis (1807–1872), while playing football at Rugby School, picked up the ball and ran with it. Such was the birth of rugby football.

ELWIN

From the Anglo-Saxon, meaning 'old friend'. A surname, now used as a first name.

EMERSON

A medieval surname, meaning 'descendant of a man called Emery', now used as a first name.

The American Ralph Waldo Emerson (1803–1882) was a famous poet, essayist and philosopher.

EMERY

From the Old German, meaning 'power'. It was brought to England by the Normans and given to both sexes until the eighteenth century, when it became exclusively male.

EMLYN

From a Welsh place name, now used as a first name. Emlyn Williams (1905–1987), actor and playwright, wrote several memorable plays, including *The Corn is Green* and *Night Must Fall*.

ERIC (Rick, Ricky)

From the Norse, meaning 'ruler of all'. The name was brought to England by the Danes. King Eric Bloodaxe fled from Norway to England in 934 and captured Northumberland from King Edred.

Dean Farrar wrote the popular Victorian children's story *Eric, or Little by Little* in 1858, which popularised the name.

Eric Blair was the real name of the novelist George Orwell (1903–1950).

ERNEST (Ernie)

From the German, meaning 'determined'. The name was brought to Britain in the eighteenth century by the Hanoverians.

The first Duke of Saxe-Gotha, Ernest the Pious (1601–1675), insisted on compulsory education for all children in his domain. A wise man.

Ernest Pontifex was the unwise hero of Samuel Butler's classic novel *The Way of All Flesh* (1903).

ERROL

A Scottish place name and surname, now used as a first name. The Tasmanian-born, swashbuckling film star Errol Flynn (1909–1959) made the name very popular.

ESMOND
From the Old English, meaning 'divine protection'. It was revived in Victorian times; perhaps influenced by the popularity of the novel by William Thackeray, *The History of Henry Esmond*, published in 1852.

ETHAN
From the Hebrew, meaning 'strong'. The Old Testament mentions four men named Ethan. One was renowned for his wisdom, only King Solomon was wiser. Another was a priest who sang as the Ark of the Covenant was brought to Jerusalem by King David.
   Ethan Frome is the title of one of the shorter novels of Edith Wharton (1862–1937).

EUGENE (Gene)
From the Greek, meaning 'noble'. Four popes and several obscure saints have borne this name.
   The American playwright Eugene O'Neill (1888–1953), who wrote *The Iceman Cometh* and *Long Day's Journey into Night* among others, won the Nobel Prize for Literature in 1936.
   Gene Kelly is famous for his singing and dancing in the classic musical, *Singin' in the Rain*.

EUSTACE
From the Greek, meaning 'fruitful'. The name was brought to England at the Norman Conquest.
   Prince Eustace was crowned King of England in 1152, during the lifetime of his father, King Stephen. Sadly, he did not live to succeed him.
   And Eustace the chorister was paid 25 shillings to sing at the coronation of King John's consort, Isabella, on 8th October 1200.

EVAN
The Welsh version of John. A very popular first name.

EVELYN
See the entry in the girls' section.

EWAN
From the Gaelic, Eoghan, a name of great antiquity. There is dispute over its derivation. Some claim it to be a version of

Eugene, q.v.; while others claim it is a Celtic name, meaning
'born of the yew'. Ewan is the Scottish version, now popular all
over Britain.

EZRA

From the Hebrew, meaning 'help'. A Hebrew priest and scribe of
the fifth century BC, Ezra gave his name to one of the books of
the Old Testament.

Ezra Pound (1885–1972), American poet and essayist, was
one of the most influential figures in modern literature.

FABIAN

From the Latin, meaning 'bean'. The name of an ancient and
illustrious Roman family, who listed among its members a
historian and a general whose tactics against Hannibal inspired
the naming of the Fabian Society. This intellectual society of
non-revolutionary socialists was founded in London in 1884.

Pope Fabian was martyred in 250 under Emperor Decius. The
name was brought to England by the Normans.

FELIX

From the Latin, meaning 'happy'. There are many saints named
Felix, including sixty-seven martyrs. The Burgundian bishop St
Felix of Dunwich (d. 648) came to preach the gospel in East
Anglia. He gave his name to the town of Felixstowe.

FERDINAND

From the German, meaning 'bold life'. Many Kings of Castile
have borne this name, the most famous of whom was Ferdinand

V of Aragon (1452–1516), who with his wife Isabella gave financial backing to the explorer Christopher Columbus.

Shakespeare gave this name to the King of Navarre in *Love's Labours Lost* and to Miranda's beloved in *The Tempest*.

FERGAL
The anglicised form of an Irish name, meaning 'man of valour'.

FERGUS
From the Gaelic, meaning 'man's strength'. Fergus is one of the heroes of Ulster in ancient Gaelic legend.

FIFE
A Scottish place name, now used as a first name. It is said to be derived from Fib, one of the seven sons of Cruithne, father of the Picts.

The Kingdom of Fife contains Dunfermline (the ancient capital of Scotland) and St Andrews (the first Scottish university and home of golf).

FINBAR
From the Gaelic, meaning 'fair haired'. An abbot and bishop, St Finbar (d. 633) founded the monastery and episcopal see of Cork. He is said to have visited St David in Wales. The hero of many legends, he is even supposed to have crossed the Irish Sea on horseback!

FINLAY (Findlay, Finley)
From the Gaelic, meaning 'fair warrior'. A Scottish surname, now used as a first name. Finlay was the father of the infamous Macbeth, King of Scotland.

FINN (Ffion, Finnian)
From the Gaelic, meaning 'fair'. Finn MacCool is a great hero in Irish folklore, the subject of tales and ballads innumerable. From his headquarters in County Kildare, Finn led a band of warriors called the Fenians, who gave help to all who required it.

St Finnian (d. 549) was the founder of Irish monasticism.

FITZROY
From the surname, meaning 'son of the king', now used as a first name.

It is the surname of the Dukes of Grafton; their family motto is '*Et decus et pretium recti*' or 'Both the glory and reward of worth'.

FLOYD

An anglicised surname, derived from Lloyd, q.v. It is now used as a first name.

Boxing fans will remember the American Floyd Patterson, World Heavyweight Champion in 1956 and 1960.

FORBES

A place name, meaning 'field', and surname, now used as a first name. The earls Granard have Forbes as their surname.

A bronze medal showing a bust of the naturalist Edward Forbes (1815–1854) can be seen at the National Portrait Gallery.

FORREST

A surname bestowed on someone who lived in, or beside, a forest. It is now used as a first name.

FOSTER

An occupational surname, denoting 'forester' or 'shearer', now used as a first name.

Stephen Foster (1826–1864), the American composer, wrote hundreds of popular songs, including *My Old Kentucky Home*, and *Massa's in the Cold, Cold Ground*. (A tearjerker, if I ever heard one!)

FRANCIS (Frank)

From the Latin, meaning 'a Frenchman'. The name of two French kings and two emperors of the Holy Roman Empire: the most famous bearer of the name is St Francis of Assisi (1182–1226), renowned for preaching to the birds, taming a wolf and beginning the tradition of the Christmas Crib.

In reality, his name was Giovanni; but he became so proficient in French that he was called 'il Francesco' (the Frenchman), and his baptismal name was forgotten, even among his followers.

Two sailors, Sir Francis Drake (1540–1596), the first English circumnavigator of the globe, and Sir Francis Chichester (1901–1972) who sailed alone around the world in *Gipsy Moth IV* in 1966–1967, add lustre to the name.

FRANK
This is now considered a diminutive of Francis (q.v.), but originally the name referred to the Teutonic tribe of Franks, led by King Clovis, who invaded Gaul in the fifth century AD and gave their name to the whole country of France. It came to England with the Normans.

FRANKLIN
From the Old French, meaning 'free citizen'. A surname, now used as a first name. The franklin was a landowner in the England of the thirteenth and fourteenth centuries who was not of noble birth.

Geoffrey Chaucer (1343–1400) included *The Franklin's Tale* in his *Canterbury Tales*.

Sir John Franklin (1786–1847), the English Arctic explorer, was lost in the attempt to discover a North-West passage to the Pacific.

FRASER (Frazer)
A French place name and a Scottish surname, now used as a first name. It is the surname of barons Lovat, Saltoun and Strathalmond.

FREDERICK (Fred, Freddie)
From the Old German, meaning 'peaceful ruler'. This has been a popular name in Britain since the eighteenth century. Frederick, Prince of Wales (1707–1751), son of George II and father of George III, was killed by a blow from a cricket ball.

The most famous bearer of the name was Frederick II (1712–1786), King of Prussia, called 'The Great'. He was a very far from 'peaceful ruler', being renowned as a soldier and a totally unscrupulous politician. (He played the flute well, too!)

FULTON
A place name, meaning 'muddy place', and surname, now used as a first name.

Robert Fulton (1765–1815), American inventor, designed the first commercially successful steamboat, the *Clermont*. This ran between New York City and Albany in 1807.

GABRIEL

From the Hebrew, meaning 'man of God'. Gabriel the Archangel announced the birth of Jesus to the Virgin Mary in St Luke's Gospel and is also mentioned in the Old Testament Book of Daniel.

Gabriel Fahrenheit (1686–1736) was a German physicist who introduced improvements to the construction of thermometers by the use of mercury. He gave his name to a temperature scale in which the melting point of ice is 32°F and boiling point is 212°F.

GARETH (Gary)

From the Welsh, meaning 'gentle'. The name of one of the knights of King Arthur's Round Table, unwittingly killed by Sir Lancelot. Alfred, Lord Tennyson (1809–1892) told the story of *Gareth and Lynette* in his hugely popular epic poem, *Idylls of the King*.

GARRICK

From the surname, meaning 'spear rule', now used as a first name. This is forever associated with the famous actor and theatre manager, David Garrick (1717–1779). He did much to revive the popularity of Shakespeare's plays.

The Garrick Theatre, named in his honour in London's Charing Cross Road, was built in the 1880s. (A stream which runs beneath it caused some problems!)

GARTH

From the Old Norse, meaning 'enclosure' or 'garden'. A surname, now used as a first name.

GARY

A diminutive form of Gareth, q.v. It was made very popular in the twentieth century by the American actor Gary Cooper (1901–1961), really Frank J. Cooper, who starred in the classic Western *High Noon*.

GAVIN

From the Welsh, meaning 'white hawk'. The Scottish form of Gawain, a knight of the Round Table and a nephew to King Arthur.

Gavin Maxwell (1914–1969) wrote the popular autobiographical book *Ring of Bright Water*.

GEOFFREY (Geoff, Jeff, Jeffrey)

From the Old German, meaning 'peace'. Brought to England by the Normans in the eleventh century.

The name was made famous by Geoffrey Chaucer (1343–1400), considered the father of English poetry, who was a secret agent, diplomat and controller of customs in addition. His *Canterbury Tales* and *Troilus and Cressida* remain in print to torment the schoolchildren of Britain. He was the first poet to be buried in Westminster Abbey, in the portion known as Poets' Corner.

GEORGE

From the Greek, meaning 'farmer'. St George, a soldier saint and martyr of whom little is known, was deeply revered in the East. The Emperor Constantine had a church erected in his honour. The Crusaders chose St George as their champion and spread his cult across Europe. Edward III made St George the patron saint of England; by 1415 his feast day was a public holiday.

The first four royal Georges, ruling from 1714 until 1830, made the name very popular and this has continued to the present day.

George Washington became first President of the United States in 1789.

GERALD

From the Old German, meaning 'spear rule'. This was introduced by the Normans and popular in the Middle Ages. It was revived in the late nineteenth century.

St Gerald of Aurillac (855–909) was a considerable land-owner, famous for his justice. St Odo of Cluny wrote a 'Life' of St Gerald which made him very popular in medieval France.

GERARD

A variant of Gerald, q.v. There have been several saints with this name. St Gerard Majella (1726–1755), an Italian Redemptorist lay-brother, is still invoked by mothers in labour for the safe delivery of their child.

Gerard Manley Hopkins (1844–1889), the English poet and Jesuit priest, wrote *The Wreck of the Deutschland* and *Pied Beauty* among others. Not one of his poems was published in his lifetime.

GERVASE

Gervase was an early martyr about whom nothing is known, but whose cult was widespread. The name has been used in England since the fifteenth century.

Sir John Beaumont (1583–1627) wrote the moving poem, *Of his Dear Son, Gervase*. This contains the line:

Whose looks could all my bitter griefs assuage.

GERWYN (Gerwen)

From the Welsh, meaning 'fair love'.

GETHIN

From the Welsh, meaning 'dark' or 'swarthy'.

GIDEON

From the Hebrew, meaning 'one who cuts down'. The name of an Israelite ruler of the Old Testament, who delivered his people from the Midianites at the instigation of an angel. Popular with the Puritans of the seventeenth century and taken by them to America.

GILBERT (Gil)

From the German, meaning 'bright pledge'. Brought to England at the Norman Conquest, the name became very popular.

St Gilbert of Sempringham (c.1085–1189) was the founder of the only specifically English religious order for both men and women. The Gilbertine Order was suppressed by King Henry VIII and all its houses appropriated.

The English writer Gilbert Keith Chesterton (1874–1936) is best remembered for creating the Roman Catholic priest and sleuth Father Brown.

GILES (Gyles)
From the Latin, meaning 'young goat'. St Giles (d. c.712) was one of the most popular saints of Western Europe. The most famous incident told about him concerns his protection of a pet deer, hunted by the Visigoth King Wamba, who loosed an arrow after it. He found St Giles himself holding the deer, wounded in the arm. St Giles Cripplegate in London and the High Kirk in Edinburgh are dedicated to him. He is the patron of the poor and of the crippled.

GILROY
A surname, meaning 'servant of the red-haired man', now used as a first name.

GLEN (Glenn, Glyn)
From the Gaelic, meaning 'narrow mountain valley'. A place name and surname, now used as a first name.

The American bandleader Glenn Miller (1904–1944), who died mysteriously over the English Channel during the Second World War, and several film stars and singers have made this name popular in modern times.

GODFREY
From the Old German, meaning 'God's peace'. This was brought to England by the Normans.

Godfrey de Bouillon was the hero of *Jerusalem Delivered*, the epic masterpiece of the Italian poet Torquato Tasso (1544–1595).

GORDON
A place name, Scottish clan name and surname, now used as a first name. Sir Gordon Richards (1904–1986) was one of the most successful flat-racing jockeys.

General Gordon (1833–1885), who was besieged by the Mahdi at Khartoum and died so dramatically when the city was stormed, made the name very popular in late Victorian England.

GRAHAM(E) (Graeme)

From the Old English, meaning 'homestead belonging to Granta'. A place name, Scottish clan name and surname, now used as a first name. The name was introduced into Scotland by the Norman William de Graham in the early twelfth century.

GRANT

From the French, meaning 'tall'. A surname, now used as a first name. Ulysses S. Grant (1822–1885) was a Union General in the American Civil War and became eighteenth President of the USA.

GRANVILLE

A place name in Normandy, meaning 'large settlement', and surname, now used as a first name. The motto of the Earls of Granville is 'Frangas non flectes', translated as 'You may break, not bend'.

GRAYDON

A variant of Gray (Grey, q.v.), now used as a first name.

GREGORY (Greg, Gregor)

From the Greek, meaning 'watchful'. A popular name in the early Christian church, sixteen popes and many saints have borne the name. It was introduced into England at the Norman Conquest and is the name of a Scottish clan.

St Gregory the Great (c.540–604) was the first monk to be elected pope. He sent missionaries to England under the charge of St Augustine in 597, and was responsible for the development of the Gregorian chant or plainsong.

Pope Gregory XIII (1502–1585) introduced the reformed Gregorian calendar on 24th February 1582.

Gregory de Rokesley (d. 1291) was eight times Lord Mayor of London.

GREVILLE

An aristocratic surname, now used as a first name. Charles Cavendish Fulke Greville (1794–1865), English diarist, was the clerk of the Council in Ordinary. His journals, the *Greville Memoirs*, are necessary to any student of the nineteenth century.

GREY (Gray)

An aristocratic surname, now used as a first name. The motto of the earls Grey is '*De bon valoir servir le roi*' or 'To serve the king with good will'.

Thomas Gray (1716–1771), poet and letter-writer, is renowned for his *Elegy Written in a Country Churchyard*.

GRIFFIN

A mythical monster, the offspring of a lion and an eagle. Considered sacred, the griffin was the guardian of the gold mines of Scythia. It is also the most magnificent of heraldic beasts.

GUSTAV (Gustave)

A Scandinavian name, now generally used. King Gustavus Vasa (1496–1560) broke away from Denmark and fashioned the modern Swedish state.

The English composer Gustav Holst (1874–1934) is well known.

GUY

From the German, meaning 'wood'. A saint's name, it was introduced by the Normans and popular, until Guy Fawkes and others made the attempt to blow up the Houses of Parliament on 5th November 1605.

Sir Walter Scott's novel *Guy Mannering* (1815) and the hero of the very popular *Heir of Redcliffe* (1853) by C. M. Yonge revitalised the name.

GWYN

From the Welsh, meaning 'fair' or 'blessed'.

HAL
A diminutive of Henry, q.v.; used most famously by Shakespeare as the pet-name of the future Henry V in the plays *Henry IV: Part I* and *Part II*.

HALLAM
A place name, meaning 'at the rocks', and surname, now used as a first name.

Alfred, Lord Tennyson, wrote the long poem *In Memoriam* in honour of his friend Arthur Hallam, who died in 1833. It is considered one of the greatest English elegies.

HALLEY
A place name, meaning 'hay meadow', and surname, now given as a first name.

Edmund Halley (1656–1742), the second Astronomer Royal, is best known for his study of comets. His star catalogue was the first to record stars in the southern hemisphere by using a telescope.

Halley's Comet, which returns approximately every 76 years, was last seen in 1986.

HAMILTON
A place name and aristocratic surname, used as a first name for nearly 200 years. It is the surname of the Dukes of Abercorn and five other peers.

HAMISH
The Gaelic version of James, q.v.

HAMO

A variant of Hamlet, which has been used in England since the sixteenth century.

HANDEL

A name bestowed since the late nineteenth century in honour of the German-born composer, George Frideric Handel.

The Handel House Museum at 25 Brook Street, London, W1 can be visited. There he lived for 36 years, composing such masterpieces as *The Messiah* and *Zadok the Priest*. And there he died in 1759.

HANS

The German form of John, taken from the Latin, Johannes. It is now given as a first name in Britain.

Sir Hans Sloane (1660–1753) endowed the Chelsea Physic Garden. More famously, his collection of books and manuscripts was purchased by the nation, providing the foundation for the British Museum. Hans Place and Sloane Square in London were named in his honour.

HARLEY

A place name and surname, meaning 'wood with hares', now used as a first name. Robert Harley, 1st Earl of Oxford (1661–1724), and his son Edward, collected the thousands of rare manuscripts and papers bought by the Government in 1754 to be preserved for the nation at the British Museum.

HAROLD

From the Old English, meaning 'army rule'. A royal name, particularly associated with Harold II (1022–1066), son of Godwin of Wessex, killed at the Battle of Hastings.

(King Harold I of Norway (850–933) unwisely vowed not to cut or comb his hair until he became sole king of that country: to achieve this took ten years! He cannot have been a wholesome companion.)

The name fell from favour until Byron's verse epic, *Childe Harold's Pilgrimage*, took Britain by storm in the early nineteenth century.

HARRISON

A surname, used as a first name since Victorian times.

HARRY
See the entry under Henry.

HARTLEY
A place name, meaning 'stag wood', and surname, now used as a first name. The poet Coleridge named his son Hartley in 1796 as a compliment to the philosopher David Hartley (1705–1757), who was famous for his book *Observations on Man*.

HARVEY
This name was brought to England at the time of the Norman Conquest. St Hervé, anglicised to Harvey, was venerated all over Brittany. He was born blind in the sixth century, and was a wandering minstrel before becoming a hermit.

This name is mentioned eleven times in the Domesday Book.

HAYDON (Hayden)
A place name, meaning 'heather hill', and surname, now used as a first name.

Benjamin Robert Haydon (1786–1846), historical painter, is better remembered for his fascinating diaries. Both Keats and Wordsworth wrote sonnets in his honour.

HEATH
A place name and surname, used as a first name since the mid-twentieth century.

John Heath was a composer of the sixteenth century. Some of his work can be found in the *Mulliner Book*, a large manuscript collection of music dating from the 1550s.

HECTOR
From the Greek, meaning 'holding fast'. In Greek legend, he was the son of Priam and Hecuba, the noblest of all the Trojan heroes. He was slain by Achilles and his body was dragged around Troy three times, lashed to Achilles' chariot.

Hector Munro (1870–1916) was the real name of the writer 'Saki'.

HEDLEY
A place name, meaning 'heather clearing', and surname. Now used as a first name.

HENRY (Harry)

From the Old German, meaning 'home ruler'. A solidly regal name, borne by eight English kings. Henry V (1387–1422) is renowned for an outstanding victory at Agincourt in 1415. His son, Henry VI (1421–1471), came to the throne at eight months and is remembered for founding Eton College and King's College, Cambridge.

Henry FitzAilwyn was the first Lord Mayor of London in 1189. His first duty was to organise the ransom of Richard the Lionheart, captured on his way home from the Third Crusade.

Sir Henry Irving (1838–1905) received a knighthood in 1895, the first actor to be so honoured.

HERBERT

From the Old German, meaning 'army bright'. St Herbert (d. 687) lived a hermit's life on the island in Lake Derwentwater. The name died out in England after this, to be reintroduced at the Norman Conquest. Herbert FitzHerbert was treasurer to Henry I (1068–1135).

Herbert Farjeon (1887–1945), the English writer and playwright, wrote *Nine Sharp* and the delightfully named *An Elephant in Arcady*, among others.

HERMAN

From the Old High German, meaning 'soldier'. This is another of the names introduced into England by the Normans. The American writer, Herman Melville (1819–1891) wrote *Moby Dick: or, The Whale*, as well as dwelling with cannibals and becoming involved in a mutiny!

HERMES

In Greek mythology, the messenger of the gods. He also invented the lyre and guided souls to Hades.

(And it is the name of a potato developed especially for use in the making of crisps!)

HERON

A surname, now used as a modern first name. John Heron was the treasurer to Henry VII in 1505.

'*Ardua petit ardea*' or 'The heron seeks high places' is the appropriate motto used by the Heron baronets.

HORACE
From the Latin, meaning 'time'. The name of an ancient Roman family and a renowned lyric poet, it was first used in England during the sixteenth century.

Horace Walpole (1717–1797), son of the first British Prime Minister, is famous for his prolific letters which proved an unrivalled view of the eighteenth century. He also wrote the earliest Gothic novel, *The Castle of Otranto* (1764).

HOWARD
An aristocratic surname, most notably of the Duke of Norfolk, Earl Marshal of England, used as a first name from Victorian times.

John Howard (1726–1790) became famous for his efforts to secure prison reforms; he died in Russia, having gone there to investigate conditions in the Russian army. The Howard League for Penal Reform is named after him.

HUBERT
From the Old German, meaning 'bright heart'. St Hubert (656–727), Bishop of Liège and patron of huntsmen, made the name popular in the Middle Ages. It was revived by the Victorians.

Hubert Lane was the perpetual enemy of the hero of the many *William* books for children, written by Richmal Crompton.

HUDSON
A surname, meaning 'son of Hudd' or 'Hugh', now used as a first name. Henry Hudson (d. 1611), an English explorer, made four voyages in search of the North-East and North-West Passages. Hudson Bay, Hudson Strait and the Hudson River are named after him. On his last voyage, he was set adrift by mutineers and never seen again.

HUGH (Hew, Hughie, Huw)
From the Old German, meaning 'bright spirit'. There are several saints bearing this name. St Hugh of Lincoln (c.1135–1200) was a Carthusian monk, later a bishop. He is famous for having a pet swan and being responsible for the rebuilding of Lincoln Cathedral.

Huw and Hew are Welsh variants of the name.

HUGO
The Latin form of Hugh, revived by the Victorians. It is mentioned in the Domesday Book.

HUMPHREY
From the Old German, meaning 'peaceful giant'. The name was introduced by the Normans. Humphrey, Duke of Gloucester (1391–1447) was the youngest son of Henry IV and brother of Henry V, with whom he fought at Agincourt. He was a great patron of literature.

The American actor Humphrey Bogart (1899–1957) played the private detective Sam Spade in the classic film *The Maltese Falcon*.

HUNTER
An occupational surname, now used as a first name. The anatomist and surgeon John Hunter (1728–1793) gathered a large anatomical and pathological collection, now the core of the Hunterian Museum of the Royal College of Surgeons. Hunter is buried in Westminster Abbey. (And his bust stands in the south-east corner of Leicester Square.)

IAN (Iain)
The Scottish form of John, q.v. The writer Ian Fleming (1908–1964) created James Bond, a secret agent for British intelligence.

INIGO
A Spanish version of the name Ignatius, regularly used in Great Britain. The English architect Inigo Jones (1573–1652) was responsible for introducing the proscenium arch to the theatre

and designed the Banqueting Hall in Whitehall and the Queen's House at Greenwich, among others.

IRA

Three Old Testament characters bear this name. Ira, son of Ikkesh, was distinguished for his bravery. He was one of twelve commanders in King David's army.

The Puritans of the seventeenth century began its use in England.

ISAAC (Izaak)

From the Hebrew, meaning 'God be kind'. The Old Testament Isaac was the son of Abraham and Sarah, born when his father was 100 years old.

Mentioned in the Domesday Book, it became generally popular after the Reformation.

Sir Isaac Newton (1642–1727), mathematician and discoverer of the law of gravity, whose magnificent tomb can be seen in Westminster Abbey, is the most famous bearer of the name.

Fishermen will never forget the writer and ironmonger Izaak Walton (1593–1683), best known for his book *The Compleat Angler* which is still in print today.

ISIDORE (Izzy)

From the Greek, meaning 'gift of Isis'. St Isidore of Seville (560–636), bishop, wrote an encyclopedia of the knowledge of his time. He was declared a doctor of the church in 1722. Dante includes him in the *Paradise* of his *Divine Comedy*.

Izzy is becoming increasingly popular as an independent name.

IVAN

The Russian form of John, used steadily in Great Britain since the late nineteenth century. Ivan III (1440–1505) was the first Russian ruler to use the title of Tsar (Caesar).

IVANHOE

A literary name, derived from the most enthralling of Sir Walter Scott's novels, *Ivanhoe* (1819).

Wilfred, Knight of Ivanhoe, son of Cedric the Saxon, finally marries Rowena. This happens after adventures involving Richard the Lionheart, Robin Hood, fair ladies, tournaments and castles aflame. A rattling good yarn!

IVO (Ives)
From the German, meaning 'yew wood'. A popular name in
Normandy, it was brought to England at the Norman Conquest.
An Englishwoman, sister of Edwin, Earl of Mercia and Morcar,
Earl of Northumbria, married an Ivo Taillebois shortly after-
wards.

IVOR (Ifor)
From the Welsh, meaning 'lord'. (David) Ivor Novello (1893–
1951), the composer and actor-manager, was a well-known
bearer of the name.

JABEZ
An Old Testament reference, 1 Chronicles 4: 9 – 'His mother
called him Jabez, saying "Because I bore him in pain" ' –
explains the use of this from the seventeenth century onwards,
when Puritans rejected non-Biblical names.

JACK
A popular diminutive of John; the name of many heroes in tales
and songs for children, including *Jack the Giant-Killer* and *Jack
and Jill* (which demonstrate its age).

JACOB (Jake)
From the Hebrew, meaning 'supplanter'. In the Bible, Jacob was
twin brother to Esau and the son of Isaac and Rebecca. He had
twelve sons, who became the fathers of the twelve tribes of
Israel.

Always a favourite in the Jewish community, it attained general popularity at the Reformation.

Jacob Flanders was the hero of the first memorable novel by Virginia Woolf, entitled *Jacob's Room* (1922).

JADON (Jayden)
From the Hebrew, meaning 'he will judge'. The Old Testament Jadon helped to rebuild the walls of Jerusalem at the time of Nehemiah, in the fifth century BC.

JAGO
The Cornish version of James, q.v., now popular all over Britain.

JAMES (Jamie, Jemmy, Jim, Jimmy)
The English form of Jacob. The apostle, St James the Great, son of Zebedee, was one of the most popular saints of the Middle Ages. His shrine at Compostella in Spain had its first pilgrimage from England in 1148.

James VI of Scotland (1566–1625) became James I of England in 1603 and the name has remained popular ever since. The English explorer Captain James Cook (1728–1779) discovered New Caledonia and the Sandwich Islands, now known as Hawaii. He was murdered there by the natives, after an altercation over a stolen boat.

JARED
From the Hebrew, meaning 'descent'. The Old Testament Jared is the father of Enoch and the grandfather of Methuselah. The name was revitalised by Puritans in the seventeenth century.

JARROLD
An old surname, derived from Gerald (q.v.), now used as a first name.

JARVIS (Jervis)
A surname derived from Gervase, now used as a first name. Mr Jarvis Lorry, clerk at Tellson's Bank in London, is a character in *A Tale of Two Cities* by Charles Dickens. He helps Lucy Manette and Charles Darnay to escape from France during the French Revolution.

JASON
The English version of Joshua (q.v.). In Greek mythology, Jason
led his band of Argonauts in the quest for the Golden Fleece.
There are two men of this name mentioned in the New Testament: the first sheltered St Paul and his followers in his home at
Thessalonica, suffering persecution for this. It seems to have
been used as a first name in Britain since the seventeenth
century.

JASPER
The English form of the name Casper (q.v.). One of Mrs Jarley's
waxwork exhibits in *The Old Curiosity Shop* by Charles Dickens
(1812–1870) is Jasper Packlemerton 'of atrocious memory, who
courted and married fourteen wives, and destroyed them all by
tickling the soles of their feet when they was sleeping in the
consciousness of innocence and virtue'. (Unforgettable!)

JAY
Now an independent name, originally used as a pet-form for
names beginning with the letter 'J'.

JEAVON
A surname, from the Latin meaning 'young man', now used as a
first name.

JED
From the Hebrew, meaning 'beloved of the Lord'. The shortened form of Jedidiah; bestowed on King Solomon as an
additional name by the prophet Nathan. It was used by seventeenth century Puritans and taken by them to America.

JEFFERY (Jeffrey)
A variant spelling of Geoffrey (q.v.).

JEREMY (Jerry)
The English version of Jeremiah, the great Hebrew prophet,
used in England from the thirteenth century.
   The English philosopher Jeremy Bentham (1748–1832) is now
best known for bequeathing his body to University College,
London, where it is preserved in a cupboard, sitting fully clothed
on a chair.

JEROME

From the Greek, meaning 'sacred name'. St Jerome (c.342–420) was a rarity among saints in being known for his bad temper. The greatest of Biblical scholars, he was responsible for translating the Bible into Latin from its original tongue. His popularity was great in the Middle Ages.

Jerome Klapka Jerome (1859–1927) wrote the incomparable *Three Men in a Boat* (1889).

JESSE

From the Hebrew, meaning 'the Lord is'. The Old Testament Jesse lived in Bethlehem, the father of eight sons, of whom the future King David was the youngest.

Jesse James (1847–1882), American outlaw, committed daring railroad and bank robberies in the Mid-West during the 1870s. Robert Ford, a member of the James gang, shot Jesse in the back to claim the large reward for his capture.

JET

A modern name. Jet is a hard, black material derived from fossilised wood. Polished and carved for jewellery and decorative objects, it has been used since the Bronze Age. Whitby in North Yorkshire was the most important centre of production in the nineteenth century.

JETHRO

From the Hebrew, meaning 'excellence'. In the Old Testament, Jethro was a father-in-law to Moses. It came into use as a baptismal name in England after the Reformation.

Jethro Tull (1674–1741), the agriculturalist, invented the seed drill, among other things.

JOACHIM

From the Hebrew, meaning 'may Jehovah exult'. Legend gives this name to the father of the Virgin Mary. It has been used in England since the thirteenth century.

JOB

From the Hebrew, meaning 'persecuted'. In the Old Testament, he endured great suffering with exemplary patience. His story was a favourite of the medieval miracle plays. *Job* is the title of a masque composed by Ralph Vaughan Williams.

JOCELYN (Joss)

Another of the names brought to England in the eleventh century by the Normans, and mentioned in the Domesday Book. Originally a masculine name only, it is now bestowed on both boys and girls.

Joscelin of Furness, an English Cistercian monk of the twelfth century, wrote several 'Lives' of the saints, including *The Life and Miracles of St Patrick.*

Jocelyn is the title of a novel by John Galsworthy (1898).

JOEL

From the Hebrew, meaning 'the Lord is God'. The Bible contains fourteen men with this name: the most famous of these was a prophet whose Book of Joel was written c.500 BC. The name has been used in Britain since the sixteenth century.

The American Joel Chandler Harris (1848–1908) wrote *Uncle Remus: His Sons and Sayings,* introducing us to Brer Rabbit.

JOHN (Ivan, Jack, Johnny, Jon)

From the Hebrew, meaning 'God is merciful'. The name of many saints and twenty-five popes, this has been one of the most popular names in Western Europe since the twelfth century. Both St John the Baptist and St John the Divine, writer of the fourth gospel, have two feast days each in the church calendar.

The unpopular King John (1167–1216) was forced by the barons to sign the Magna Carta at Runnymede on 15th June 1215, outlining royal powers and the rights of free men.

The first English novel, *Euphues: the Anatomy of Wit,* was written by John Lyly in 1578.

The Scottish writer and physician to Queen Anne, John Arbuthnot (1667–1735), wrote *The History of John Bull;* a name which personifies the 'typical' Englishman.

JOLYON

A medieval version of the name Julian (q.v.), made popular by the hero of *The Forsyte Saga,* written by John Galsworthy (1867–1933), and later televised.

JONAH (Jonas)

From the Hebrew, meaning 'dove'. The Old Testament Jonah had been told by God to preach repentance in the wicked city of

Nineveh. He refused and boarded a ship going in the opposite direction. When storms arose, the sailors threw Jonah into the sea to avert catastrophe.

Being swallowed by a whale, he lived in its belly for three days until deposited on dry land. Wisely, he then went to Nineveh and caused the city to repent. The story was very popular in the Middle Ages.

Jonas is the Greek version of the name. St Jonas was martyred in Iran in 327.

JONATHAN (Johnny, Jon)
From the Hebrew, meaning 'God's gift'. The Biblical Jonathan is best remembered as a friend to King David. It has been used in Britain since the thirteenth century.

The clergyman Jonathan Swift (1667–1745), satirist and political writer, is best remembered for his novel *Gulliver's Travels*.

JORDAN
The name of the principal river in Israel, where Christ was baptised by John the Baptist. Twelfth century Crusaders brought back a flask of Jordan water to be used in the baptism of their children and bestowed the name on both boys and girls, as now.

JOREN
A Dutch version of George (q.v.), now generally used.

JOSEPH (Joe, Joey)
From the Hebrew, meaning 'may Jehovah add'. The Old Testament Joseph was the favourite son of Jacob and famed for his 'coat of many colours', before being sold into slavery in Egypt by his jealous brothers. The most renowned Joseph in the New Testament was husband to the Virgin Mary.

And heartfelt thanks to Joseph Lister (1827–1912), the founder of antiseptic surgery; and to the civil engineer Sir Joseph Bazalgette (1819–1891), who designed London's main drainage system.

JOSHUA (Josh)
From the Hebrew, meaning 'Jehovah saves'. The Biblical Joshua led the Israelites into the Promised Land after the death of Moses. It came into general use after the Reformation.

Sir Joshua Reynolds (1723–1792), the English portrait painter, was a founding member of the Royal Academy and its first president.

JOSIAH
From the Hebrew, meaning 'God heals'. The Old Testament Josiah (c.639–609 BC), King of Judah, came to the throne at the age of 8 and was killed at Megiddo, fighting the Egyptians. The name came into use after the Reformation.

Josiah Wedgwood (1730–1795), the founder of the pottery company, is the most well-known bearer of the name.

JUBAL
From the Hebrew, meaning 'sound'. The Old Testament son of Lamech and Adah, and a descendant of Cain, Jubal was the first musician. He is said to have invented wind and string instruments.

JUDE
From the Hebrew, meaning 'praise'. St Jude the apostle, writer of an Epistle in the New Testament, reputedly preached and was martyred in Persia. He is invoked as an intercessor for those in desperate situations.

The miserable Jude Fawley is the hero of Thomas Hardy's tragic novel, *Jude the Obscure* (1895). It is not a book to raise the spirits!

JULIAN
Derived from Julius, the name of an ancient Roman family, the most famous member of which was Julius Caesar (100–44 BC).

There are many saints named after Julian: St Julian the Hospitaller is the patron of ferrymen and innkeepers. The name has been used in England since the thirteenth century.

JULIUS
The name of an ancient Roman family, now increasingly popular as a first name in the twenty-first century.

Giuliano della Rovere became Pope Julius II in 1503, aged 60. (Age did not deter him from leading the papal army.) Julius founded the Vatican Museum, began the construction of St Peter's Basilica, and employed the artists Raphael and Michelangelo. He died in 1513.

JUSTIN
From the Latin, meaning 'just'. A name popular among the early Christians in Rome. St Justin (100–165) was beheaded for refusing to sacrifice to idols. His *Dialogues* and *Apologies* survived and have been translated into English.

KAI
A Welsh name, derived from Caius, increasingly popular. In the Welsh story, *Kulhwch and Olwen* (1100), Sir Kai (or Kay) is a great hero. No physician can heal a wound inflicted by his sword. Arthurian legend makes him King Arthur's steward.

KANE
A French place name, meaning 'field of combat' and surname, now used as a first name.

KARL
Karl is the popular German version of Charles, q.v.

KEIR
From the Gaelic, meaning 'swarthy'. A surname, now used as a first name. (James) Keir Hardie (1856–1915), who did not go to school and began work in the coalmines at the age of 10, is renowned as the first Labour Member of Parliament.

KEITH
From the Gaelic, meaning 'forest'. A Scottish place name and surname, used as a first name all over Britain from the late nineteenth century.

KELLY
See the entry in the girls' section.

KELSEY (Kelcey)
An English place name and surname, used as a first name since the 1870s.

KELVIN
The name of a Scottish river, used as a first name since the 1920s. The physicist Lord Kelvin (1824–1907) is a notable bearer of the name.

And, remembering your science lessons, absolute zero stands at 273 Kelvin.

KEMP
A surname, meaning 'athlete', now used as a first name. An actor in Shakespeare's company, William Kemp is famous for morris-dancing from London to Norwich. He published a booklet to commemorate this, *Kemps nine daies wonder* (1600).

KENDALL
A place name, meaning 'valley of the River Kent', and surname. It has been used as a first name from mid-Victorian times.

KENDRICK
A surname, meaning 'chief man', now used as a first name.

KENNETH (Ken, Kenny)
From the Gaelic, meaning 'handsome'. A Scottish royal name, it has been used all over Britain since the late nineteenth century.

Kenneth I MacAlpin was the first King of Scotland, and invaded England six times. Kenneth Grahame (1859–1932), Governor of the Bank of England, is more famous for writing *The Wind in the Willows*.

KENTON
A place name, meaning 'royal manor', and surname. It is now given as a first name.

KERR
A place name, meaning 'marsh', and surname, now used as a first name.

Kerr is the surname of the Marquesses of Lothian.

KESTER
An abbreviation of Christopher, popular in the seventeenth century and now enjoying a revival.

KEVIN
From the Irish, meaning 'handsome at birth'. St Kevin (d. 618) was the founder of the monastery at Glendalough, County Wicklow. Always a popular name in Ireland, it became generally used in the 1920s.

KIAN
A popular modern name which may derive from Cian, meaning 'ancient' in Gaelic.

KIERAN (Kieron)
From the Irish, meaning 'dark-haired'. Over twenty Irish saints have borne this name. St Kieran of Clonmacnois (516–549) was once dismissed from a monastery for too great a generosity to the poor. There was nothing left for the monks to eat. This name has been generally popular since the 1950s.

KILLIAN (Kilian)
From the Gaelic, meaning 'warlike'. St Kilian was an Irish monk, sent to preach the gospel in Bavaria. He and two companions were beheaded in 689. His feastday is celebrated on July 8th.

KIMBALL
This is derived from a pre-Conquest personal name, later a surname. It is once again used as a first name.

The hero of Rudyard Kipling's novel *Kim* (1901) is an orphaned Irish boy, Kimball O'Hara. He roams India with a Tibetan lama, his geographical knowledge making Kimball a valuable asset to the English Secret Service.

KINGSLEY
An Old English place name, meaning 'king's wood', and surname, now used as a first name. The novelist Charles Kingsley (1819–1875) wrote *Westward Ho!* and *The Water Babies*. Kingsley Amis (1922–1995) wrote, among other novels, the very funny *Lucky Jim*, which has been filmed and televised.

KIPPS (Kippy)
A surname, now used as a first name. *Kipps* (1905), the novel by
H. G. Wells, must always spring to mind. Suddenly acquiring
wealth, the humble draper's apprentice Arthur Kipps finds it
difficult to fit into his new world. All ends happily when he
marries the housemaid and returns to a simple life.

And Kipp's apparatus is used in the laboratory for generating
gas. This was invented by a German chemist of the same name.

KIRK
From the Old Norse, meaning 'church'. A place name and
surname, now used as a first name. Sir John Kirk (1832–1922),
the Scottish administrator and naturalist, distinguished himself
by helping to abolish slavery in Zanzibar (now Tanzania) and
was one of the first white men to see Lake Nyasa.

KIT
A pet form of Christopher (q.v.), used independently and
increasingly popular.

Kit Marlowe (1564–1593), dramatist and poet, wrote *The
Tragical History of Dr Faustus* and *Tamburlaine*, among others.
He was killed in a quarrel over the payment of a tavern bill.

KJELL (Chell)
From the Old Norse, meaning 'sacrificial cauldron', now generally used.

KOBE (Kobi)
From the Japanese city, now bestowed as a first name. Situated
in the region of Western Honshu, the port of Kobe has been
trading since the eighth century. And Kobe beef is the world's
most expensive meat!

KOLYA
A Russian pet form of Nicholas (q.v.), now generally used.

KURT (Curt)
A German name, derived from Conrad, used in Britain since the
late twentieth century.

Kurt Weill (1900–1950), the German composer, is well known.
The Nazi regime condemned his works as decadent, so Weill left
his country in 1933 and went to America.

KYD (Kidd)
A surname derived from Christopher, now a modern first name. Thomas Kyd (1557–1594) was the author of the most popular drama of his time, the extremely violent revenge-play *The Spanish Tragedy*.

KYLE
From the Gaelic, meaning 'channel between islands'. A place name and a surname, now used as a first name for both boys and girls.

The Kyles of Bute, very narrow straits between the Scottish coast and the island of Bute, are noted for their beautiful surroundings.

LACHLAN
From the Gaelic, meaning 'warlike'.

LAMBERT
From the Old German, meaning 'shining land'. St Lambert of Maastricht (635–705) was martyred at Liège. Many churches, especially in Belgium, are dedicated to him. He was greatly revered in medieval England.

Henry VII (d. 1509) punished Lambert Simnel, who claimed to be the *true* king of England, in an unusual fashion. He put him to work in the royal kitchens, turning the spit!

LANCE
A diminutive of Lancelot, the hero of Arthurian legend, whose affair with Queen Guinevere brought disaster.

Lance has been used as a first name in England since the thirteenth century.

LAURENCE (Laurie, Lawrence)
From the Greek, meaning 'laurel'. This was a popular name among the early Christians and the name of a saint much revered in the Middle Ages. St Laurence (d. 258) was martyred in Rome by being roasted on a gridiron. The Saxon church of St Laurence in Bradford-upon-Avon, Wiltshire, dates from 700 and is the most complete example to survive.

The actor Laurence Olivier (Lord Olivier) was the best-known bearer of the name in modern times.

LEANDER
A name now bestowed on both boys and girls. In Greek legend, Leander of Abydos nightly swam the Hellespont to meet his beloved, Hero. She was a priestess of Sestos. When Leander drowned, she threw herself into the sea.

LEE
From the Old English, meaning 'field' or 'pasture'. A place name and surname, now used as a first name.

LEIGHTON
From the Old English, meaning 'herb garden'. A place name and surname, used as a first name since the late 1800s.

The British painter and sculptor Frederic Leighton (1830–1896) is the only English painter to be raised to the peerage: unfortunately, this happened only days before his death. His home in Holland Park Road, London is open to the public as the Leighton House Museum.

LEO (Leon)
From the Latin, meaning 'lion'. The name of thirteen popes, of which five are saints. St Leo I (390–461), known as 'the Great', induced Attila the Hun and his army to withdraw beyond the River Danube, after confronting them in person.

Leo is a northern constellation of stars (as in Leo Minor) and the fifth sign of the zodiac. The name has been used in England since the thirteenth century. Leon is the Greek version.

LEONARD (Len, Lenny)

From the Old German, meaning 'bold as a lion'. St Leonard was a French hermit in the sixth century. Many miracles were attributed to him and he became very popular during the Middle Ages in France and England. Crusaders revered him as the patron saint of prisoners.

Leonardo da Vinci (1452–1519), artist and sculptor, also designed a flying-machine and parachute, a fore-runner of the tank, and nearly discovered the circulation of blood!

LEOPOLD (Leo)

From the German, meaning 'people bold'. The name became popular in Britain in the nineteenth century. Leopold, the King of the Belgians, was Queen Victoria's favourite uncle: she named her fourth son in his honour.

LEROY

From the French, meaning 'the king'. A surname originally bestowed on servants of a king, it has been used in Britain as a first name since the beginning of the twentieth century.

The French horologist Pierre Le Roy (1717–1785) did much work on the chronometer and made many fine clocks and watches.

LESLIE

A Scottish place name (in Aberdeenshire) and a surname, used as a first name since the end of the nineteenth century. It is the surname of the Earls of Rothes.

LESTER

A contraction of Leicester (the English place name) and a surname, now used as a first name.

Whether or not you follow the sport of kings, the jockey Lester Piggott is the best-known bearer of this name.

LEVI

From the Hebrew, meaning 'joined'. This name is now bestowed on both boys and girls.

The Old Testament Levi, third son of Jacob and his wife Leah, had three sons from whom the priestly caste of Levites are descended.

LEWIS
See the entry under Louis.

LIAM
The Irish form of William, now generally popular.

LINCOLN
A place name, meaning 'colony at the pool', and surname. It has been used as a first name since the nineteenth century.

   The city of Lincoln was founded long before Julius Caesar visited our shores. And Lincoln Cathedral possesses the Lincoln Imp, hidden away in the Angel Choir, now on his best behaviour! (The second corbal from the east on the north side, should you wish to find him.)

LINDSAY
A place name and surname, now given as a first name to both boys and girls. It is the surname of the Earls of Crawford, whose motto – *'Astra castra, numen lumen munimen'* – translates as 'The stars my camp, God my light and protection'.

LINUS
From the Greek, meaning 'flax'. St Linus, who is venerated as a martyr, succeeded St Peter as the second pope. He reigned from AD 67 to 76.

LIONEL
From the Greek, meaning 'little lion'. Edward III (reigned 1327–1377) named his third son Lionel in honour of the gallant Sir Lionel, one of King Arthur's legendary knights of the Round Table. The name was very popular in the Middle Ages. The composer Lionel Bart wrote the musical *Oliver*.

LLEWELLYN (Llewelyn)
From the Welsh, meaning 'leader' or 'lion'. Llywelyn ap Gruffydd, or Llewelyn the Last, died in 1282 fighting Edward I of England, and Welsh independence was lost.

LLOYD
From the Welsh, meaning 'grey'. A Welsh surname and first name, now used all over Britain. David Lloyd George (1863–1945) was Prime Minister 1916–1922.

LOCKHART
From the Old English, meaning 'herder of sheep'. A surname, now used as a first name.

John Gibson Lockhart (1794–1854) wrote the definitive seven-volume biography of his father-in-law, the writer Sir Walter Scott.

LOGAN
From the Gaelic, meaning 'small hollow'. A Scottish place name and surname, now used as a first name. Mount Logan is the highest mountain in Canada.

LORIMER
An occupational surname, meaning 'spurrier' or 'bit-maker', now used as a first name.

The Loriners' Guild was first mentioned in 1261, the name derived from the Latin *lorum*, meaning 'bridle thong'. The company colours are blue and white, and the Guild ranks as number 57 in the order of precedence.

LOUIS (Lew, Lewis, Lou, Louie)
From the Old German, meaning 'renowned warrior'. The name of eighteen French kings (the first of whom, Louis the Fair (778–840), was the son of Charlemagne), it was brought to England at the Norman Conquest. Lewis is the anglicised version of the name, used since the thirteenth century.

The French-born sculptor Louis Roubiliac (1702?–1762) spent all his working life in England. He is most famous for funeral monuments erected in Westminster Abbey.

LUCA
The Italian form of Luke, recently becoming popular in Britain.

LUCAS
A surname, and Latin form of Luke (q.v.), used in Britain as a first name since the mid-twentieth century.

The sailor Charles Lucas was the very first man to win the Victoria Cross, on 21st June 1854, during the Crimean War.

A live Russian bomb landed on the deck of HMS *Hecla*. Mate Lucas, although the fuse was still burning, carried it to the side and threw it overboard, where it immediately exploded. Lucas rose to the rank of rear-admiral. His Victoria Cross can be seen at the National Maritime Museum, Greenwich.

LUCIAN
From the Latin, meaning 'light'. Two early Christian martyrs bore this name. The Greek writer Lucian (AD 125–180) is best remembered for his entertaining satirical dialogues.

LUDOVIC
The Latin version of Louis, q.v.

LUKE
From the Greek, meaning 'coming from Lucania', a place in southern Italy. St Luke was the author of the third gospel and the Acts of the Apostles. A Greek physician from Antioch, he was a constant companion to St Paul. The name was brought to England at the Norman Conquest.

LUTHER
A name bestowed in honour of Martin Luther (1483–1546), leader of the Protestant Reformation in Germany. He translated the Bible into German and composed many popular hymns.

Martin Luther King (1929–1968), the campaigner for racial equality in America, is well known.

LYNDON
From the Old English, meaning 'lime-tree hill'. A place name and surname, now used as a first name.

LYNTON (Linton)
From the Old English, meaning 'place on the torrent'. A place name and surname, now used as a first name.

LYSANDER
A venerable name, from the Greek, meaning 'free'. The Spartan naval commander Lysander (d. 395 BC) defeated the Athenians in 405 BC, ending the Peloponnesian War.

And in Shakespeare's *A Midsummer Night's Dream*, Lysander escapes to the woods with Hermia to prevent her marrying Demetrius.

MACKENZIE

A Scottish clan name and surname, now given as a first name. It is the surname of the Earls of Cromartie.

And Kenneth Mackenzie, Earl of Seaforth, raised that illustrious fighting force, the Seaforth Highlanders, in 1778.

MAGEN

From the Hebrew, meaning 'protector'.

MAGNUS

From the Latin, meaning 'great'. A royal name in Norway and Denmark: Magnus VI, King of Norway sold the Isle of Man to Scotland in 1266. A popular first name in Scotland, it is now used all over Britain.

MALACHY (Malachi)

From the Hebrew, meaning 'my messenger'. The Book of Malachi is the last of the prophetical books in the Old Testament.

St Malachy (1094–1148), bishop, founded the first Cistercian monastery in Ireland, at Mellifont. His friend, St Bernard of Clairvaux, said, 'There was nothing in his behaviour that could offend *anyone*.'

MALCOLM

From the Gaelic, meaning 'disciple of Columb'. There have been four Scottish kings with this name: Malcolm IV (1141–1165) was the last Gaelic-speaking monarch. Sir Malcolm Sargent (1895–1967) was the chief conductor at the Promenade concerts at the Royal Albert Hall from 1948 until his death.

MARCUS
The Latin form of Mark (q.v.), which came into use in Britain in the nineteenth century.

The Roman Emperor Marcus Aurelius (AD 121–180) wrote his famous *Meditations* in Greek as he rested between battles.

MARK (Marc)
Derived from the name of Mars, the Roman god of war. The Biblical St Mark was the writer of the second gospel. A martyr, his body was enshrined in the original church of San Marco in Venice.

In Arthurian legend, Mark was the King of Cornwall. The name was popular throughout the Middle Ages.

MARLEY
From the Old English, meaning 'pleasant wood'. A place name and surname, now used as a first name.

The reggae musician Bob Marley (1945–1981) made his surname a popular choice for music-loving parents.

MARMADUKE
A name of uncertain origin, perhaps meaning 'servant of Madoc'. It has been used in England since the sixteenth century.

MARSHALL
An occupational surname, given to one who looked after horses, now used as a first name.

The Duke of Norfolk, hereditary Earl Marshal of England, is still responsible for the ceremonial at royal coronations and funerals. It is the only one of the medieval Great Offices of State still functioning.

MARTIN (Martyn)
From the Latin, meaning 'belonging to Mars'. St Martin of Tours (c.315–397) was one of the first holy men not martyred to be venerated as a saint. The story of his dividing his cloak with a beggar was a favourite subject with medieval artists and many churches are dedicated to him.

MASON
An old occupational surname, now used as a first name. The Mason-Dixon Line, the boundary line popularly used to distinguish the northern from the southern states of America, is

named after two British astronomers. Charles Mason and Jeremiah Dixon surveyed it between 1763 and 1767 to put an end to land disputes.

MATTHEW (Matt)
From the Hebrew, meaning 'gift of the Lord'. In the New Testament, St Matthew was the writer of the first gospel. He was a tax-collector until called to be an apostle. The name was brought to England at the Norman Conquest.

MATTHIAS
The Latin form of Matthew, q.v. In the New Testament, the name of the disciple chosen to replace Judas Iscariot.

MAURICE (Morris)
From the Latin, meaning 'a Moor' or 'dark skinned'. St Maurice was a member of a Roman legion serving in Gaul in the third century, all of whom were martyred for refusing to take part in heathen sacrifices. The name was brought to England at the time of the Norman Conquest.

MAXIMILIAN (Max, Maxim)
From the Latin, meaning 'greatest'. A European royal name, popular in Germany, now used worldwide. The Viennese born Maximilian, Emperor of Mexico (1832–1867) caused a civil war and was executed by firing squad.

Maxim de Winter is the romantic hero of *Rebecca* (1938), the novel written by Daphne du Maurier.

MAXWELL
A Scottish place name, meaning 'Magnus's stream', and surname, now used as a first name.

MELVILLE
A French place name and surname, used as a first name from the late nineteenth century.

Melville Island is situated off the coast of Northern Australia.

MELVIN (Melvyn)
A modern name, possibly derived from Melville.

MERLIN
From the Welsh, a contraction of Carmarthen, meaning 'sea-hill fort'. A great figure of Arthurian Legend, Merlin had charge of

the infant Arthur and ensured his future greatness as a king. A seer and magician, he transported Stonehenge from Ireland to Salisbury Plain in one night. Nothing now remains of him but his voice, thanks to the enchantment of the Lady of the Lake.

MERVYN (Mervin)
The English form of Merlin, q.v.

MICHAEL (Mick, Micky, Mike)
From the Hebrew, meaning 'Who is like God?' The Bible speaks of the Archangel Michael as leader of the heavenly hosts. Tradition states that he drove the rebel angels from heaven: St Michael and all Angels is the most popular church dedication in Britain. The name has been a favourite since the twelfth century.

Michael Faraday (1791–1867), a blacksmith's son, became a famous chemist and a pioneer in the science of electricity.

MILES (Milo)
From the Old German, meaning 'merciful'. The name was brought to England by the Normans and became popular. It was revived by the Victorians.

Miles is a character in the famous Coventry Mystery Plays of the fifteenth century.

MILTON
An Old English place name, meaning 'mill farm', and surname, used as a first name from the nineteenth century.

The poet and writer John Milton (1608–1674) is famous for the epic poem *Paradise Lost* (1667) and for *Samson Agonistes*. Latin secretary to Oliver Cromwell, the strain of the work caused him to lose his sight.

MITCHELL (Mitch)
A surname derived from the medieval French version of Michael, now used as a first name. Reginald Mitchell (1895–1937), a leading designer in the history of aviation, was responsible for the Spitfire.

MOHAMMED (Muhammad)
From the Arabic, meaning 'the praised one'. The prophet (570–632), founder of Islam, was a rich merchant of Mecca. A vision in the cave of Mount Hera told him to teach the true religion.

MONTAGUE (Monty)

A French place name, meaning 'pointed hill', and surname, now used as a first name. Drogo de Montaigu accompanied William the Conqueror to England.

Montague Rhodes James (1862–1936), Provost of Eton, was the writer of the finest ghost stories in English literature, notably *Casting the Runes* and *The Tractate Middoth*.

MONTGOMERY (Montgomerie)

This was brought to England at the Norman Conquest, the name of a Norman baron. It has been used as a first name since the late nineteenth century.

Field Marshal Montgomery of Alamein (1887–1976) made the name well known. Montgomerie is the surname of the earls Eglinton.

MORDRED

In Arthurian legend, the nephew of King Arthur, and the treacherous knight of the Round Table. He is finally slain by his uncle, but deals Arthur his death blow as they fight.

The poet Dante names him as a traitor in his *Divine Comedy*.

MORGAN

From the Welsh, meaning 'sea-bright'. A surname, now used as a first name for both boys and girls.

MORLEY

A place name, meaning 'moor clearing', and surname. Now used as a first name.

Henry Morley (1822–1894), Professor of Literature at University College, produced a massive ten-volume history, entitled *English Writers*. This reaches only to the death of Shakespeare!

MORTIMER

A French place name and surname, now used as a first name. The archaeologist Sir Mortimer Wheeler, who fought long and hard to establish archaeology as an academic subject in the University of London, is the best-known bearer of the name.

MORTON

An Old English place name, meaning 'farm on the fen', and surname, used as a first name since the mid-nineteenth century.

MOSS

A place name, meaning 'swamp', and a surname, now a very modern first name.

Moss is fascinating. It has fine stalks, on which are little capsules. These release spores as a fine dust which flies through the air. The dust finds a home in tiny cracks and grows into *more* moss. Sphagnum moss, suitably sterilised, is still used to dress wounds.

MOSTYN

A Welsh place name, meaning 'field of the fortress', and surname. Now given as a first name.

'*Heb Dhuw, heb ddim, Duw a dygon*', meaning 'Without God, without anything, God and enough', is the motto of the barons Mostyn, of Mostyn Hall, Mostyn, Flintshire.

MUNGO

This is the Celtic nickname, meaning 'most dear', for St Kentigern, founder of the church in Glasgow. The Scottish explorer Mungo Park (1771–1806) navigated the river Niger in West Africa, finally dying in the rapids at Bussa after great hardships.

MUNRO

A Scottish surname, now used as a first name.

MURDOCH (Murdo)

From the Gaelic, meaning 'sailor'. A surname, now used as a first name.

MURRAY (Moray)

A Scottish place name, meaning 'settlement beside the sea', and surname, now used as a first name. It is the surname of the Dukes of Atholl, the only family in Britain permitted to keep a private army.

MYRON

From the Greek, meaning 'myrrh'. The Greek sculptor Myron of Eleutherae is famous for his statue Discobolus or Discus-Thrower, made around 450 BC. Many copies of this exist.

NATHAN

From the Hebrew, meaning 'gift'. In the Old Testament, the prophet Nathan rebuked King David for sending Uriah to his death in battle so that David could marry his widow, Bathsheba.

The name came into general use in the seventeenth century when Puritan parents rejected non-Biblical names.

NATHANIEL (Nat)

From the Hebrew, meaning 'God has given'. In the New Testament, the personal name of the apostle Bartholomew (which means 'son of Talmai'), who tradition states was martyred by being flayed alive in Armenia. The name became common after the Reformation.

The Scarlet Letter is the best-known work of the American writer Nathaniel Hawthorne (1804–1864). He also wrote the delightful *Our Old Home* while American consul in Liverpool.

NAUGHTON

A place name, meaning 'new homestead', and surname, now used as a first name.

NED

A pet-form of Edward (q.v.). Common in the Middle Ages, it is now enjoying a revival.

NEIL (Neal, Niall)

From the Gaelic, meaning 'champion'. Well-known before the Norman Conquest, the name travelled from Ireland to Scandinavia and on to England.

In 1969 Neil Armstrong was the first man to step upon the moon.

NELSON
Originally a surname, meaning 'son of Neil' or 'Nell'. Its use as a first name was in honour of Admiral Lord Nelson (1758–1805), who defeated the French and Spanish at the Battle of Trafalgar and died in action. He was given a state funeral and lies buried in the crypt of St Paul's Cathedral in London.

NEVILLE (Nevil)
A French place name and aristocratic surname, used regularly as a first name from the mid-nineteenth century. Gilbert de Nevil came to England as a companion to William the Conqueror. (Arthur) Neville Chamberlain, Prime Minister of Great Britain 1937–1940, had the melancholy task of taking the country into the Second World War.

NEVIN
From the Gaelic, meaning 'servant of the saint'.

NICHOLAS (Nick, Nicky, Nicol, Nicolas)
From the Greek, meaning 'people's victory'. The patron saint of children, sailors, merchants and pawnbrokers; venerated in both East and West; St Nicholas, fourth century Bishop of Myra, is best known as the original 'Father Christmas', taken from the Dutch Sinte Claus. It has been a favourite name in England since the twelfth century. Nicol is the medieval version of the name.

Nicholas of Cusa (1401–1464), a German theologian, suggested that the earth rotated around the sun approximately fifty years before the theory was formulated by Copernicus.

NIGEL
The Latin version of Neil (q.v.), introduced to England by the Normans and mentioned in the Domesday Book. It was revived by the Victorians. Sir Nigel Loring is a heroic character in *The White Company* (1891), a historical romance by Sir Arthur Conan Doyle.

NILES (Nyles)
A variant of Nicholas (q.v.), now independently used.

NIMROD

The Old Testament Nimrod, great-grandson of Noah, was renowned as a mighty hunter and ruled over a large kingdom, now Iraq.

Edward Elgar's *Nimrod*, part of his *Enigma Variations*, was first performed in 1899.

NINIAN

St Ninian (d. 432) was a British bishop who evangelised the Picts in southern Scotland. He is included in the writings of the Venerable Bede.

Sir Ninian Comper (1864–1960), church architect, is responsible for many buildings. His masterpiece is agreed to be St Mary's, Wellingborough. He wished to be buried there, but a grateful nation sent him to Westminster Abbey.

NOAH

From the Hebrew, meaning 'long-lived'. The name of the Biblical hero who built the ark, at the behest of the Almighty, to ensure the survival of the patriarch, his family and two of each kind of animal at the time of the Great Flood. It was used by Puritans in the seventeenth century and taken to America by them.

Noah Claypole brings about the murder of Nancy by Bill Sikes in Charles Dickens' novel *Oliver Twist*.

NOËL

From the French, meaning 'Christmas'. Used as a baptismal name for both boys and girls born on Christmas Day during the Middle Ages, it has been a male name from the seventeenth century.

Noël Coward (1899–1973), writer, actor and playwright of such plays as *Blithe Spirit* and *Private Lives*, is a well-known bearer of the name.

NOLAN

An Irish surname, meaning 'descendant of a noble', now used as a first name.

NORBERT

From the Old German, meaning 'famous in the north'. St Norbert (1080–1134) was a German courtier who became a bishop and founder of the Premonstratensian Canons. The name has been used in Britain since the late nineteenth century, when there was great enthusiasm for medieval names.

NORMAN
From the Old English, meaning 'Northman'. The name was popular in England before the Norman Conquest and continued so until the 1300s. It was revived by the Victorians.

The British actor Norman Wisdom (b. 1915) and the fashion designer Norman Hartnell (1901–1979) are well-known bearers of the name.

NORRIS
From the Old French, meaning 'northerner'. A surname, now used as a first name.

OCTAVIUS
From the Latin, meaning 'eighth'. It was the name of an ancient Roman family.

Gaius Octavius (63 BC–AD 14), son of Gaius Octavius, was posthumously adopted by his great-uncle, Julius Caesar. In 31 BC he became the first Roman Emperor, using the name Caesar Augustus. The most talented administrator the world has known, he was also 'remarkably handsome, with yellow curly hair', according to Suetonius.

OLIVER
From the Old Norse, meaning 'ancestor'. Oliver is a close friend to the eponymous hero of *Song of Roland*, the popular medieval romance, in which both are knights of Charlemagne.

Oliver Cromwell (1599–1658), Puritan leader and Lord Protector of the Realm after the execution of Charles I, caused the name to fall into disfavour until the nineteenth century.

Oliver Twist, or The Parish Boy's Progress (1837), which tells of a boy who emerges unscathed from the criminal underworld to be happy ever after, remains one of the most popular of the novels of Charles Dickens.

ORLANDO

The Italian form of Roland (q.v.). The English composer Orlando Gibbons (1583–1625) was organist at Westminster Abbey. His church anthems, keyboard works and madrigals are still performed today.

OSBERT

From the Old English, meaning 'god-bright', one of the names surviving from pre-Conquest times.

The writer Sir Osbert Sitwell (1892–1969) is renowned for his autobiography in five volumes, *Left Hand, Right Hand!*

OSBORNE

From the Old English, meaning 'god bear', used as both surname and first name.

John Osborne, the playwright and 'angry young man', is remembered for his savage first play, *Look Back in Anger* (1956).

OSCAR

From the Old English, meaning 'god-spear'. James Macpherson (1736–1796) published poems purporting to have been composed by the mythical Gaelic bard Ossian, who had a son named Oscar. The popularity of this work revived the name.

Napoleon bestowed it on his godson, who went on to become Oscar I, King of Sweden and Norway.

Oscar Fingal O'Flahertie Wills Wilde (1854–1900), writer and playwright, penned the delightful *The Importance of Being Earnest*, now considered his masterpiece.

OSMOND

From the Old English, meaning 'God's protection'. This is the Norman version of a name used in England before the Norman Conquest.

St Osmond (d. 1099) came to England as Chancellor to William the Conqueror, later becoming a bishop. The name was revived in the late nineteenth century.

OSWALD

From the Old English, meaning 'divine power'. St Oswald I of Northumbria (605–641), who was the first Anglo-Saxon king to be canonised, and St Oswald, Archbishop of York, ensured the popularity of the name. It was revived by the Victorians.

Oswald Bastable is the hero of several classic books by the children's writer Edith Nesbit (1858–1924). If you have not already read these, you have a treat in store.

OTIS

From the Old German, meaning 'riches'. A surname derived from Otto, now used as a first name.

OTTO

From the Old German, meaning 'riches'. The nomadic tribe of Magyars was defeated by King Otto the Great of Germany in 955 and settled down to farm the land which we call Hungary. The name was introduced to England by the Normans and is mentioned in the Domesday Book. The name was revived in the mid-nineteenth century.

OTTOKAR

A German name, now increasingly bestowed in Britain. Ottokar, King of Bohemia, gained possession of what is now Austria in 1252, losing it to the Hapsburgs in 1278.

And *King Ottokar's Sceptre* is the title of one of the popular Tintin books, written by Hergé (real name Georges Remi).

OWEN (Owain)

A Welsh name, derived from Eugene, now in general use. Owen Glendower (1359–1416) was a Welsh chieftain who fought for Welsh independence from the English. He was defeated by the future Henry V in 1405.

OZZIE (Ozzy)

The pet-form of Oswald (q.v.), now used independently.

PASCAL
From the Old English, meaning 'Easter'. Given to boys born in the Easter season, this has been used as a baptismal name since the Middle Ages, particularly in Cornwall.

PASCOE
A medieval variant of Pascal, revived in the late nineteenth century.

PATRICK (Paddy, Pat)
From the Latin, meaning 'nobleman'. The patron saint of Ireland, St Patrick (c.385–461), whose original name was Succat, was taken as a slave to Ireland at the age of 16 from his home on the Severn Estuary. After six years he managed to escape, but was called in a dream to go back to Ireland as an evangelist. Thought of as an Irish name, it has been used in the north of England since the twelfth century and is now generally popular.

Patrick Macnee is well-known as John Steed, the male hero of the cult television series *The Avengers*, first shown in the 1960s.

PAUL
From the Latin, meaning 'small'. St Paul, Apostle to the Gentiles, converted to Christianity by a vision while on the road to Damascus and writer of fourteen Epistles included in the New Testament, made the name very popular among the early Christians. The name occurred in England before the Norman Conquest and has been used steadily since then.

PAVEL
The Czech and Russian version of Paul, now increasingly popular.

PAXTON
A surname, now given as a first name. Sir Joseph Paxton (1801–1865), gardener and architect, designed the Crystal Palace, erected in Hyde Park for the Great Exhibition of 1851. (The Exhibition was visited by over six million people, including an 84-year-old lady who walked all the way from Penzance.)

PEDRO
The Spanish version of Peter (q.v.), now generally used. Pedro II (1825–1891), Emperor of Brazil, alienated the land-owning class by abolishing slavery in 1888. The next year he was forced to abdicate.

PERCIVAL
This seems to have been invented by Chrétien de Troyes, a French poet of the twelfth century, for the hero of his epic poem *Perceval, le Conte du Graal*, written c.1175. Alfred, Lord Tennyson (1809–1892) included Sir Percival in his immensely popular poem *Idylls of the King*, which led to a great resurgence in the name.

PERCY
A place name and aristocratic surname, now used as a first name. The Percy family are descended from William de Perci who accompanied William the Conqueror to England.

The great Romantic poet Percy Bysshe Shelley (1792–1822) was born near Horsham and went to Eton. He was a friend of Lord Byron and John Keats; his second wife, Mary, wrote *Frankenstein*. Shelley drowned off Viareggio in Italy at the age of 29, leaving behind a large amount of poetry to give him immortality.

PEREGRINE
From the Latin, meaning 'stranger'. A name common among the early Christians, it has been the name of three saints and used in England since the Middle Ages.

Peregrine Pickle, written by Tobias Smollett in 1751, made the name well-known.

PERRY
A surname, meaning 'a man who lives by a pear tree', now used as a first name.

PETER (Pete)
From the Greek, meaning 'rock'. An apostle of Christ and the first pope, St Peter wrote two Epistles included in the New Testament. Tradition states that he was martyred in Rome in AD 67, by being crucified upside down. There are over 1,000 British churches dedicated to St Peter and it was the commonest name to be given to boys in the Middle Ages.

The play *Peter Pan: or The Boy Who Would Not Grow Up* (1904), written by James Matthew Barrie, made the name immensely popular and this has continued.

PETROC
Originally considered an exclusively Cornish name, it is now generally used.

The remains of the Welsh St Petroc (d. 564) are enshrined in the church dedicated to him in Bodmin, Cornwall. Stolen several times, St Petroc's casket is now set into the south wall. Dating from 1170, it is made of gold and ivory.

PHILIP (Phil, Pip)
From the Greek, meaning 'fond of horses'. It was the name of an apostle and several saints and is a regal name, especially in France and Spain. Philip II, King of Macedonia (382–336 BC), was father to Alexander the Great.

The poet, scholar and soldier Sir Philip Sidney, who died so nobly at Zutphen in 1586, was considered the perfect Renaissance gentleman. His poem *Astrophel and Stella* made the sonnet very fashionable.

PHILO
From the Greek, meaning 'love'. It is the name of a second century saint, about whom little is known.

PHINEAS
From the Egyptian, meaning 'the Nubian'. There are three Old Testament characters bearing this name. One was a priest who weighed the gold, silver and precious stones brought to the Temple from Babylon.

Phineas Finn (1869) is the title of the first of the parliamentary novels by Anthony Trollope. The eponymous hero is a poor young Irishman, elected an MP.

PHOENIX
A modern first name, taken from a mythical Arabian bird, the only one of its kind. At the end of 500 years, the phoenix sang a dirge and immolated himself on a pyre of spices. After being reduced to ashes, the bird arose from the flames, re-born. The phoenix was regarded as a symbol of immortality.

PIERCE
A variation of Piers, much used in the nineteenth century. The film star Pierce Brosnan has made the name popular.

PIERS
This is the French version of Peter, brought to England by the Normans. William Langland wrote the long and rambling poem *The Vision of Piers Plowman* c.1362 which begins when the poet falls asleep in the Malvern Hills.

PIRAN
The name of a sixth century Cornish saint, patron of miners. The Domesday Book mentions a piece of land in Cornwall belonging to the monks of St Piran. There was great devotion to him in Brittany.

St Piran's Round, near the village of Rose, is an artificial amphitheatre once used for the performance of Cornish miracle plays.

PITT
A place name and surname, now used as a first name. William Pitt the Younger (1759–1806) was the greatest of Britain's Prime Ministers. He remained in office from 1783 to 1801, the longest in British history.

PRESTON
An Old English place name, meaning 'priest's farm', and surname, used as a first name since the nineteenth century. It is the surname of the Viscounts Gormanston.

Oliver Cromwell defeated the Royalists at Preston in 1648, and the Old Pretender was proclaimed king in its town square.

PRICE
A surname, meaning 'son of Rhys', now used generally as a first name.

QUENTIN
From the Latin, meaning 'fifth'. St Quentin was martyred in the third century and gave his name to the town of St Quentin in northern France. The Normans introduced the name to England at the Norman Conquest.

Quentin Durward, the romantic novel set in fifteenth century France, written by Sir Walter Scott (1771–1832), revitalised the name.

RAFFERTY
An Irish surname, meaning 'prosperous', now a modern first name. 'Rafferty rules', in Australian slang, means absolutely *no* rules at all!

RALEIGH
From the Old English, meaning 'clearing with roe deer'. A place name and surname, now used as a first name.

The flamboyant Sir Walter Raleigh (c.1552–1618), favourite of Elizabeth I, poet and pirate, writer and explorer, ended a tumultuous life in Old Palace Yard, Westminster, where he was beheaded.

RALPH (Rafe)
From the Old English, meaning 'wolf counsel'. This has been used in England since before the Norman Conquest. The Eton headmaster Nicholas Udall (1505–1556) wrote the first English comedy, entitled *Ralph Roister-Doister*, for his pupils. The swaggering hero attempts to make a wealthy marriage.

Rafe was a popular medieval variant of the name, now enjoying a resurgence.

RALSTON
A place name and surname, used as a first name since the nineteenth century.

RAMSAY
A place name and aristocratic surname, now used as a first name. Allan Ramsay (1713–1784) was a Scottish painter much favoured by George III. He is most famous for his portraits of women: the National Gallery of Scotland has the fine *Margaret Lindsay, the Painter's Wife* in its collection.

James Ramsay MacDonald (1866–1937) became the first Labour Prime Minister in 1924.

RANDAL (Ranulph)
From the Old English, meaning 'wolf shield'. Both Randal and Ranulph were the popular medieval forms of Randolph, now used in their own right.

RAOUL
The French version of Ralph (q.v.), used regularly in Britain. Raoul Island is one of a group of uninhabited volcanic islands off the cost of the North Island of New Zealand.

RAPHAEL
From the Hebrew, meaning 'God heals'. The Archangel Raphael is patron of doctors and travellers.

The great painter Raphael Santi (1483–1520) was born in Urbino and studied under Perugino. He worked for many patrons, producing portraits, altarpieces and frescoes. Ten of his masterpieces, including *The Madonna of the Pinks*, can be seen at the National Gallery in London.

RAVEN
From the bird, a modern first name. The raven (*Corvus corax*) is the largest member of the crow family in Europe.

Norse mythology saw them as symbols of wisdom. The god Odin was accompanied by two ravens, Hugin (Thought) and Munin (Memory).

And did you know that a collection of ravens is called an unkindness?

RAYMOND (Ray)
From the Old French, meaning 'wise protection'. Another of the names brought to England at the Norman Conquest, two saints have borne this name. St Raymond Nonnatus (d. 1240) voluntarily sold himself into slavery to save others and was later made a cardinal in Rome. He is the patron saint of midwives.

The American writer Raymond Chandler (1888–1959) created the private detective Philip Marlowe. *The Big Sleep* and *Farewell, My Lovely* are two of his best-known novels.

REGINALD (Reg, Reggie)
From the Old English, meaning 'power force'. This is a medieval name revived in the nineteenth century. Reggie is a character in the once-popular Victorian novel *Love Me Little, Love Me Long* (1859) written by Charles Reade.

REID
A surname, meaning 'red-haired', now used as a first name. The British novelist Thomas Mayne Reid (1818–1883) was a popular writer of 'rattling good yarns' for boys, such as *The Scalp Hunters* and *The Headless Horseman*.

REMY
From the Latin, meaning 'oarsman'. St Rémy, Bishop of Rheims, was a great preacher. His early biographers said that, 'By his signs and miracles he brought low the heathen altars everywhere.' He died in 533.

REUBEN

From the Hebrew, meaning 'behold a son'. In the Bible, the name given to the eldest son of Jacob and one of the twelve tribes of Israel. Always popular in the Jewish community, the Puritans brought it into general use in the seventeenth century.

The drunkard Reuben Smith came to a bad end in the classic children's story *Black Beauty* written by Anna Sewell (1820–1878).

REX

From the Latin, meaning 'king' or 'ruler'. Its use as a first name seems to have begun in the twentieth century.

Rex Harrison (1908–1990; real name Reginald Carey Harrison), the British actor who starred in the classic films *Blithe Spirit* and *My Fair Lady*, made the name known worldwide.

RHODRI

From the Welsh, meaning 'crowned ruler'. Rhodri Mawr (the Great) succeeded his father in AD 844 as King of Gwynedd; he extended his kingdom to include Powys and Ceredigion before his death in 878. Rhodri was believed to have been killed by the English.

The name was revived in the twentieth century.

RHYS (Reece)

From the Welsh, meaning 'ardour'. A name famous in Welsh history: King Rhys ap Tewdwr ('son of Tewdwr') paid William the Conqueror £40 per annum to ensure that his position as ruler was acknowledged.

RICHARD (Dick, Rick, Ricky, Rik)

From the Old German, meaning 'powerful ruler'. Brought to England at the time of the Norman Conquest, it has remained popular since then. St Richard of Chichester (1197–1253) was a reforming bishop, merciless towards nepotism and very generous to the poor.

Richard I (1157–1199), Coeur de Lion, led the Third Crusade and is the complete antithesis of Richard III (1452–1485), who has become the archetypal royal villain, thanks to the play by William Shakespeare.

Richard Steele (1672–1729) founded the periodicals *The Tatler* and *The Spectator*, and wrote plays and essays. Sir Richard Arkwright (1732–1792) invented the spinning frame for cotton mills.

Richard A. Butler (1902–1982), Education Minister in 1944, instigated free education for all.

RIDLEY
A place name, meaning 'cleared land', and surname, now used as a first name.

Nicholas Ridley (1500–1555), Bishop of London, was burnt at the stake in Oxford, a Protestant martyr. A cross set in the road in the middle of Broad Street, opposite Balliol College, marks the spot.

RILEY
A place name, meaning 'rye meadow', and surname. It is now used as a first name.

The painter John Riley (1646–1691) is renowned for his unidealised portraits of servants. The most famous of these is *The Scullion at Christ Church*, still a prized possession of the Oxford college.

RIO
From the Spanish, meaning 'river'. A modern first name.

The American Rio Grande rises in the San Juan Mountains of Colorado and empties into the Gulf of Mexico, a journey of 1,885 miles.

RIORDAN
An anglicised version of a Gaelic name, meaning 'royal poet'.

RIVER
A modern British name. In Greek mythology, Oceanus and his wife Tethys bore 3,000 sons, the Rivers, and 3,000 daughters, the Water Nymphs.

ROBERT (Bob, Bobby, Rob, Robbie, Robby)
From the Old German, meaning 'fame bright'. The French form of an Anglo-Saxon name, it has remained popular since the Middle Ages. Robert, nicknamed 'the Devil', was the father of William the Conqueror, and brother-in-law to King Canute.

Sir Robert Peel (1788–1850) was twice Prime Minister, but is famous for forming the Metropolitan Police, nicknamed 'Bobbies'.

Rob Roy was the title of a novel by Sir Walter Scott, based on a true character, Robert MacGregor (1671–1734), a legendary Scottish outlaw.

Robert Bridges (1844–1930) was appointed Poet Laureate in 1913. His most famous work is a long poem entitled *The Testament of Beauty*.

ROBIN

A popular pet-form of Robert (q.v.) in the Middle Ages, this name is now seen as independent.

English literature, from the stories of the famous outlaw Robin Hood down to Christopher Robin Milne, owner of Winnie the Pooh, shows its popularity. Robin Goodfellow is a mischievous sprite in Shakespeare's play *A Midsummer Night's Dream*.

RODERICK (Rod, Roddy)

From the Old German, meaning 'famous rule'. Roderick was the last Visigoth King of Spain, dying in battle against the Saracens in AD 711. He is the hero of a novel by Sir Walter Scott and a poem by Robert Southey (1774–1843), entitled *Roderick, the Last of the Goths*. (On a lighter note, Sir Roderick Glossop is a perpetual enemy to Bertie Wooster, hero of the stories by P. G. Wodehouse.)

RODNEY

A place name and surname, now used as a first name. It was made popular by Admiral Lord Rodney (1719–1792), who defeated the French at Le Havre and beat the Spanish fleet off Cape St Vincent. Sir Arthur Conan Doyle wrote the novel *Rodney Stone* (1896).

ROGER

From the Old German, meaning 'illustrious warrior'. The name was brought to England at the Norman Conquest and remained a favourite throughout the Middle Ages. It was revived in the nineteenth century.

Roger of Salerno, an Italian surgeon, wrote the first textbook of surgery in 1170. Sir Roger de Coverley is the name of an English country dance and a character who typified an eighteenth century gentleman in the writings of Steele.

ROHAN

A French place name and aristocratic surname, now used as a first name.

ROLAND (Rollo, Roly, Rowland)

From the Old German, meaning 'famous throughout the land'. The nephew of Charlemagne, Roland was a chivalrous knight about whom many stories were told. The twelfth century *Song of Roland* made the name very popular. Sir Rowland Hill (1795–1879) was the originator of the penny post in 1840.

ROLF

The Scandinavian version of Rudolph, now generally used. Rolf, son of Rognvald of Norway, sailed to France and besieged Paris. He was given the land now known as Normandy and ruled it well. He died in 932. William the Conqueror is descended from him.

ROMAN

A Polish name derived from 'Romanus', meaning 'citizen of Rome', now generally used.

Romanus the Melodist, a Byzantine saint of the sixth century, is credited with having written 1,000 hymns. Unfortunately, only eighty of these have survived.

The film maker Roman Polanski is well known.

RONALD (Ron)

The Scottish version of the medieval name Reynold, used generally since the nineteenth century.

Two film stars, Ronald Colman (1891–1958) and Ronald Reagan (1911–2004), the latter better known as a former President of the USA, kept the name before the public.

RONAN

From the Irish, meaning 'little seal'. The Irish St Ronan worked as a missionary in Cornwall in the fifth century. He was later consecrated bishop by St Patrick.

RORY

From the Gaelic, meaning 'red'. Originally a Scottish name, it is now generally used.

ROSCOE
A place name, meaning 'roe deer wood', and surname, now used
as a first name.

William Roscoe, banker and botanist, wrote the early children's classic *The Butterfly's Ball and the Grasshopper's Feast*
(1806).

And American slang gives the name of Roscoe to a revolver!

ROSS
A Scottish place name, meaning 'promontory', and a surname,
now used as a first name. The British physician Sir Ronald Ross
(1857–1932) received the Nobel Prize for Medicine in 1902 for
his work on discovering the cause of malaria.

Sir John Ross and his nephew Sir James Ross discovered the
north magnetic pole in 1831.

ROWAN
Either derived from the Gaelic, meaning 'red', or from the
rowan tree (mountain ash), notable for its small scarlet berries.

ROY
Experts disagree over this name, so you may choose to believe
that it is either the anglicised version of Rory or it is taken from
the French word for 'king' (*roi*).

ROYSTON
A place name and aristocratic surname, it has been used as a
first name since the late nineteenth century.

RUFUS
From the Latin, meaning 'red-haired'. William Rufus (1056–
1100), third son of William the Conqueror and Matilda of
Flanders, became King of England on his father's death. A
warlike man, he was murdered while out hunting in the New
Forest, shot in the back by an arrow. He is buried in Winchester
Abbey. The name was revived in the nineteenth century.

RUPERT
The anglicised version of Rupprecht, introduced to England by
Prince Rupprecht of the Rhine (1619–1682), who came to help
his uncle, the unfortunate Charles I, in the English Civil War. He

was decisively beaten at Marston Moor in 1644 and Naseby in 1645, but, more happily, was a founder member of the Royal Society.

Rupert Brooke (1887–1915) was the most famous poet of the First World War, remembered for *The Great Lover* and *Grantchester*. (And children are very fond of Rupert the Bear, who lives in Nutwood.)

RUSSELL
From a French nickname, meaning 'a little man with red hair', which became an aristocratic surname and is now used as a first name. It is the surname of the Dukes of Bedford and four other peers.

RYAN
An Irish surname, now used as a first name. The port of Stranraer is situated on Loch Ryan in Dumfries.

RYDER
An occupational surname, now given as a first name. Ryder is the surname of the earls Harrowby. Their motto, '*Servata fides cineri*', translates as 'The promise made is faithfully kept'. (A most excellent motto for us all!)

SACHEVERELL
A Norman name of disputed origin, either 'without leather' or 'roebuck leap'.

The writer Sacheverell Sitwell (1897–1988) made the name known.

SAMUEL (Sam)

From the Hebrew, meaning 'name of God'. The prophet Samuel lived in the eleventh century BC. He anointed the shepherd boy David to be successor to Saul as the King of Israel. The name became popular at the Reformation and has been given to many famous men. Samuel Johnson (1709–1784), the English lexicographer, essayist and poet (and prodigious tea drinker) was the most famous literary character in the eighteenth century.

Samuel Pepys (1633–1703), politician and diarist; Samuel Richardson (1689–1761), writer of *Clarissa Harlowe*, the longest novel in the English language; Samuel Palmer (1805–1881), landscape painter; and Samuel Morse (1791–1872), American inventor of Morse code are just a few of many who added lustre to the name.

SANDY

The medieval pet-form of Alexander (q.v.), now considered an independent name. It was particularly popular in Scotland.

SCOTT

A surname describing nationality – 'a Scot' – now used as a first name.

The English explorer Robert Falcon Scott (1868–1912) died with his companions after failing to be the first to reach the South Pole. His son, Sir Peter Scott, was an artist, writer and founder of the Wildfowl Trust.

The American (Francis) Scott Fitzgerald (1896–1940) wrote novels and short stories of the 'Jazz Age' or 1920s, notably *The Great Gatsby*.

SEAN (Shaun)

The Irish version of John, q.v. The Irish writer Sean O'Casey (1880–1964) is best remembered for the play *Juno and the Paycock*.

SEBASTIAN

St Sebastian was a Roman army officer, martyred in 288 for declaring himself to be a Christian. He was sentenced to death, by being shot with arrows; and the scene was a popular subject with medieval artists.

Sebastian is the name given to two characters in Shakespeare's *Twelfth Night* and *The Tempest*.

SELWYN
From the Old French, meaning 'savage'. A surname, used as a first name since the nineteenth century.

Selwyn College, Cambridge was named after the Englishman George Augustus Selwyn (1808–1878), who went to be the first Bishop of New Zealand.

SERGEI
A Russian name, derived from Sergius, now generally used. A third century saint, Sergius was a Roman officer who refused to sacrifice to Jupiter. He was martyred at Resapha in Syria. The desert nomads considered him their patron saint.

The composers Sergei Rachmaninov (1873–1943) and Sergei Prokofiev (1891–1953) ensure the name is well known.

SETH
From the Hebrew, meaning 'founder'. Seth was the third son of Adam and Eve, born after his eldest brother Cain had killed Abel.

The Bible states that he was born when Adam was 130 years old. It was used as a first name after the Reformation.

SEYMOUR
A French place name and aristocratic surname, now used as a first name. It is the surname of the dukes of Somerset.

Sir Seymour Hicks (1871–1949), actor-manager and playwright, is best remembered as son-in-law to the actor William Terriss who was assassinated by a madman in 1897 and reputedly haunts Covent Garden tube station!

SHANE
An anglicised version of Sean, q.v. This was made popular by the classic Western film *Shane* (1953), starring Alan Ladd.

SHERIDAN
An Irish surname, used as a first name since the mid-nineteenth century. The playwright Richard Brinsley Sheridan (1751–1816) is best known for his brilliant comedies of manners *The School for Scandal* and *The Rivals*. Arrested for debt in 1813, seriously ill for several years before his death, he found a last resting place in Westminster Abbey.

SHERMAN

An occupational surname, now used as a first name. The American Union General, William Tecumseh Sherman (1820–1891), is best remembered for saying, 'There is many a boy here today who looks on war as all glory, but boys, it is all hell'.

SHOLTO

From the Gaelic, meaning 'sower'.

SIDNEY (Sid, Syd, Sydney)

A French place name and aristocratic surname, now used as a first name. The family came to England in 1154 with the French-born King Henry II – William Sidney was his Chancellor. '*Quo fata vocant*', translated as 'Wherever fate may summon me', is the appropriate family motto.

Sir Philip Sidney (1554–1586), the poet and soldier fatally wounded at Zutphen, gave his own water bottle to a dying foot soldier, saying 'Thy necessity is greater than mine.'

Sydney Carton, the dissipated hero of Dickens' novel *A Tale of Two Cities* (1859), dies on the guillotine with the lines, 'It is a far, far better thing that I do, than I have ever done; it is a far, far better rest that I go to, than I have ever known,' ensuring floods of tears from the reader.

SILAS

From the Aramaic, meaning 'asked of God'. In the New Testament, Silas, a Roman citizen, accompanied Paul on his second journey to Corinth. Later he became secretary to St Peter. The name came into use after the Reformation.

SIMON

From the Greek, meaning 'snub-nosed'. The New Testament mentions nine men with this name, the most famous being Simon Peter, the chief Apostle. The Syrian St Simon Stylites (c.390–459) spent thirty-six years on top of a pillar in prayer and fasting.

The dashing Simon Templar is the hero of 'the Saint' novels by Leslie Charteris, the first of which, *Enter the Saint*, appeared in 1930.

SINCLAIR

A French place name and aristocratic surname, used as a first name since the nineteenth century.

Sinclair Lewis (1885–1951), the first American writer to be awarded the Nobel Prize for Literature in 1930, is best known for his novel *Elmer Gantry*, later filmed.

SOLOMON

From the Hebrew, meaning 'peaceable'. The Old Testament King Solomon, renowned for his wisdom, son of King David, reigned from 970–931 BC.

In Westminster Abbey can be seen one of the few remaining sculptures from the time of Edward the Confessor. The eleventh century carving shows the Judgment of Solomon, the king adjudicating between two women, both of whom claim to be the mother of the same baby.

SORLEY

A surname, derived from Somerled, the founder of the Clan MacDonald, greatest of the Highland clans. He freed his country-men from the Norsemen, and died in 1164.

Charles Hamilton Sorley (1895–1915), war poet, left only 37 complete poems. The best known of these is *The Song of the Ungirt Runners*.

SPENCER

From the Old English, meaning 'steward' or 'butler'. An aristo-cratic surname, now used as a first name. The British politician Spencer Perceval (1762–1812) became Prime Minister in 1809 and was assassinated in the lobby of the House of Commons on 11th May 1812 by a bankrupt merchant named John Belling-ham.

STAFFORD

A place name, meaning 'ford by a landing place', and surname, now used as a first name.

'*Abstulit qui dedit*', meaning 'He who gave has taken away', is the motto of the barons Stafford.

STANFORD (Stamford)

An English place name, meaning 'stony ford', and surname, now regularly used as a first name. The extremely prolific British composer Sir Charles Stanford (1852–1924) is the best-known bearer of the name.

STANLEY (Stan)

A place name, meaning 'stony meadow', and aristocratic surname, now used as a first name. Its popularity began in the 1870s when Henry Morton Stanley (*real* name John Rowlands) greeted the long-lost African explorer David Livingstone with the famous words, 'Doctor Livingstone, I presume!'

Sir Stanley Matthews (1915–2000) was the first footballer to receive a knighthood.

STEPHEN (Stefan, Steve, Steven, Stevie)

From the Greek, meaning 'crown'. The name of the first Christian martyr and several other saints, it was made popular by the Normans. William the Conqueror dedicated the Abbey built at Caen to St Stephen.

Stephen I (c.977–1038) was the first Christian ruler of Hungary and later canonised. Stephen Bathory was elected King of Poland in 1575 and ruled for eleven years.

STUART (Stewart)

From the Old English, meaning 'steward'. The Stuart family were rulers of Scotland from 1371 until 1603 and of both England *and* Scotland from 1603–1714. It became popular as a first name in the nineteenth century.

TAI

From the fish, a most unusual modern first name. The tai is a Pacific sea bream, a deep red in colour. It is particularly valued in Japan, being known as the King of Fish.

TALBOT
An aristocratic surname, now used as a first name. Richard Talbot came to England with William the Conqueror. It is the surname of the Earls of Shrewsbury.

TANCRED
From the Old German, meaning 'thought counsel'. Tancred (d. 1112) took part in the Siege of Jerusalem in the First Crusade. He went on to become ruler of Antioch.

And a more macabre character of the same name in *The Revenge of Tancred* by Boccaccio sends his daughter her lover's heart in a goblet of gold. Naturally, this drives her to drink poison!

TARQUIN
The family name of a legendary line of early Roman kings, seven in number. Lucius Tarquinius Superbus, the seventh and last King of Rome, was sent, with his family, into exile in 510 BC and a republic established.

TATE
A surname of disputed meaning, from 'lock of hair' to 'hilltop'. It is now used as a first name.

Nahum Tate was Poet Laureate from 1692 until 1715. Sir Henry Tate (1819–1899), philanthropist, built the Tate Gallery (now Tate Britain), which opened in London in 1897.

TAYLOR ✳
An occupational surname, now a first name bestowed on both boys and girls. John Taylor (1580–1653) was a poet who achieved fame by sailing from London to Queensborough in Kent in a paper boat. (He also walked from London to Edinburgh.)

TERENCE (Terry)
The anglicised version of the Irish Turlough. Terence (185–159 BC), the comic playwright of ancient Rome, was taken to Rome from Carthage as a slave to the senator Terentius Lucanus. The senator helped him to study and freed him: the former slave then took the owner's name as a mark of gratitude.

THANE
From the Old English, meaning 'servant'. A thane held land given by the king and ranked with an earl's son. It was the title of a clan chief in Scotland. Used as a first name since the nineteenth century.

THEL
An unusual modern first name, perhaps bestowed in honour of the twentieth century American jazz pianist Thelonious Monk.

The Book of Thel, written by the mystic William Blake, first appeared in 1789. This encapsulates his personal mythology, so is rather a complex tome. (Even the maiden Thel returns shrieking to the Vales of Har!)

THEODORE (Theo)
From the Greek, meaning 'God's gift'. It was a popular name with the early Christians and borne by several saints. St Theodore of Canterbury (602–690) was a Greek monk sent by Pope St Vitalian to be Archbishop of Canterbury in 667. The name was revived by the Tractarians in the mid-nineteenth century and now seems to be gaining in popularity.

THOMAS (Tom, Tommy)
From the Aramaic, meaning 'twin'. The name of one of the Twelve Apostles and many saints, it was made popular by St Thomas à Becket (1118–1170), murdered in Canterbury Cathedral as a result of some harsh words by Henry II. Thomas has been one of the commonest names for boys, as is shown in the expression 'every Tom, Dick and Harry'.

The poet Thomas Gray (1716–1771), who wrote *Elegy written in a Country Churchyard*; Thomas Hardy (1840–1928), poet and author of *Tess of the D'Urbervilles* and *Far from the Madding Crowd*; and Thomas Gainsborough (1727–1788), portrait and landscape painter, are just three of those who have borne the name with distinction.

TIMOTHY (Tim, Timmy)
From the Greek, meaning 'honouring God'. The New Testament St Timothy was converted by St Paul, whose helper and companion he became.

Tradition states that he was beaten to death by a mob in AD 97 for opposing the worship of the goddess Diana. The name came into use in England after the Reformation. *The Tale of Timmy Tiptoes* (1911) by Beatrix Potter is the story of a fat grey squirrel.

TIRIAN (Tirion)
A modern Welsh name, meaning 'gentle'. King Tirian (inseparable from his friend, Jewel the Unicorn) is an important character in the seventh and final *Narnia* book by C. S. Lewis, *The Last Battle* (1956).

TITUS
The Biblical St Titus was a gentile disciple of St Paul. The Roman Emperor Titus (40–81), who served as a military tribune in Britain, captured and destroyed Jerusalem in AD 70. He was responsible for the building of the Colosseum in Rome. The name was used in England after the Reformation.

TOBY (Tobias, Tobin)
Toby is the anglicised version of Tobias, from the Hebrew meaning 'the Lord is good'. The apocryphal story of 'Tobias and the Angel' was a favourite with Renaissance artists.

The surgeon and novelist Tobias Smollett (1721–1771), notorious for becoming involved in controversy and being outrageously malicious, is remembered for the novels *Roderick Random*, *Peregrine Pickle* and *Humphrey Clinker*.

TODD
A surname, meaning 'fox', now used as a first name.

TORQUIL
From the Old Norse, meaning 'Thor's cauldron'. It was brought into England by the Danes before the Norman Conquest.

TRAVIS
An occupational surname for a toll-keeper, now used as a first name.

TREVOR
A place name, meaning 'large settlement', and surname, now used as a first name. The actor Trevor Howard, best remembered for his part in the film *Brief Encounter* (1945), helped to make the name known.

TRISTRAM

An anglicised version of the Celtic Tristan, used in England since the twelfth century.

Sir Tristram of Lyoness was one of the bravest knights of the Round Table, second only to Sir Lancelot. Sent by his uncle, King Mark of Cornwall, to collect his intended bride the beautiful Princess Isolt from Ireland, Tristram and Isolt drank a potion that caused them to fall eternally in love with each other. Alfred, Lord Tennyson, included the story in his immensely popular poem *The Idylls of the King*.

The English novelist and clergyman Laurence Sterne (1713–1768) wrote the chaotic classic novel *Tristram Shandy*.

TROY

A surname, meaning 'descendant of a foot soldier', now used as a first name. (Should you love the classics, you will ignore the mundane and think only of the ancient city in Asia Minor, besieged by the Greeks for ten years and immortalised by Homer.)

TUDOR

The Welsh version of Theodore. Edmund Tudor, 1st Earl of Richmond, was the father of Henry VII (1457–1509), the first Tudor king.

TYLER

An occupational surname for someone who tiled roofs, now used as a first name for both boys and girls.

The Dartford blacksmith Wat Tyler, leader of the Peasants' Revolt against a poll tax in 1381, was killed by William Walworth, the Lord Mayor. The dagger used can still be seen at Fishmongers' Hall.

TYRONE

The name of a county in Northern Ireland, 'Owen's land'. The name was popularised by the American film star Tyrone Power (1913–1958), swashbuckling star of *The Mark of Zorro* and many others.

ULICK
A Gaelic name, meaning 'mind reward'.

ULRIC
From the Old English, meaning 'wolf power'. Mentioned in the Domesday Book, it has been the name of three saints.

The English St Ulric (d. 1154) was a priest in Wiltshire who ended his life as a recluse at Haselbury.

URBAN
From the Latin, meaning 'of the town'. The Urban of the New Testament was greeted by St Paul in his letter to the Romans. Several early saints and eight popes have borne the name.

URIEL
From the Hebrew, meaning 'God is my light'. The Old Testament Uriel was one of the priests ordered by King David to carry the Ark of the Covenant to Jerusalem.

John Milton's epic poem *Paradise Lost* (1667) includes the angel Uriel, describing him as 'the sharpest-sighted spirit of all in heaven'.

URQUHART
A place name, meaning 'at the woodside', and surname, now given as a first name.

The Scottish clan Urquhart takes its name from a district in Ross-shire. The clan badge is the wallflower; its motto 'Mean, speak and do well'.

VALENTINE

From the Latin, meaning 'strong'. A third century martyr, about whom little is known, inextricably liked to Valentine cards and treacly endearments in the 'Personal' columns of newspapers on his feast day, 14th February.

Valentine and Orson was a French romance about twin brothers published in England in 1550 and much imitated. Abandoned in a forest, Orson was carried off and raised by a bear while the rescued Valentine grew up at the court of King Pepin, later marrying the sister of a giant.

VASCO

Vasco Da Gama (1469–1524), the famous Portuguese navigator, was the first European to discover a sea route to the East. Rounding the Cape of Good Hope in November 1497, he sailed along the coast of Africa and crossed the Indian Ocean, reaching Calicut in May 1498. Named viceroy of India in 1524, he is the hero of Meyerbeer's opera *L'Africaine*.

VAUGHAN

A Welsh surname, meaning 'little', now used as a first name. The English composer Ralph Vaughan Williams (1872–1958), noted especially for *Fantasia on a Theme by Thomas Tallis* and *The Lark Ascending*, is a well-known bearer of the name. (He also wrote the music for the 1948 film *Scott of the Antarctic*!)

VERE
A French place name and aristocratic surname, used as a first name since the seventeenth century.

VERNON
A French place name, meaning 'place of alders', and aristocratic surname, now used as a first name. It is the surname of the barons Lyveden.

Richard de Vernon was yet another companion to William the Conqueror at the Norman Conquest in 1066.

VICTOR (Vic)
From the Latin, meaning 'conqueror'. Popular with the early Christians, it has been the name of several early martyrs and a pope. Rare in the Middle Ages, it became more popular in the nineteenth century, presumably in honour of Queen Victoria.

The pianist and comedian Victor Borge (1909–2000) is a well-known bearer of the name.

VINCENT (Vince)
From the Latin, meaning 'to conquer'. There are several saints with this name, the most revered being the Frenchman St Vincent de Paul (c.1580–1660). He devoted his life to the service of the poor, especially abandoned children and galley-slaves, and founded the Daughters of Charity.

The world-famous Dutch painter Vincent Van Gogh (1853–1890), who sold only one painting in his lifetime, is remembered for *Sunflowers*, *The Yellow Chair* and *Starry Night*.

VIVIAN
From the Latin, meaning 'alive'. The name of an obscure Christian martyr of the fifth century, it has been used in England since the Middle Ages. Originally the masculine form, it is now bestowed on both boys and girls.

Vivian Grey (1826) was the first novel of the future Tory Prime Minister, Benjamin Disraeli.

WADE
An Old English place name, meaning 'ford', and surname, used as a first name since the nineteenth century.

WALLACE
A Scottish surname, meaning 'stranger', used generally since the nineteenth century.

The Scottish patriot William Wallace (c.1270–1305), known as 'the Scourge of England', fought for Scottish independence but was betrayed to the English and hanged, drawn and quartered in Westminster Hall.

WALTER (Wally, Walt)
From the Old German, meaning 'folk-ruler'. This was a popular name with the Normans and brought by them to England.

The British Impressionist painter Walter Sickert (1860–1942) is well-known for his portraits and pictures of the London streets.

WARD
An occupational surname, meaning 'watchman', and aristocratic surname, used as a first name since the nineteenth century. It is the surname of the Earls of Dudley.

WARNER
A surname, Norman in origin, now used as a first name. The 'warner' of eighteenth century Bristol had to possess a good head for heights. The name was given to the man who watched for sailing ships as they approached harbour.

WARREN

The name of a noble French family, brought to England at the Norman Conquest. The English statesman Warren Hastings (1732–1818) made the name popular in England. Governor General of India, he was impeached at the bar of the House of Lords for corruption and cruelty. After a trial lasting seven years, he was found innocent.

The actor Warren Beatty (b. 1937), star of *Bonnie and Clyde*, *Shampoo* and *Dick Tracy* among others, has kept the name a favourite.

WARWICK

A place name, meaning 'farm beside a weir', and aristocratic surname, used as a first name since the nineteenth century.

WAYNE

An occupational surname, meaning 'carter'. Its use as a first name in the twentieth century appears to rest on the great popularity of the American actor Marion Michael Morrison, far better known as John Wayne, the star of so many Westerns and war films. His stage name was derived from a general of the American Revolution, Anthony Wayne (1745–1796).

WEBSTER

An occupational surname, meaning 'weaver', now used as a first name.

John Webster (1580–1625), dramatist, is most famous for his extremely violent plays, including *The White Devil* and *The Duchess of Malfi*. (The body count is high!)

WELDON

A place name, meaning 'hill with a spring', and surname, now used as a first name.

John Weldon (1676–1736), organist and prolific composer, was a pupil of Purcell. He became a Gentleman of the Chapel Royal, and organist to three London churches.

WENDELL

From the Old German, meaning 'wandering man'. A surname, now given as a first name.

The American doctor, professor and writer, Oliver Wendell Holmes (1809–1894) made the name well known in Britain. He was honoured by the universities of Oxford, Cambridge and Edinburgh. His son of the same name was equally famous in the law.

WENSLEY

A place name, meaning 'clearing sacred to Woden', and surname. It is now used as a first name.

And it is North Yorkshire we must thank for the excellent Wensleydale cheese.

WESLEY

An English place name, meaning 'western wood', and surname, now used as a first name. This was made popular by John Wesley (1703–1791), the founder of Methodism. His nephews Charles and Samuel Wesley were well-known organists and prolific composers who did much to spread a knowledge of Bach in England.

WILFRED (Wilfrid)

From the Old English, meaning 'desiring peace'. St Wilfred of York (634–709), about whom it was said 'a quick walker, expert in all good works, with never a sour face', was made Bishop of York in 669 and was the first Englishman to carry a lawsuit to the Roman courts. A delightful legend states that he taught the men of Sussex to fish. There are fifty churches dedicated to him in Britain. The name was revived by the Tractarians of the nineteenth century.

WILLIAM (Bill, Billy, Will, Willy)

From the Old German, meaning 'helmet of resolution'. William Duke of Normandy, later William I, known as the Conqueror (1027–1087), first cousin once removed to Edward the Confessor, fought the only battle known to everybody ('Battle of Hastings 1066' all in one breath) on 14th October and killed Harold II. He was crowned King of England on Christmas Day of the same year at Westminster Abbey.

Unfortunately, William IV lingers in the memory for being nicknamed 'Silly Billy' and having a head shaped like a pineapple.

A royal name past and present, it has been borne by many famous men. William Shakespeare (1564–1616), William Wordsworth (1770–1850), the visionary poet and painter William Blake (1757–1827), William Makepeace Thackeray (1811–1863),

William Camden the historian (1551–1623), the politician William Gladstone – who was notorious for addressing Queen Victoria, 'as if I were a public meeting!' – William Wilkie Collins (1824–1889), writer of *The Woman in White* and the first English detective story *The Moonstone*, . . . the list of luminaries seems endless.

WILLOUGHBY
A place name, meaning 'farm beside the willow trees', and aristocratic surname, now used as a first name.

The fickle Willoughby is the most interesting character in *Sense and Sensibility* (1811) by Jane Austen.

WINSTON
An Old English place name, meaning 'friend's farm', and surname, now used as a first name.

The first Winston Churchill was born in 1620, his mother's maiden name being bestowed upon him at baptism: he became the father of the great Duke of Marlborough, victor at the Battle of Blenheim.

WOLF (Wolfie)
A modern first name. Native American storytellers made wolves the heroes of many sacred tales.

The Rocky Mountain Blackfeet followed the Wolf Trail – known to us as the Milky Way – to the spirit world.

Wolf Solent (1929) was the first major success for the novelist John Cowper Powys.

WOODY
The pet-form of Woodrow, meaning 'row of cottages in a wood', now independently used.

The American folksinger Woody Guthrie (1912–1967) and film maker Woody Allen are well known.

WYATT
A surname, meaning 'wide forest', now used as a first name. The poet Sir Thomas Wyatt (1503–1542) is credited with introducing the sonnet into England.

Employed by George III and George IV, the architects James Wyatt and his nephew, Jeffrey Wyattville, are mainly responsible for the Windsor Castle we visit today.

WYNDHAM

A Norfolk place name, meaning 'Wyman's homestead', and surname, used as a first name since the nineteenth century.

(Percy) Wyndham Lewis (1882–1957), novelist and painter, is a well-known bearer of the name. 'John Wyndham' was the pen name of John Beynon Harris, the writer of the science fiction novel *The Day of the Triffids* (1951).

WYSTAN

From the Old English, meaning 'battle-stone'. The name of a ninth century boy saint, King of Mercia. The best-known bearer of the name in modern times is Wystan Hugh Auden (1907–1973), the English poet and dramatist.

XAVIER

From the Arabic, meaning 'bright'. St Francis Xavier (1506–1552), the great Basque missionary to India, Sri Lanka and Japan, popularised the name. His feast day is 3rd December.

YALE
A Welsh place name, meaning 'fertile upland', and surname. Now used as a first name.

Yale University, the third oldest in the USA and founded in 1701, was named after Elihu Yale whose family came from Denbighshire.

YURI
The Russian version of George (q.v.), now generally used. The first man in space was the Russian Yuri Gagarin (1934–1968). He orbited the earth on 12th April 1961.

ZACHARY (Zak)
From the Hebrew, meaning 'Jehovah has remembered'. The elderly Zachary was the father of John the Baptist.

St Zachary (d. 742) was elected pope in 741. He was an implacable enemy to the trade in Christian slaves.

ZANE

A surname, now given as a first name. The erstwhile dentist and American novelist Zane Grey (1872–1939) was a tremendously successful writer of cowboy stories. *Riders of the Purple Sage* was his first bestseller.

He took his first name from an ancestor, Ebenezer Zane, who founded the town of Zanesville, Ohio.

ZENO

A classical name, derived from Zeus, the king of the gods. Zeno of Citium (334–262 BC) was founder of the Stoics.

St Zeno was one of three Christian brothers, martyred c.362, for destroying a heathen temple in Gaza.

And in the apocryphal Gospel of the Infancy, the boy Zeno is raised from the dead by the Christ Child.

GIRLS' NAMES

ABIGAIL (Abbie, Abby)

From the Hebrew, meaning 'father rejoices'. The Old Testament contains two Abigails: one the sister and the other the second wife of King David.

Popular in England since the Reformation, it fell from favour when the name was given to a servant in a play by Beaumont and Fletcher, *The Scornful Lady* (1616), and became the slang term for a lady's maid.

Mrs Abigail Masham was the influential confidante of Queen Anne in the eighteenth century.

ADA

From the Old German, meaning 'noble'. Originally a pet-form of Adelaide (q.v.), it has been used independently since the late eighteenth century.

Ada Lovelace (1815–1852), only legitimate daughter of Lord Byron and mathematician, worked with Charles Babbage on the forerunners to the calculator and computer.

ADELA

From the Old German, meaning 'noble'. This was brought to England by the Normans, the name of the fourth daughter of William the Conqueror. It was revived by the Victorians.

ADELAIDE

From the Old German, meaning 'noble one'. St Adelaide (931–999) was married to Otto the Great and became Empress of the Holy Roman Empire. St Odilo described her as 'a marvel of beauty and goodness'. The name became popular in England when Princess Adelaide of Saxe-Meiningen married the future William IV in 1818. The city of Adelaide, capital of South Australia, was named in her honour.

ADÈLE

The French diminutive of Adelaide, now generally used. Adèle is the name of the ward of Edward Rochester, hero of *Jane Eyre* (1847), written by Charlotte Brontë.

ADRIANA (Adrienne)

The feminine form of Adrian, q.v. Adriana is the wife of Antipholus of Ephesus in *The Comedy of Errors* by William Shakespeare.

AGATHA

From the Greek, meaning 'good'. A Sicilian martyr of the third century, St Agatha is the patron saint of bell-founders. Although greatly venerated, little is known of her life. Her feast day is 5th February.

The name was brought to England at the Norman Conquest by a daughter of William the Conqueror.

Agatha Christie (1890–1976) is famous for her many detective novels, including *The Murder of Roger Ackroyd* and *Murder on the Orient Express*.

(And P. G. Wodehouse created an unforgettable literary character in the terrifying Aunt Agatha, scourge of Bertie Wooster.)

AGNES

From the Greek, meaning 'pure'. St Agnes was the most famous of all Roman Christian martyrs, executed by being stabbed in the throat in 304, aged 13. Her emblem in art is a lamb. There are five churches dedicated to her in Britain. Agnes was one of the commonest English names in the Middle Ages.

Agnes Grey (1847), the story of an ill-treated governess, was one of two novels written by Anne Brontë.

AILEEN

The anglicised form of the Irish name Aibhlin, used generally since the beginning of the twentieth century.

AILSA

The Ailsa Craig is an island rock in the Firth of Clyde on the west coast of Scotland. Originally bestowed by Scottish parents on their daughters, the name is now generally used.

AINE

From the Gaelic, meaning 'brightness'. Celtic mythology gives this name to the queen of the fairies.

AISHA (Ayesha)

From the Arabic, meaning 'woman'. It was the name of the Prophet Mohammed's favourite wife.

Sir Henry Rider Haggard wrote of Ayesha, 'She who must be obeyed', in the novels *She* (1887) and *Ayesha* (1905).

AISLING

From the Gaelic, meaning 'dream'. This name has been popular since the mid-twentieth century.

ALANA (Allanah, Lana)

A twentieth century feminine version of Alan (q.v.).

ALANDA

A modern feminine version of Alan (q.v.), now popular.

ALETHEA

From the Greek, meaning 'truth'. This was first used by the Puritans in the seventeenth century: another example of their adopting abstract virtues as names for their daughters.

ALEXANDRA (Alex, Alix, Lexie)

The feminine form of Alexander, used in England since the thirteenth century. The beautiful Princess Alexandra of Denmark (1844–1925), daughter of King Christian IX, made the name very popular when she came to England to marry the future Edward VII in 1863. She founded the Queen Alexandra's Royal Army Nursing Corps and the charitable Alexandra Rose Day.

The Princess Alexandra, Mrs Angus Ogilvie (b. 1936), cousin to Elizabeth II, continues the royal connection.

ALEXIS

The Russian version of Alexander. This name is given to both boys and girls, but is usually considered feminine in this country.

St Alexis (d. 430) lived by begging, sharing all he received with other poor people. On his death it was discovered that he was a Roman nobleman, who left his bride on his wedding day to live in poverty in Syria. St Alexis was a favourite saint in the Middle Ages.

ALICE (Alicia, Alisha, Alys)

From the Old German, meaning 'nobility'. The name was brought to England by the Normans, remaining popular throughout the Middle Ages in the form of Alys.

It was revived in the nineteenth century. Queen Victoria gave the name to her third child in 1843. Lewis Carroll (Charles Lutwidge Dodgson) wrote *Alice's Adventures in Wonderland* (1865) and *Through the Looking Glass* (1871) to please Alice Liddell, the daughter of Henry Liddell, Dean of Christ Church, Oxford.

ALIDA

The Hungarian pet-form of Adelaide (q.v.), now generally used.

ALINE

Used originally in the Middle Ages as a pet-form of Adeline, it now stands as an independent name.

ALISON

A pet-form of Alice, used as an independent name since the thirteenth century. Alison is a character in the *Miller's Tale*, a part of *The Canterbury Tales* by Geoffrey Chaucer (1343–1400).

ALIYAH

From the Hebrew, meaning 'to ascend'.

ALLEGRA

From the Italian, meaning 'cheerful, sprightly'. The best-known bearer of the name was Lord Byron's illegitimate daughter by Claire Clairmont, Shelley's sister-in-law. Born in Bath in 1817, her short and turbulent life ended in Italy in 1822, where she succumbed to typhus.

ALMA

From the Latin, meaning 'kindly'. The name became fashionable in Britain after the Battle of Alma (1854), so called from the Russian river, during the Crimean War.

(It is also the Spanish word for 'soul' or 'ghost'.)

ALOISE
The female version of Aloysius, used in England since the seventeenth century.

The Italian St Aloysius (1568–1591), son of the Marquis of Castiglione, was intended for a military career. He chose instead to become a Jesuit priest, dying of plague while working to assist those stricken with the disease in a Roman hospital.

ALTHEA
From the Greek, meaning 'to heal'. A venerable name, Althea is the mother to Meleager in *The Iliad*.

Revived in the seventeenth century, it has been used steadily since then.

Richard Lovelace (1618–1658) wrote the poem *To Althea, From Prison*, containing the lines:

> Stone walls do not a prison make,
> Nor iron bars a cage;

AMABEL
From the Latin, meaning 'lovable'. A very common name in the twelfth and thirteenth centuries, it was revived in the nineteenth century when the passion for medieval names was at its height.

AMANDA (Mandy)
This seems to have been invented by the architect and playwright Sir John Vanbrugh (1664–1726) for the heroine of his play *The Relapse*. Another literary Amanda married the eponymous hero of *Peregrine Pickle* (1751) by Tobias Smollett.

AMBER
From the gemstone, one of the jewel names which became popular in the late nineteenth century. Amber beads have been prized in England since the thirteenth century – for their sweet smell as well as their beauty!

AMELIA (Emelia)
From the Old German, meaning 'work'. Shakespeare includes a character named Aemilia in *A Comedy of Errors*, but the name became popular in the eighteenth century with the birth of Princess Amelia (1783–1810), the youngest daughter of George III.

Amelia Edwards (1831–1892) was 43 when she visited Egypt for the first time; from this adventure came a book, the founding (with Sir Erasmus Wilson) of the Egypt Exploration Society and funding for the first Chair of Egyptology in Britain.

AMINTA
A literary invention of the seventeenth century. The opera *Il re pastore*, composed by Mozart in 1775 when he was 19 years old, has the shepherd Aminta as hero. This male character is played by a lady, which adds to the confusion of a very complicated drama!

AMITY
From the Latin, meaning 'friendship'.

AMORET
From the Latin, meaning 'beloved'. It was used in the Middle Ages to refer to love songs.

Edmund Spenser (c.1552–1599) includes Amoret in the fourth book of his masterpiece, *The Faerie Queene*. Daughter of the nymph Chrysogne, Amoret is married to Sir Scudamour; imprisoned by the enchanter Busirane, she is rescued by the female knight Britomart.

The name has gained in popularity recently.

AMY (Aimée)
From the Old French, meaning 'loved'. Used in Britain since the Middle Ages, the name became popular in the nineteenth century on the publication of *Little Dorrit* (1855) by Charles Dickens. Amy Dorrit was the saintly little seamstress of the Marshalsea Prison.

Amy Johnson (1903–1941) was the first woman to fly solo from England to Australia in 1930.

ANAIS
The Catalan version of Anne (q.v.), now used in Britain. The Parisian born writer and diarist Anaïs Nin (1903–1977) wrote avante-garde novels in the surrealist style.

ANASTASIA
From the Greek, meaning 'resurrection'. A fourth century martyr, the name was popular in the Middle Ages when legend attributed the name to the midwife of the Virgin Mary.

More recently, the ill-fated Russian Grand Duchess Anastasia (1901–1918) was executed with her family in the cellar at Ekaterinburg by the Bolsheviks.

ANDREA
The female form of Andrew (q.v.), used since the seventeenth century.

ANGELA
From the Greek, meaning 'messenger'. St Angela of Brescia (1474–1540) founded the Ursuline nuns, the first teaching order of women. The name Angel or Angela was sometimes given to children born on the feast of St Michael and All Angels, 29th September. It was revived by the Tractarians in the nineteenth century.

ANGELICA
From the Latin, meaning 'angelic'. Princess Angelica is the object of desire in the epic *Orlando Furioso* by the Italian poet Ludovico Ariosto (1474–1533).

ANGHARAD
From the Welsh, meaning 'much loved'. Angharad is the lady of *Peredur, son of Efrawg*, a medieval Welsh tale included in the *Mabinogion*.

ANITA (Nita)
The popular Spanish version of Anne, used all over Britain.

ANNA
The Greek version of Hannah (q.v.). Anna is the sister of Dido, Queen of Carthage in the *Aeneid* of Virgil, and the unwitting cause of the queen's death. Henri I of France (1031–1060) married the Russian princess Anna, which made the name popular in Europe.

Anna Sewell (1820–1878) wrote the classic children's novel *Black Beauty*, which did so much to improve the treatment of horses.

ANNABEL (Annabella)
A medieval variant of Amabel (q.v.), now considered an independent name. Annabella Drummond (d. 1401) was married to the crippled Scottish king, Robert III.

Edgar Allan Poe (1809–1849) wrote the haunting poem *Annabel Lee* on the death of his young wife, Virginia.

ANNE/ANN (Annette, Annie)

The French form of Hannah (q.v.), used since the Middle Ages and interchangeable with Ann. Fourteenth century devotion to St Ann, traditionally the mother of the Virgin Mary, made the name very popular indeed from then on.

Queen Anne (1665–1714), sadly remembered for bearing seventeen children, of whom only one survived to the age of 11, was the last Stuart monarch.

A Canadian novelist, Lucy Maud Montgomery (1874–1942) wrote *Anne of Green Gables*, and a string of sequels, which became a success worldwide.

The Princess Royal, christened Anne Elizabeth Alice Louise (b. 1950), is the most eminent modern bearer of the name.

ANNELIES

The German version of Anne, now generally popular. Annelies Marie Frank (1929–1945) is the full name of the girl who wrote *The Diary of Anne Frank* which has sold many millions of copies worldwide since being published in 1947.

ANNIKA

The Swedish pet-form of Anna (q.v.), now generally used.

ANNIS

The medieval version of Agnes (q.v.), now used independently.

ANTHEA

From the Greek, meaning 'flowery'. Used in Classical Greece as a name applied to the goddess Hera, wife of Zeus, it was used by English poets of the seventeenth century. *To Anthea Who May Command Him Anything* by Robert Herrick (1592–1674) is a typical example.

ANTIGONE

From the Greek, meaning 'contrary born'. In Greek mythology, Antigone was the daughter of Jocasta, born of the unknowing incestuous marriage to Oedipus.

Creon, King of Thebes, uncle to Antigone, had her buried alive when she disobeyed his order to leave her brother, Polynices, unburied. A very strong character!

ANTONIA (Toni, Tonya)

The feminine form of Anthony, q.v. The daughter of Mark Antony and great-grandmother of Nero, Antonia Augusta was the most influential Roman matron of her time.

Antonia Fraser, writer of historical biographies such as *Cromwell, Our Chief of Men*, is the best-known modern bearer of the name.

ANUSHKA

The Russian pet-form of Anne (q.v.) now used in Britain.

APHRODITE

From the Greek, meaning 'born of the foam'. In Greek mythology, the goddess of love and beauty, a daughter of Zeus and mother to Eros.

She first stepped ashore on the isle of Cythera. Paris judged her the most beautiful of all the goddesses; in return, she assisted him in abducting Helen, causing the siege of Troy.

APRIL (Avril)

A name which became popular in the early twentieth century, mostly for girls born in that spring month. Avril, the French word for April, is equally favoured.

ARABELLA

Originally a medieval Scottish name, meaning 'moved by prayer', now generally used. It was at its most popular in the eighteenth century, when Lord Petre cut off a lock of hair belonging to Arabella Fermor. This prompted Alexander Pope (1688–1744) to write his well-known poem *The Rape of the Lock*.

ARAMINTA

The name was invented by Sir John Vanbrugh (1664–1726), architect of Blenheim Palace and playwright, for his comedy *The Confederacy*.

ARIADNE

From the Greek, meaning 'very holy one'. In Greek mythology, Ariadne fell in love with Theseus, who came to Crete to kill the Minotaur. She gave him a sword, and a ball of thread with which to trace his path through the labyrinth. Ariadne later married the god Dionysus. There is an obscure early Christian martyr with the name.

ARIANNA
The Italian version of Ariadne (q.v.), now independently popular.

ARLINE
A modern name which seems to have come from America, possibly derived from Marlene or Charlene.

ARTEMIS
One of the twelve deities who lived on Mount Olympus, twin sister to Apollo, Artemis was the goddess of hunting and defender of children and all weak things. She is a main character in three plays by Euripides. The name has been used in England since the eighteenth century, when the love for the classical was at its height.

ASHLEIGH
From the Old English, meaning 'ash wood'. A place name and a surname, now used as a first name for both girls and boys, although the spelling Ashley is preferred for boys.

ASIA
The continent, a popular modern name. Asia, daughter of Ocean, was the beloved wife of Prometheus; he who stole fire from heaven to benefit mankind.

ASPEN
A modern name. The aspen (*Populus tremula*) is the most widespread of European poplar trees. It ranges from the Arctic to the Mediterranean and crosses Asia.

As suggested by its Latin name, the leaves flutter in the slightest breeze.

ASTARTE
The Phoenician goddess of love. *Manfred*, a poetic drama by Lord Byron published in 1817, has the eponymous hero in love with his sister, Astarte.

ASTER
From the Latin, meaning 'star'. The only indigenous *British* flower of this type is the Michaelmas daisy. (And it is an obsolete seventeenth century English word for the stars.)

ASTRID
From the Old Norse, meaning 'divinely beautiful'. Astrid was the wife of St Olaf (995–1030), King of Norway, and it has remained a popular royal name in that country. It has been used in Britain since the beginning of the twentieth century.

ATALANTA
In Greek mythology, Atalanta was a beautiful huntress who said that she would marry any suitor who could out-run her, but anyone who could not do so must die. She was finally beaten by Melanion, who dropped three golden apples given to him by Aphrodite. Atalanta stopped to pick them up and so lost the race and married the winner. Algernon Charles Swinburne wrote a famous poem, *Atalanta in Calydon* (1853), about her.

ATHENE
The name of the 'pale-eyed' Greek goddess of wisdom, daughter of the nymph Metis. She sprang fully formed from the head of Zeus, her father.

AUDREY
From the Old English name, Etheldreda, used as an independent name since the sixteenth century. St Etheldreda (630–679) founded a monastery for both monks and nuns at Ely: the present Ely Cathedral stands on its site. She was the most revered of all Anglo-Saxon women saints. Audrey is a country lass in *As You Like It* by Shakespeare.

AUGUSTA
The female form of Augustus, q.v. Popular as an aristocratic name in Germany, it was brought to England by the Hanoverians.

George III named two daughters, Charlotte Augusta Matilda, Princess Royal (b. 1766), and Augusta Sophia (b. 1768), after his mother, Augusta of Saxe-Gotha-Altenburg. The name became very popular in the nineteenth century and has been used steadily since then.

AURIEL (Aurial)
From the Latin, meaning 'golden'. A name used in ancient Rome, it was revived in the nineteenth century.

AURORA
The Roman goddess of the Dawn, sister to the Sun and the Moon. This has been used in Europe since the Renaissance.

Lady Aurora Sydney was travelling in a carriage stopped by the highwayman Claude Duval. Part of his plunder was restored to her on condition that she dance a coranto with him on the heath. (He was hanged at Tyburn in 1670.)

AVA
A name of obscure origin, possibly a variation of Eve. The film star Ava Gardner seems to have been responsible for its initial popularity.

AVRIL
The French word for the month of April, used as a first name since the early twentieth century.

BAILLIE
A modern female version of Bailey (q.v.). Joanna Baillie (1762–1851) was a Scottish dramatist and poet. Her home in Hampstead was a meeting place for many famous literary figures. She was dubbed 'the immortal Joanna'.

BARBARA (Barbra)

From the Greek, meaning 'strange' or 'foreign'. (The ancient Greeks believed that the language of foreigners was unintelligible, sounding like nothing but 'bar-bar-bar'.) St Barbara, probably martyred in the third century, became very popular in the Middle Ages. The patron saint of architects and miners, she was invoked for protection against lightning. The name was revived in the late nineteenth century.

BEATRICE/BEATRIX

From the Latin, meaning 'bringer of joy'. The name of a Christian martyr in the fourth century, it was common in England during the Middle Ages and is mentioned in the Domesday Book. Princess Beatrice (1857–1944) was the youngest daughter of Queen Victoria, and is the name of the elder daughter of Prince Andrew, Duke of York.

Beatrice Portinari was the guide through Paradise to God for the Italian poet Dante Alighieri (1265–1321) in his epic poem *The Divine Comedy*. A painting in the Tate Gallery in London, entitled *Beata Beatrix*, by Dante Gabriel Rossetti, depicts her death. And the writer and illustrator Beatrix Potter (1866–1943), of 'Peter Rabbit' fame, should not be forgotten.

BELINDA

It was used by Alexander Pope as the name of the beautiful heroine of his epic poem *The Rape of the Lock* (1712), which made it fashionable.

> If to her share some female errors fall,
> Look on her face and you'll forget 'em all.

The name has been used regularly since then.

BELLE

From the French, meaning 'beautiful'. Charles Perrault (1628–1703) included *La Belle au bois dormant* (The Sleeping Beauty) in his book of fairy tales.

BERENICE (Bernice)

From the Greek, meaning 'bringer of Victory'. Popular in ancient Greece and Rome, the New Testament Berenice was the daughter of Herod Agrippa. It has been used in Britain since the Reformation. *Bérénice* was the title of a tragedy by the French playwright Jean Racine (1639–1699).

BERNADETTE
The French female version of Bernard. This became well-known when the very poor and sickly Bernadette Soubirous (1844–1879) had several visions of the Virgin Mary in 1858 at the grotto in Lourdes, now celebrated as a place of pilgrimage for the sick. St Bernadette was canonised in 1933.

BERYL
A green gemstone, first used as a name for girls by the Victorians. (Medieval Parisian jewellers sometimes pretended that these stones were diamonds, which did not please the buyers at all!)

BETHANY (Bethan)
A modern name taken from a town situated on the Mount of Olives. It was the Biblical home of Lazarus, whom Christ raised from the dead.

BETONY (Bettony)
A botanical name, used for girls since the late twentieth century.
   Our Anglo-Saxon ancestors seem to have found this plant indispensable. It cured toothache, and illness in both ears and eyes. Nightmares were repelled by its use; and it was an antidote to both snake bite and injuries bestowed by rabid dogs. Invaluable!

BETSY/BETTY
An abbreviation for Elizabeth, q.v.

BEULAH
From the Hebrew, meaning 'married'. This was the name given to the land of Israel by the prophet Isaiah.
   In John Bunyan's book *The Pilgrim's Progress* (1678), the land of Beulah was 'beyond the valley of the Shadow of Death and also out of the reach of Giant Despair'.
   The Puritans of the seventeenth century made this popular.

BEVERLEY
A Yorkshire place name, meaning 'beaver stream', and surname, used as a first name since the eighteenth century. It is given to both boys and girls.

BIANCA
The Italian version of Blanche, meaning 'white'. In Shakespeare's play *The Taming of the Shrew* Bianca is the younger

sister of Katharina, as gentle and meek as her sister is irascible; while in Shakespeare's *Othello*, Bianca is a courtesan.

BIBA
Always associated with Barbara Hulanicki, the fashion illustrator. She began Biba as a postal boutique in 1961. The enormous success of one of her designs, a pink gingham dress, led on to the opening of the legendary Biba department store in 1973. A seven-storey epitome of Swinging London!

BIBI
From the French, meaning 'toy'.

BIJOU
From the French, meaning 'jewel'.

BLANCHE
From the French, meaning 'white'. The name was brought to England by Blanche of Artois on her marriage to Prince Edmund (d. 1296), a son of Henry III. It was revived in the nineteenth century.

BLATHNAT
From the Gaelic, meaning 'flower'. It is the name of an Irish queen.

BLODWEN
From the Welsh, meaning 'white flower'.

BLOSSOM
From the Old English, meaning 'tree in flower'. First used as a given name in the nineteenth century, it appears to be enjoying a revival.

BLUEBELL
Another flower name which appears to be gaining in popularity. In bloom from April to June, almost half the world's bluebells are to be found in Britain's ancient woods.

The bluebell was supposed to ring to summon the fairies to their revels.

BONNIE
An affectionate Scottish term, meaning 'pretty', now used as a first name. Two films may have helped to popularise the name.

Scarlett O'Hara's daughter was given the nickname Bonnie in *Gone with the Wind*; while Bonnie Parker was the murderous accomplice to Clyde Barrow in *Bonnie and Clyde* (1967).

BRENDA
From the Norse, meaning 'sword'. Popular in Scotland, it became generally used in the nineteenth century. Sir Walter Scott gave the name to a character in his novel *The Pirate* (1822).

BRIDGET (Biddy, Brigitte)
The anglicised version of the Irish Brighid, meaning 'the high one'. St Bridget (450–523), patroness of Ireland, founded the first religious community for women in that country. Her cult spread to England and Scotland, where churches were dedicated in her honour in the medieval form of St Bride. (A well-known example, 'the printers' church', stands in Fleet Street in London.)
  Brigitte is the French version, the best-known bearer of the name being Brigitte Bardot (b. 1934), the former film star and animal lover.

BRITTANY
A French province of north-west France, an independent duchy until 1532, now used as a first name.

BRONWEN
From the Welsh, meaning 'white breast'. Bronwen is the daughter of the sea god in ancient legend.

BROOKE
A place name, meaning 'dweller by a stream', and surname, now used as a first name by both girls and boys.

BRYONY (Briony)
A botanical name, used as a first name since the beginning of the twentieth century. A climbing plant, the white bryony has large yellow flowers and poisonous red berries.

CAITLIN
The Gaelic form of Catherine (q.v.), now generally used.

CALLIOPE
From the Greek, meaning 'beautiful face'. Ancient Greek mythology made her the Muse of Epic Poetry; one of the daughters of Zeus and Mnemosyne, and mother to Orpheus. Her symbols are a writing tablet and stylus.

CALLISTO
From the Greek, meaning 'most beautiful'. In Greek mythology she was a nymph, changed into a bear for displeasing Artemis. Zeus placed her and her son in the heavens, where they are known as the Great and Little Bear.
   Callisto is also the name of several early saints. The catacomb of San Callisto on Rome's Appian Way can still be visited.

CALYPSO
From the Greek, meaning 'to conceal'. In Greek mythology Calpyso was a sea nymph, who kept Odysseus on the isle of Ogygia for seven years. He refused to remain, rejecting her offer of immortality.

CAMILLA (Camille)
The feminine form of Camillus, a family name of ancient Rome. In Virgil's *Aeneid*, Camilla was a warrior maiden so fleet of foot that she could run across a field of corn without bending a single blade. She was killed in battle with the Trojans. The name was first used in England in the thirteenth century. Fanny

Burney (1752–1840) wrote the novel *Camilla* (1796) which helped to revive the name. The best-known modern bearer of the name is Camilla, Duchess of Cornwall.

Camille is the French version, now generally used.

CANDACE (Candice, Candy)
A title given to the Queens of Ethiopia, also mentioned in the New Testament. The name has been used in Britain since the seventeenth century.

CANDIDA
From the Latin, meaning 'white'. The name of an early Christian martyr, not used in Britain until the twentieth century. Candida Morell is the heroine of the play *Candida*, written by George Bernard Shaw (1856–1950), which brought the name into favour.

CAPRICE
From the French, meaning 'whim' or 'fancy'. A modern name.

The musical term denotes a lively composition. (Appropriate for the memorable *Caprice Bohémian* by Sergei Rachmaninov.)

And Ronald Firbank wrote *Caprice* (1917), the story of a short and dazzling theatrical career.

CARA (Carina, Kara)
From the Italian, meaning 'dear'. A popular modern name.

CAREY
A place name, meaning 'pleasant stream', and surname, used as a first name since the mid-nineteenth century.

CARLA (Carly, Karli)
The feminine version of Carl, the German for Charles, q.v.

CARMEL
From the Hebrew, meaning 'garden'. It is the name of a mountain near the city of Haifa in Israel. The monastic Carmelite order – begun when hermits living on the mountain formed themselves into a community in the early thirteenth century – has spread worldwide.

CARMEN
The Spanish form of Carmel (q.v.), now generally used.

Carmen is the eponymous heroine of Bizet's opera, first performed in 1875, based on a novel by Prosper Mérimée. As is usual in classic opera, the end is tragic, with Carmen stabbed to death.

CAROL (Carole)
Originally a pet-form of Caroline, used independently since the late nineteenth century. This is sometimes given to girls born in the Christmas season, in association with the carol, a song for the festivity.

CAROLINE (Carolyn, Carrie)
Derives from the Italian feminine form of Charles. Caroline Wilhelmina of Brandenburg-Ansbach (1683–1737), wife of George II, made the name a great favourite in the eighteenth century and this popularity has continued. Another royal Caroline was married to George IV; her turbulent life included an abortive attempt at divorce and being forcibly excluded from her husband's coronation at Westminster Abbey.

CARSON
A surname, now a first name for both girls and boys. The American novelist Carson McCullers (1917–1967) gained fame with her very first novel, *The Heart is a Lonely Hunter* (1940).

CASEY
An Irish surname, now used as a first name by both girls and boys. See the entry in the boys' section.

CASSANDRA (Cassie)
In Greek legend, she was the beautiful daughter of King Priam. When she rejected the god Apollo, he cursed her so that her prophecies would never be believed. She died in the fall of Troy. The story was popular in the Middle Ages and has been used regularly since then.

Cassandra was the beloved elder sister of the novelist Jane Austen (1775–1817), the recipient of many of her surviving letters.

CATHERINE/KATHERINE (Cath, Catharine, Cathie, Cathy, Catrina, Kate, Katerina, Katey, Kath, Katharine, Kathy, Katie, Katrina, Katy)
From the Greek, meaning 'pure'. The name of many saints, the most famous of whom is St Catherine of Alexandria (d. 307).

Refusing to deny her faith, a vain attempt was made to break her on a wheel (thus giving us the firework 'Catherine wheel') and she was beheaded. The angels carried her body to Mount Sinai, where the monks of the orthodox monastery there still guard her shrine. Her cult was brought to England by returning Crusaders and many churches were dedicated to her.

Henry VIII (1491–1547) was particularly partial to the name. Catherine of Aragon, Catherine Howard and Catherine Parr were unfortunate enough to be married to him.

The name has been, and remains, a great favourite.

CATRIONA
The Gaelic diminutive of Catherine, now used all over Britain. *Catriona* (1893) is the name of a novel written by Robert Louis Stevenson, sequel to the more famous *Kidnapped*.

CECILIA (Cecily, Cicely)
From the Latin, meaning 'blind', the feminine form of Cecil. An early Christian martyr in Rome, St Cecilia has been revered in Europe since the sixth century. She is the patron saint of musicians. The name was brought to England at the Norman Conquest by a daughter of William I.

Cecily Cardew is the ward of Jack Worthing in the classic play *The Importance of Being Earnest* (1895) by Oscar Wilde.

CELESTE
From the Latin, meaning 'heavenly'. The name of two (male) saints, but considered exclusively feminine in Britain.

CELIA
The feminine name of an ancient Roman family, the name became popular when Shakespeare included it in *As You Like It*. Celia is the daughter of Duke Frederick.

The poet Ben Jonson (1572–1637) wrote the well-known poem *To Celia*, which includes the lines:

> Drink to me only with thine eyes,
> And I will pledge with mine.

CERIAN
From the Welsh, meaning 'love'.

CERYS
From the Welsh, meaning 'to love'.

CHANEL
The world-famous French perfume, now used as a first name. The French dress designer Gabrielle ('Coco') Chanel (1883–1971) opened her first fashion house in 1914. Her life was portrayed in a musical comedy entitled *Coco* in 1969.

CHANTAL (Chantelle)
This name was originally used in honour of St Jeanne de Chantal (1572–1641), the charming co-founder of the Order of the Visitation. She was described by another saint as 'one of the holiest people I have ever met on this earth'. It has been used in Britain since the beginning of the twentieth century.

CHARIS
From the Greek, meaning 'grace'. Charis was one of the three Graces, attendants to Aphrodite, mentioned in Homer's *Iliad*. She was married to Hephaestus, the lame god of fire and metal-working. The name was used after the Reformation.

CHARLENE
A feminine version of Charles, in use since the 1950s.

CHARLOTTE (Charlie, Lottie)
The French feminine form of Charles. The name was unusual in Britain until the marriage of Charlotte Sophia of Mecklenburg-Strelitz (1744–1818) to George III in 1761 made it fashionable. Her grand-daughter, Princess Charlotte (1796–1817), daughter of the Prince Regent, died in childbirth, generating a great wave of public grief. There is a beautiful monument to her in St George's Chapel, Windsor.

The writer Charlotte Brontë (1816–1855), author of *Jane Eyre*, *The Professor*, *Shirley* and *Villette*, is a famous bearer of the name, as is the poet Charlotte Mew (1869–1928).

CHARMIAN
From the Greek, meaning 'delight'. Shakespeare gives the name to a kind-hearted attendant to Cleopatra in his play *Antony and Cleopatra*. After the queen's death, she kills herself by applying an asp to her arm.

CHELSEA (Chelsie)
A place name in west London, meaning 'a landing place for limestone', now used as a first name. The singer Joni Mitchell had a success with her song *Chelsea Morning*, which may have helped.

CHERRY (Cherie, Cherrie, Cheryl)
Sometimes considered the anglicised form of the French word
for 'darling' (cherie), it was originally a pet-form of Charity.
Charity and Mercy, daughters of Mr Pecksniff in *Martin Chuz-
zlewit* (1843), are called Cherry and Merry.

CHLÖE
From the Greek, meaning 'green shoot'. The New Testament
Chlöe lived in Corinth and was mentioned by St Paul. It was
popular with the Puritans of the seventeenth century as they
searched the Bible for names for their children.
   Daphnis and Chlöe, a Greek pastoral poem of the fourth
century by Longus, has inspired many imitations. Maurice Ravel
wrote the music for a ballet of the same name.

CHRISTA
A pet-form of Christine (q.v.), originating in Germany, now
generally used.

CHRISTABEL
This appears to have been coined by the poet Samuel Taylor
Coleridge in his fragmentary poem *Christabel* (1816).
   The most famous bearer of the name was Dame Christabel
Pankhurst (1880–1958), suffragette. She is included on the
memorial to her mother in the Victoria Tower Gardens near the
House of Lords.

**CHRISTINA/CHRISTINE (Chris, Chrissie, Christen, Christy,
Krystyna, Tina)**
The feminine abbreviation of Christian (q.v.), used regularly
since the eighteenth century. The enigmatic poet Christina Ros-
setti (1830–1894) must be the most famous bearer of the name.
In the Bleak Midwinter, now used as a carol, was written by her.
   Christine is the French version of the name, favoured in
Britain since the end of the nineteenth century.

CINDY
The pet-form of Cynthia or Lucinda, now used as an independent name.

CIRCE
A sorceress of Greek mythology, daughter of the sun, she lived
on the isle of Aeaea. When Odysseus landed, she turned his

companions into swine. (He avoided this ghastly fate by means of a herb, given to him by Hermes.)

Reinhard Keiser's opera *Circe* was first produced in 1702.

CLARE (Claire)

From the Latin, meaning 'bright'. St Clare of Assisi (1194–1253), the friend of St Francis and founder of the Poor Clare contemplative nuns, made the name well-known. She is the patron saint of television; owing to her having seen and heard a mass being celebrated far away, which illness had prevented her from attending.

CLARISSA

From the Latin, meaning 'renowned'. A form of Clarice, made famous by the book *Clarissa Harlowe* by Samuel Richardson (1689–1761), the longest novel in the English language. Clarissa rejects the man her tyrannical family wish her to marry, elopes with the unsuitable Robert Lovelace and it all ends in tears.

CLAUDIA (Claudette, Claudine)

The feminine form of Claudius, the name of an ancient Roman family. The name is mentioned in the New Testament as that of a Roman convert. It has been used in England since the seventeenth century.

Claudine is the heroine of four semi-autobiographical novels written by 'Colette' (Sidonie Gabrielle Colette) between 1900 and 1903.

CLEA

From the Greek, meaning 'praise'. *Clea* (1960) is the fourth novel in Lawrence Durrell's *Alexandria Quartet*. The eponymous heroine is a painter, loved by Darley, the narrator.

CLEMENCY (Clemmie, Clementine)

From the Latin, meaning 'merciful', the feminine form of Clement. The name has been used in England since the thirteenth century; seventeenth century Puritans liked the abstract nouns of Clemency, Prudence and Patience.

CLIO

From the Greek, meaning 'praise'. In Greek mythology, the inventor of heroic and historical poetry, one of the nine Muses, daughters of Zeus and Mnemosyne.

CLODAGH
From the river in County Tipperary. A modern first name.

CLOTILDE
From the Old German, meaning 'renowned in battle'. Daughter of King Chilperic, Clotilde (474–545) married Clovis, King of the Franks, converting him to Christianity.

Clotilde Peploe (1915–1997), the daughter-in-law of Scottish colourist Samuel Peploe, was a talented painter who exhibited rarely. Her first retrospective took place in London in 2006.

CLOVER
A botanical name, used as a first name since the nineteenth century. Clover Carr is the sister of the eponymous heroine of the classic children's books *What Katy Did* and *What Katy Did Next* by Susan Coolidge (1835–1905; real name Sarah Chauncey Woolsey).

COLETTE
The French feminine diminutive of Nicholas (q.v.). St Colette (1381–1447) was born when her mother was 60 years of age. She became a hermit and, later, a reformer of the Poor Clares. The name has been used in England since the thirteenth century.

CONSTANCE
From the Latin, meaning 'firmness'. A saint's name, it was brought to England by the Normans, the name of a daughter of William the Conqueror.

Lady Constance Lytton (1869–1923) was a militant suffragette whose health was permanently impaired by forcible feeding; she wrote a book about her experiences.

CORA (Corah)
From the Greek, meaning 'maiden'. The name was not used until the nineteenth century, apparently brought to public attention by a character in James Fenimore Cooper's novel *The Last of the Mohicans* (1826). Cora Munro is in love with Uncas, the last of the Mohicans, and it ends in suicide.

CORAL
Used as a girl's name since the late nineteenth century, when there was a passion for jewel names. Italian babies of the

fourteenth century wore pieces of coral mounted with silver around their necks; this can be seen in several medieval paintings of the Virgin and Child.

CORDELIA

From the Latin, meaning 'heart'. Cordelia is the only faithful daughter of Shakespeare's *King Lear* and marries the King of France. To her are applied the lines:

> Her voice was ever soft, gentle and low,
> An excellent thing in a woman. (!)

CORINNA (Corinne)

From the Greek, meaning 'maiden'. Corinna was a Greek poet of the fourth century BC. Robert Herrick used the name in his well-known poem *Corinna's Going A-Maying* (1648). The French writer Madame de Staël (1766–1817) wrote the romantic novel *Corinne*.

CORNELIA

Daughter of Scipio the Elder (237–183 BC), Cornelia was considered the ideal Roman matron. Once visited by a wealthy woman who boasted of her jewels, she responded by pointing to her sons, 'These are my jewels'.

COSIMA

From the Greek, meaning 'harmony'. Cosima Wagner (1837–1930), the daughter of Franz Liszt and wife of Richard Wagner, is the best-known bearer of the name.

COURTNEY

An aristocratic surname, originating from Courtenay in France, now bestowed as a first name on both girls and boys.

CRESSIDA

Both Chaucer and Shakespeare wrote about the legend of 'Troilus and Cressida'. Cressida, the daughter of a Trojan priest, vowed eternal fidelity to Troilus but threw him aside for Diomedes, thus making herself a byword for infidelity. A favourite name in the twentieth century.

CRYSTAL (Chrystal, Krystle)
Another of the gem names, popular since the late nineteenth century. The word is derived from the Greek 'krystallos', meaning 'ice'.

CYNTHIA
A title of the goddess Diana, meaning 'of Cynthus', the mountain on which she was born. It has been used in England since the sixteenth century.

DAGMAR
From the Scandinavian, its meaning in hot dispute. On the marriage of Alexandra of Denmark to the Prince of Wales in 1863, she brought as part of her dowry the Dagmar necklace, still part of the Royal Collection.

It consists of 2,000 diamonds, 118 pearls and a facsimile of the eleventh century Dagmar cross; the original of which had belonged to the beloved Queen Dagmar (d. 1212), wife of King Waldemar the Victorious.

DAISY
From the flower, which in Old English means 'the eye of day'. The Victorians began the vogue for flower names in the latter part of the nineteenth century.

Daisy Miller is the eponymous, unsophisticated, American heroine of a novelette by Henry James (1843–1916).

And 'top of the pops' c.1902 was:

> Daisy, Daisy, give me your answer do,
> I'm half crazy, all for the love of you.

DAMARIS

From the Greek, meaning 'heifer', implying gentleness. In the New Testament, Damaris was an Athenian woman converted by St Paul. Along with Priscilla and Dorcas, it was one of the most popular of all Puritan names in the seventeenth century.

DANIELLE (Dannie)

The French feminine form of Daniel (q.v.), very popular indeed since the 1960s.

DAPHNE

From the Greek, meaning 'laurel'. In Greek mythology, Daphne, the daughter of a river-god, was loved by Apollo. Pursued by him, she appealed to her father to save her and was transformed into a laurel tree. This was believed to be so holy as to protect all beneath its shade from lightning. The name came into fashion in Britain in the late nineteenth century and is now enjoying a revival.

Daphne du Maurier (1907–1989), author of such popular novels as *Rebecca* and *Jamaica Inn*, is the best-known bearer of the name.

DARA

From the Hebrew, meaning 'pearl of wisdom'. A male name in the Old Testament, shown in a genealogical list as 'one of the five sons of Zerah, grandson of Judah' (I Chronicles 2: 6), it is used as a girls' name in modern times.

DARCEY/DARCY

A French place name and surname, brought to England by Norman d'Arcy, a companion of William the Conqueror.

It is now bestowed on both girls and boys; a compliment to the fine ballerina Darcey Bussell, perhaps.

DARIA

The feminine form of Darius. Darius I (558–486 BC) was one of seven Persian chiefs who overthrew the usurper Smerdis and won the throne by a trick. He invaded Greece and was defeated at the Battle of Marathon in 490 BC.

DARRYL

Generally considered a male name, but occasionally bestowed on girls.

DAVINA
The Scottish feminine version of David (q.v.), now generally used.

DAWN
This name has been used since the early twentieth century; the English version of the goddess Aurora, who was married to the Titan Astraeus and gave birth to the stars, the winds and Eosphorus, the Morning Star.

DEBORAH (Debbie, Debra)
From the Hebrew, meaning 'bee'. In the Old Testament there are two women with this name. The first was nurse to Rebecca and accompanied her when she married Isaac. The second Deborah was the prophetess, whose wisdom made her leader of the Israelites as they fought successfully against the Canaanites.

The Puritans of the seventeenth century favoured the name and it has been used since then. The blind poet John Milton (1608–1674) bestowed it on his youngest daughter.

DEIRDRE
The heroine of Irish legend, Deirdre, the most beautiful woman in the land, fled to Scotland with the man she loved and his two brothers. Persuaded to return and betrayed, the three men were murdered and *Deirdre*, by the poet W. B. Yeats (1865–1939), and *Deirdre of the Sorrows* by J. M. Synge (1871–1909), have made the name popular since the early years of the twentieth century.

DELIA
From the Greek island of Delos, birthplace of the goddess Diana. Delia was the shepherdess in the *Eclogues* of Virgil (70–19 BC) and the name was used in many poems of the seventeenth and eighteenth centuries, including *Sonnets to Delia* by Samuel Daniel (1562–1619).

DELPHI
From the Greek, meaning 'dolphin'. An ancient oracle on the southern slope of Mount Parnassus, Delphi was regarded as the final authority in religious matters. Associated with the shrine was the omphalos, a sacred stone considered the navel of the world.

Some of the most famous Greek myths hinge on oracles issued from Delphi.

DELPHINE

From the Latin, meaning 'woman from Delphi'. The Provençal Blessed Delphine (1284–1358) was married to St Elzear of Sabran. At the age of 70, she had the rare experience of being required to give evidence as to her late husband's sanctity.

Madame de Staël wrote the romantic novel *Delphine* (1802).

DEMELZA

A Cornish place name, meaning 'hill fort', used as a first name since the mid-twentieth century.

Demelza is the heroine of Winston Graham's *Poldark* novels.

DEMI

A pet-form of Demeter, Greek goddess of agriculture. This has been made popular by the actress Demi Moore.

DENA

From the Old English, meaning 'valley'. This is considered to be the feminine version of Dean and has been used since the 1950s.

DENISE

The French feminine form of Dennis, q.v. The name was brought to England at the Norman Conquest and in use until the eighteenth century when it disappeared to be revived in the early twentieth century.

DESIRÉE

From the French, meaning 'desired'. The Puritans of the seventeenth century gave the name Desire to their daughters, but it was never popular. The French version appears to have been used in Britain since the beginning of the twentieth century. (It is also the name of the rather delicious potato!)

DESTINY

From the Middle English, meaning 'fate'. A modern first name, seemingly initiated in America.

Wordsworth's lines from his epic poem *The Prelude*, completed in 1805, spring to mind:

> Whether we be young or old,
> Our Destiny, our being's heart and home,
> Is with infinitude . . .

DETTA
The Italian pet-form of Bernadette (q.v.), now generally used.

DEVON
The name of a beautiful county, used as a first name since the late twentieth century.

Sir Henry Newbolt's bracing patriotic poem *Drake's Drum* states that Drake would 'quit the port o'Heaven' should his beloved Devon fall into danger.

DIANA (Diane)
The Latin name for the goddess of the moon, it became fashionable in England in the sixteenth century when there was much interest in classical literature.

Diane de Poitiers (1499–1566) was the mistress of the French king, Henry II, and allowed unlimited power when he ascended the throne. She was created Duchesse de Valentinois, but expelled from court on his death.

Diana of the Crossways (1885) was a novel by George Meredith; the heroine of which disliked her 'pagan' name!

Diana, Princess of Wales (1961–1997) greatly increased the name's popularity.

DIDO
The legendary founder and Queen of Carthage, whose husband was murdered by her brother, Pygmalion.

In Virgil's *Aeneid*, she falls in love with Aeneas when he and other Trojans are shipwrecked on her shores. Finally abandoned by him, she commits suicide.

Christopher Marlowe and Thomas Nashe collaborated on the play *Dido, Queen of Carthage* (1593) and the English Baroque composer Henry Purcell (1659–1695) wrote one opera, *Dido and Aeneas*.

DILYS
From the Welsh, meaning 'genuine'. It has been used as a name since the latter part of the nineteenth century.

DINAH
From the Hebrew, meaning 'judged'. In the Old Testament, the unhappy daughter of Jacob and Leah. Another of the names

adopted by the Puritans of the seventeenth century and used regularly since then. (An unusual literary Dinah was the cat of Alice in Wonderland fame!)

DIONNE (Dione)
In Greek mythology, Dione was a consort of the god Zeus and the mother of Aphrodite. Another of the same name was a daughter of Atlas who married the unfortunate Tantalus. The American singer Dionne Warwick brought the name back into the limelight.

DOLORES (Lola)
From the Spanish, meaning 'sorrows'. A title of the Virgin Mary, 'Maria de los Dolores', which commemorated seven sad episodes in her life.

DONNA
From the Italian, meaning 'lady', literally mistress of the household. An Italian title, it has been used as a first name in Britain since the 1930s.

DORA (Dorrie)
A shortened form of Theodora and Dorothy, used as an independent name since the beginning of the nineteenth century.

David Copperfield, the eponymous hero of the novel by Charles Dickens (1812–1870) is hopelessly in love with Dora Spenlow who appears to be besotted only with her dog, Jip. He later marries his 'child-wife', who fortunately does not long survive. This rather idiotic character made the name very popular.

DORCAS
From the Greek, meaning 'gazelle'. In the New Testament, Dorcas is the Greek translation of the Aramaic name Tabitha, a woman who was 'full of good works and almsdeeds', and raised from the dead by St Peter (Acts 9: 36–41). This was first used by the Puritans of the seventeenth century.

DOREEN
An Irish version of Dora. It has been used in Britain since the beginning of the twentieth century, possibly prompted by the novel *Doreen* (1894) written by Edna Lyall.

DORINDA
A name invented in the eighteenth century, used by both poets and playwrights. Dorinda, the daughter of Lady Bountiful, marries Thomas Aimwell, one of the two beaux in the play *The Beaux' Stratagem* by the comic dramatist George Farquhar (1678–1707).

DORIS
From the Greek, meaning 'of the sea'. In Greek mythology, Doris was married to the sea-god Nereus, and mother to fifty daughters known as Nereids or sea-nymphs.

For reasons unfathomable the name became very popular in Britain in the late nineteenth century.

The American film star Doris Day (b. 1924) is well-known.

DOROTHY (Dorothea, Dot)
From the Greek, meaning 'gift of God'. St Dorothy (d. 303) was martyred during Diocletian's persecution of the Christians. On her way to execution a lawyer mocked her, asking her to send him fruit and flowers from Paradise: a child promptly appeared and gave him a basket of apples and roses. The lawyer became a Christian and a martyr himself.

The name has been used in England since the fifteenth century. It was so common in the sixteenth century that the diminutive Doll was given to the child's toy.

The English detective-story writer Dorothy L. Sayers (1893–1957) created Lord Peter Wimsey and wrote the religious play *The Man Born to be King* (1942).

DOVE
A modern name, symbolising peace and gentleness. It is also a term of affection.

Alfred, Lord Tennyson, encapsulates this in his lines from *Maud*: 'She is coming, my dove, my dear'.

DULCIE
From the Latin, meaning 'sweet'. This was a name coined in the late nineteenth century, perhaps based on the medieval Dowsabel, now obsolete.

DYMPHA
From the Gaelic, meaning 'fawn'. A Christian martyr, whose feast day is celebrated on 15th May, Dymphna is patron of those suffering from mental disorders.

Her cultus began at Gheel, near Antwerp, in the thirteenth century. The medieval hospital dedicated to her there has grown into the largest in the world for the mentally ill.

EBONY

A modern first name, adopting the name of a very hard, black wood, imported from the exotic East in the very earliest times.

The *Ebony Concerto*, a work by Stravinsky for clarinet and orchestra, was first performed by Woody Herman and his band in 1946.

ECHO

In Greek mythology, the goddess Hera was infuriated by the incessant chatter of a nymph named Echo. As a punishment, the goddess deprived her of speech, allowing her only the ability to repeat the last words spoken by someone else. Echo fell in love with the beautiful youth Narcissus, but her love was unrequited. She pined away, leaving nothing behind but her voice.

EDDA

From the Old Norse, meaning 'poetry'. This was the name given to two Icelandic collections of Scandinavian mythology: the *Elder Edda* (ninth to twelve century), and the *Prose Edda* (thirteenth century). The second was written by the magnificently named Snorri Sturluson (1178–1241), Icelandic historian.

EDEN

From the Hebrew, meaning 'delight'. Originally bestowed on boys, it is now equally popular for girls.

The writer George Meredith (1828–1909) included these lines in his poem *Woodland Peace*:

Sweet as Eden is the air,
And Eden-sweet the ray.

EDIE
The pet-form of Edith (q.v.), now independently used.

EDITH
From the Old English, the two syllables meaning 'wealthy' and 'war'. The name of three Anglo-Saxon saints, it survived the Norman Conquest and has been used regularly since then.

Queen Edith (d. 1075), daughter of the Earl of Wessex, was married to St Edward the Confessor.

The actress Dame Edith Evans (1888–1976), famous for her Lady Bracknell in Oscar Wilde's *The Importance of Being Earnest*, and the writer and poet Dame Edith Sitwell (1887–1964), are the best-known modern bearers of the name.

EDNA
From the Hebrew, meaning 'delight'. Edna was married to Raguel, a relative of Tobit, in the apocryphal Book of Tobit. It came into use in Britain in the mid-nineteenth century.

Two bestselling literary ladies have borne the name: the Victorian novelist Edna Lyall and Edna Ferber, the American writer remembered for *Show Boat* and *Giant*.

EDWINA
The feminine form of Edwin, q.v., first used in the nineteenth century.

EGLANTINE
A flower name, first used in the late nineteenth century, and included in the famous lines from Shakespeare's *A Midsummer Night's Dream*:

I know a bank whereon the wild thyme blows
... With sweet musk-roses, and with eglantine

EILEEN
The Irish form of Helen (q.v.), used in England since the late nineteenth century. Ruth McKenney wrote the amusing *My Sister Eileen* (1938), later filmed, which helped to popularise the name.

EIRWEN
From the Welsh, meaning 'golden fair', used since the early years of the twentieth century.

ELAINE
The Old French form of Helen (q.v.), now used independently. Arthurian romance mentions two ladies named Elaine. The first, daughter of King Pelles, fell in love with Sir Lancelot and assumed the likeness of Queen Guinevere for one night in order to deceive him. Sir Galahad was the result of their union.

The second died of unrequited love for Sir Lancelot; her story is included in the poems *Idylls of the King* and *The Lady of Shalott* by Alfred, Lord Tennyson (1809–1892). These poems made the name a favourite with parents.

ELEANOR (Elinor, Nell)
A variant of Helen (q.v.), brought to England by the ebullient Eleanor of Aquitaine (1122–1204), who married Henry II at Bordeaux Cathedral. She was mother to Richard the Lionheart and the 'baddie', King John.

Queen Eleanor of Castile (1244–1290), wife of Edward I, accompanied her husband on the Crusades and saved his life by sucking poison from a wound. Twelve memorial crosses (of which four remain) were erected by him to mark her body's resting place at each halt on her last journey from Harby in Nottinghamshire to burial in Westminster Abbey.

Elinor Dashwood is the heroine of *Sense and Sensibility* (1811) by Jane Austen.

ELECTRA
In Greek mythology Electra's father, Agamemnon, King of Argos, was murdered by her mother, Clytemnestra. Her tragic life has been an inspiration throughout the ages.

The compelling *Electra at the Tomb of Agamemnon*, painted by Lord Leighton in 1868, can be seen at the Ferens Art Gallery, Hull.

ELFRIDA
From the Old English, meaning 'elf strength'. Queen Elfrida (c.945–1002) was crowned with her husband, Edgar, at Bath Abbey on 11th May 973. This was the first coronation of a queen in England.

ELGIVA
A truly royal name, bestowed on many ladies: these include St Elgiva, wife of Edmund I, who was buried at Shaftesbury Abbey, Dorset.

ELIZABETH (Bess, Bessie, Beth, Betsy, Bette, Betty, Elise, Eliza, Lisette)
From the Hebrew, meaning 'God's promise'. The Biblical Elizabeth was cousin to the Virgin Mary and mother to John the Baptist.

Queen Elizabeth I (1533–1603) made the name immensely popular, which is indicated by the very many variants used. In the twentieth century, the name continued firmly regal when borne by Elizabeth Bowes Lyon (1900–2002), wife of George VI, and bestowed upon Queen Elizabeth II (b. 1926). The poet Elizabeth Barrett Browning (1806–1861), whose tyrannical father prompted the most famous elopement in literary history, is just one of the many famous bearers of this favourite name.

ELLA
From the Old German, meaning 'all'. This was brought to England at the Norman Conquest and was popular during the Middle Ages. It was revived in the nineteenth century, chiefly by the Pre-Raphaelites in their enthusiasm for the medieval.

The jazz singer Ella Fitzgerald is a well-known modern bearer of the name.

ELLEN
An English form of Helen (q.v.), used as an independent name since the thirteenth century. Ellen Montgomery was the heroine of the Victorian tearjerker *The Wide, Wide World* by Elizabeth Wetherell.

ELLERY (Ellerie)
A surname, now used as a first name by both girls and boys.

ELLIE (Elle)
A pet-form of Eleanor (q.v.), now used independently.

ELSA
From the Old German, meaning 'noble maiden'. Elsa, Princess of Brabant, is a heroine of German romances. Lohengrin, the Knight of the Swan, marries her on the understanding that she

should know neither his name nor his lineage. Of course, on her wedding night she *does* ask, is told, and Lohengrin leaves, accompanied by a swan.

Richard Wagner wrote an opera, *Lohengrin* (1850), on the subject.

ELSIE
A Scottish diminutive of Elizabeth (q.v.), used as an independent name since the eighteenth century.

Oliver Wendell Holmes wrote *Elsie Venner: A Romance of Destiny* (1861), whose heroine has the qualities of a snake and a repellent nature!

And Elsie Marley is the girl of nursery rhyme who refuses to feed the pigs and

> Lies in bed till eight or nine.
> Lazy Elsie Marley.

Who can find it in their heart to blame her?

ELSPETH
Another Scottish diminutive of Elizabeth (q.v.), in use since the nineteenth century.

ELVIRA
A Spanish name, brought to public attention as the wife of Don Juan in the opera *Don Giovanni* (1787) by Mozart.

Elvira is the deceased first wife of the novelist Charles Condomine in the Noël Coward play *Blithe Spirit* (1941), later a highly successful film.

ELYSIA (Elise)
From the Greek, meaning 'blissful'. In Greek mythology, Elysium was the abode of the blessed dead.

EMERALD
From the gem stone, another of the jewel names so liked by the Victorians. Dr William Drennan (1754–1820) was the first to describe Ireland as the 'Emerald Isle' in his poem *Erin*. The Emperor Nero (AD 37–68) wore emerald spectacles to aid his sight.

EMILY (Amelie)
From the Latin, meaning 'eager'. It is derived from Aemilius, the name of an ancient Roman family and was a popular name with the early Christians.

Geoffrey Chaucer (1343–1400) included a character named Emelye in *The Knight's Tale*, part of *The Canterbury Tales*.

Two writers, Emily Brontë (1818–1848), author of *Wuthering Heights*, and the reclusive American poet, Emily Dickinson (1830–1886), who had only seven poems published in her lifetime, add lustre to the name. And Emily Davies (1830–1921), founder of Girton College, Cambridge, should not be forgotten.

EMMA
From the Old German, meaning 'universal'. The name was brought to England by Emma of Normandy (d. 1052) who married King Ethelred II ('the Unready') in 1002. A widow, she married King Canute in 1017. She was the mother of St Edward the Confessor.

Emma by Jane Austen (1775–1817) has the delightful and infuriating Emma Woodhouse as a heroine. Gustave Flaubert's *Madame Bovary* (1857) is a very different character. Emma Bovary is an adulteress, overwhelmed by debt, who finally commits suicide. A classic novel, naturally.

ENA
A pet-form of Helena. Queen Victoria's granddaughter, Princess Victoria Eugenie Julia Ena, always known as Ena (1887–1969), became Queen of Spain, marrying Alfonso XIII.

ENID
From the Welsh, meaning 'life'. Alfred, Lord Tennyson included Enid and her husband Geraint in his verse epic *Idylls of the King* (1859), thus popularising the name.

The phenomenal children's writer Enid Blyton (1897–1968) created Noddy and The Famous Five and published over 700 books!

ERICA (Erika)
The feminine version of Eric, q.v. Erica is the Latin botanical name for heather.

The Swedish form, Erika, has been used in Britain since the nineteenth century.

ERIN
From the Gaelic, meaning 'isle of the west', a poetic term for Ireland. The name became popular during the Celtic revival of the nineteenth century. *Erin* was the title of a poem written by Dr William Drennan (1754–1820).

ESME
From the French, meaning 'esteemed'. Introduced to England in the sixteenth century by the Duke of Lennox, Esme Stuart (1542–1583), it is now considered a purely feminine name.

ESTELLE (Estella)
From the French, meaning 'star'. Estella is the haughty ward of Miss Havisham in Dickens' novel *Great Expectations* (1860). The hero, Pip, remains hopelessly in love with her, even when he discovers that she is the illegitimate daughter of the convict Magwitch and Jagger's housekeeper, Molly the murderess.

ESTHER
From the Persian, meaning 'star'. The Biblical Esther became the favourite of the Persian king Ahasuerus and managed to save her fellow Jews from death, thwarting the plans of the evil Haman, who was hanged. Orthodox Jews celebrate this deliverance at the Feast of Purim.

Esther Summerson is the kindly narrator of Dickens' *Bleak House* (1852), the illegitimate daughter of Lady Dedlock.

ESYLLT
The Welsh version of Isolde (q.v.), meaning 'fair aspect'.

EUGENIE
The French feminine form of Eugene (q.v.), revived by Princess Eugenie (b. 1990), the daughter of the Duke of York.

Empress Eugenie (1826–1920) was the wife of Napoleon III of France. After he surrendered to the Prussians at Sedan, she fled to England, living first at Chislehurst, then Farnborough.

EULALIE
From the Greek, meaning 'sweetly spoken'. Devotion to a young Spanish martyr made this name popular from the eighth century onwards. It was revived by the Victorians.

And, should you enjoy the P. G. Wodehouse novel *The Code of the Woosters*, you will recall how Bertie Wooster is able to control the amateur tyrant, Roderick Spode. The very mention of Eulalie terrifies him!

EUNICE (Younice)
From the Greek, meaning 'good victory'. The New Testament Eunice was the mother of St Timothy, first bishop of Ephesus. The name came into use in England in the seventeenth century, a favourite of the Puritans.

EUPHEMIA
From the Greek, meaning 'fair speech'. Euphemia was martyred during the persecution of the Emperor Diocletian in the fourth century. Many churches were dedicated in her honour.

The name has been used in Britain since the twelfth century, being particularly popular in Scotland.

EVANGELINE
This name appears to have been invented by Henry Wadsworth Longfellow (1807–1882) for his long narrative poem, *Evangeline, a Tale of Acadie* (1847). This tells the story of Evangeline Bellefontaine and Gabriel Lajeunesse, star-crossed lovers separated by the British.

Evangeline St Claire (better known as 'little Eva') was cared for by the noble Uncle Tom in *Uncle Tom's Cabin* (1852) by Harriet Beecher Stowe.

EVE (Eva, Evie)
From the Hebrew, meaning 'life'. The Biblical first woman, helpmate to Adam, the first man. It has been used in England since the twelfth century. Eva is a character in *Die Meistersinger*, an opera by Richard Wagner (1813–1883).

EVELYN (Evelina, Eveline)
From the Old German, meaning 'hazel nut'. The name was brought to England by the Normans. It is bestowed upon both girls and boys.

Evelina (1778) is the name of the bestselling novel by Fanny Burney (1752–1840), in which the heroine, Evelina Anville, is introduced into high society and marries Lord Orville after many trials.

EVONNE
An alternative spelling for Yvonne (q.v.).

FABIENNE
The French feminine form of Fabian (q.v.), now increasingly used.

FAITH
First used after the Reformation, when the abstract virtues of Faith, Hope and Charity became favourite names.

FALLON
An Irish surname, meaning 'grandchild of the ruler', now a popular first name.
    This is also the name of a town in Nevada.

FAUSTINA
From the Latin, meaning 'fortunate'. Two Roman empresses have borne the name; one the wife of Marcus Aurelius, who believed her to be the best of women. Algernon Swinburne (1837–1909) wrote the poem *Faustine* with these ladies in mind.
    (And on a whimsical note: a cow named Faustina Gwynne is commemorated on a gravestone at Rousham House, Oxfordshire. She died in 1882, aged 22.)

FAY (Faye)
A shortened version of Faith, first used in the late nineteenth century. The wicked sorceress Morgan le Fay disclosed the liaison between Queen Guinevere and Sir Lancelot to her brother, King Arthur.

Fay Wray, the American film star, is best remembered for screaming so piercingly at the sight of the great ape who loved her in the original *King Kong* (1933).

FELICITY (Felicia)
From the Latin, meaning 'happy'. St Felicity (d. 203), a slave girl, was a Christian martyr who died in the arena at Carthage with her friend, St Perpetua. *The Passion of Saints Perpetua and Felicity* is the most moving of all the authentic narratives of early martyrs.

It came into use in England in the seventeenth century, the Puritans taking it to their hearts in its Latin meaning.

FENELLA
The anglicised version of an Irish name, meaning 'white shoulder', used since the nineteenth century.

Fenella Fielding, the actress with a truly memorable voice, is a well-known bearer of the name.

FERN
This has been used as a first name since the late nineteenth century, when the passion for botanical names was at its height. There are over 10,000 species of the beautiful non-flowering plant.

Shakespeare, in *Henry IV, Part I*, mentions the old belief that fern seed bestowed invisibility on whoever carried it.

FIONA
From the Gaelic, meaning 'fair'. The Scottish writer William Sharp (1855–1905) wrote under the pen-name 'Fiona Macleod', a name he invented as a feminine version of Finn.

FLAVIA
From the Latin, meaning 'yellow', the feminine form of the name of an ancient Roman family.

St Flavia Domitilla was a Christian of the first century AD, exiled and put to death for her faith during the persecution of the Roman Emperor Domitian, of whose family she was a member.

FLEUR
From the French, meaning 'flower'. This was made popular by Fleur Forsyte, a main character in a series of novels called *The Forsyte Saga* by John Galsworthy (1867–1933).

FLORA
The ancient Roman goddess of flowers, whose festival was celebrated from 28th April until 3rd May. The name has been used in England since the Renaissance.

Flora MacDonald (1722–1790) helped Prince Charles Edward Stuart to escape after his defeat at the battle of Culloden, disguised as her maid. She went to live in America, where her husband fought on the English side during the American Revolution of 1776.

FLORENCE (Florrie, Flossie)
From the Latin, meaning 'flourishing'. The capital of Tuscany, an old Roman colony rebuilt by Julius Caesar in 59 BC to guard the river crossing. (During the Middle Ages, the name was used for both girls and boys.)

'The Lady with the Lamp', Florence Nightingale (1820–1910), received the name because she was born in the city. After her pioneering work for the sick and injured of the Crimean War, she founded the school of nursing at St Thomas's Hospital, London. Her statue can be seen on the Crimean War Memorial off Pall Mall.

FOULA
A place name, one of the Shetland Isles, now used as a first name.

FRANCES (Fran, Francesca)
The feminine version of Francis, q.v. St Frances Cabrini (1850–1917), foundress of the Missionary Sisters of the Sacred Heart, was the first citizen of the United States of America to be canonised.

Francesca da Rimini fell in love with her husband's brother, Paolo, and both were put to death; their history is included in Dante's *Inferno*. The name has been used in England since Tudor times.

FREDA
A pet-form of Winifred or Frederica, used as an independent name since the late nineteenth century.

FREYA
The anglicised version of the Swedish name Freja, used in Britain in the twentieth century and now very popular.

Freya was the Nordic goddess of love, wife of Odin. She travelled in a chariot drawn by cats and wept tears of gold when her husband was absent.

FRITH
A surname, and place name, meaning 'woodland', now used as a first name.

The artist William Powell Frith (1819–1909) painted the magnificent *Derby Day*, which can be seen at Tate Britain.

GABRIELLE (Gabriella, Gaby)
The first is the French, the second the Italian feminine version of Gabriel (q.v.), both generally popular.

Gabrielle Adorno is a character in *Simon Boccanegra,* the opera by Giuseppe Verdi (1813–1901).

GAIA
From the Greek, meaning 'earth'. Greek mythology made Gaia, daughter of Chaos, mother to the earth and the Titans.

GAIL
A shortened form of Abigail (q.v.), used as an independent name since the mid-twentieth century.

GALA
The Russian pet-form of Galina, now generally used. We may also think of it as a time of festivity and rejoicing.

GARNET
From the Latin, meaning 'pomegranate', indicating the deep red colour of the stone.
   New York claims the garnet as its 'state gem'.

GAYNOR (Gayna)
A medieval form of Guinevere, the name of the wife of King Arthur, now enjoying a revival.

GEMMA
From the Italian, meaning 'precious stone'. St Gemma Galgani (1878–1903), an Italian stigmatic and visionary, brought the name to public attention. It was first used in England in the thirteenth century. Gemma Craven (b. 1950) is a well-known actress.

GENEVA
A modern name, taken from the capital of the Swiss canton. The Geneva Convention established the necessity of humane treatment for prisoners of war.

GENEVIEVE
Popular in France as the name of the saintly patroness of Paris, it has been used in Britain since the nineteenth century.
   Genevieve is a character in the opera *Pelléas and Mélisande* by Achille Claude Debussy (1862–1918).

GEORGINA (Georgia, Georgiana)
The feminine version of George, q.v. This has been popular in Britain since the eighteenth century, when the very first of the six British King Georges arrived reluctantly from Hanover,

speaking only French and German, to be crowned at Westminster Abbey on 20th October 1714.

GERALDINE
The feminine form of Gerald; supposedly invented by Henry Howard, Earl of Surrey (1517–1547), in his poems to the 'fair Geraldine' (really Lady Elizabeth Fitzgerald, grand-daughter of the ninth Earl of Kildare). The name came into general use at the beginning of the nineteenth century.

GERMAINE
A French name, now generally used. The shepherdess St Germaine of Pibrac (1579–1601) was accused of stealing bread to feed a beggar by her wicked stepmother. On opening her apron, it was found to be full of spring flowers. Her grave continues to be a place of pilgrimage.

The writer Germaine Greer is well known.

GERTRUDE
From the Old German, meaning 'ruler of the spear'. The German mystic St Gertrude the Great (1256–1302) made the name popular in the Middle Ages. It was revived in the nineteenth century.

The writer and artist Gertrude Jekyll (1843–1932) is best known for her garden design, collaborating with the architect Edwin Lutyens for a 'Lutyens house' with a 'Jekyll garden'. Her portrait hangs in the National Portrait Gallery in London.

GIGI
A French pet-name, now generally used. Leslie Caron played the eponymous heroine in the film *Gigi* (1958).

GILLIAN (Gill, Gilly)
The English form of Juliana, common in the Middle Ages. It came back into favour in the twentieth century.

Gillian Avery is a well-known modern writer for children; *The Warden's Niece* (1957) and *The Elephant War* (1960) have become classics.

GINA
A pet-form of Georgina, used independently since the early twentieth century. Gina Lollobrigida (b. 1927), the Italian actress, is a well-known bearer of the name.

GINEVRA
The Italian version of Genevieve (q.v.), now generally used. Ginevra is a Scottish princess in Ariosto's *Orlando Furioso* (1516), unjustly accused of murder.

GISELLE
From the Old German, meaning 'pledge'. The Adam ballet, *Giselle* (1841), made the common French name widely known.

GLADYS
The anglicised version of a Welsh name, meaning 'princess'. It came into general use in the second half of the nineteenth century, helped by being bestowed on the heroines of several popular novels of the time.

GLENDA
From the Welsh, meaning 'holy and good'. Glenda Jackson (b. 1936), the fine actress, turned to politics and became a Labour MP.

GLORIA
From the Latin, meaning 'glory'. Gloria was a character in the play *You Never Can Tell* by George Bernard Shaw, and the name appears to have been coined by him.

GLYNIS
From the Gaelic, meaning 'narrow valley'. The actress Glynis Johns is best remembered for her portrayal of the mermaid heroine in the film *Miranda* (1948).

GOBNAIT
A traditional Gaelic name of unknown derivation.

GRACE (Gracie)
The name came into use after the Reformation and was favoured by the Puritans. In Roman mythology, the Three Graces embodied charm and beauty and have been a favourite subject for painters.

Grace Darling (1815–1842) was the daughter of the light-house keeper on Longstone, one of the Farne Islands. At great risk to themselves, she and her father rescued nine people from the *Forfarshire*, sailing from Hull to Dundee, when wrecked off the Longstone lighthouse in 1838. Her heroism engendered an immense fame which popularised the name.

GRANIA
The anglicised version of the Irish name Grainne, used since the 1970s. In Irish legend, Grainne was the second wife of Finn MacCool and eloped with his nephew.

GRISELDA
From the German, meaning 'grey battlemaid'. Griselda is the epitome of the perfect medieval wife, the heroine of the final tale in Boccaccio's *Decameron* (1353). Her patience became proverbial.

Geoffrey Chaucer included this story in the *Canterbury Tales*, told by the Clerk.

GWEN
From the Welsh, meaning 'white'. A shortened form of Gwendolen, now generally used.

The artist Gwen John (1876–1939), born in Wales and a graduate of the Slade School of Art who spent most of her working life in France, was described as 'the greatest woman artist of her age'.

GWENDOLEN (Gwenda, Gwendolyn)
An ancient Welsh name, used in Britain since the mid-nineteenth century. George Eliot's last novel, *Daniel Deronda* (1876), has a heroine named Gwendolyn Harleth who is hopelessly in love with the eponymous hero, to no avail.

And Gwendolen Fairfax, daughter of Lady Bracknell in Oscar Wilde's play *The Importance of Being Earnest* (1895), carried her diary with her at all times in order to have something sensational to read!

GWYNNETH
From the Welsh, meaning 'happiness'.

HALINA
The Polish version of Helen (q.v.), now generally used.

HANNAH
From the Hebrew, meaning 'grace'. In the Old Testament, Hannah was the mother of the prophet Samuel. It has been used in Britain since the seventeenth century.

Hannah More (1745–1833), writer, dramatist and philanthropist, was a friend of Dr Johnson, Horace Walpole and Joshua Reynolds. Her play *Percy* was performed at Drury Lane for fourteen nights – a long run in those days. Her later years were spent in attempts to improve conditions for the poor of Somerset.

HARPER
An occupational surname, now used as a first name. The reclusive American novelist Harper Lee, writer of *To Kill A Mockingbird* (1960), is well known.

HARRIET (Hattie)
The feminine version of Harry, used regularly since the eighteenth century. The writer Harriet Martineau (1802–1876) worked very hard, producing nearly fifty books on subjects as diverse as education, hypnotism and the abolition of slavery. She is renowned as a political economist and feminist.

Harriet Smith is an ingenuous young girl who suffers from the attempts of Emma Woodhouse to improve her and to find her a husband in Jane Austen's *Emma* (1816).

HAYLEY
A place name, meaning 'hay field', and surname, popularised as a first name by the actress Hayley Mills, daughter of Sir John Mills, who made her début in *Tiger Bay* (1959).

HAZEL
Another of the botanical names first bestowed upon girls in the late nineteenth century. The hazel-wand represented both protection and wisdom in ancient times.

HEATHER
From the plant name, first used in the late nineteenth century and now very popular.

HEBE
The Greek goddess of youth, daughter of Zeus and Hera. Cupbearer to the gods, she married the deified Heracles and both were worshipped in Athens. (Her Latin name was Juventas, now more familiar as a football team!) The name has been used in Britain since the nineteenth century and is now enjoying a revival.

HEIDI
The pet-form of the German name Adalheid, more familiar in Britain as Adelaide, q.v. The children's classic *Heidi*, written by the Swiss author Johanna Spyri (1829–1901), inspired its use.

HELEN (Helena, Nell, Nellie)
From the Greek, meaning 'light'. In Greek mythology, the beautiful Helen was wife of King Menelaus of Sparta. Her elopement with Paris precipitated the Trojan War. St Helena (c.255–330), mother of Constantine the Great, is best remembered for her reputed discovery of the True Cross and was much revered in the Middle Ages.

Helen Adams Keller (1880–1968), deaf and blind since the age of 19 months, learned to speak, wrote several books and lectured all over the world on behalf of the blind.

HÉLOISE (Eloisa, Eloise)
Héloise (1101–1164) is remembered as the beloved of Pierre Abelard, a French philosopher and theologian. Their tragic lives and famous love letters made their history a popular romantic subject in literature.

Jean-Jacques Rousseau's bestselling novel *La Nouvelle Héloise* (1761) revived the name and it has been used steadily since then.

HENRIETTA (Etty, Hettie)
The name was brought to England by the daughter of Henry IV of France, Henrietta Maria (1609–1669), who married the unfortunate Charles I in 1625.

HEPHZIBAH
From the Hebrew, meaning 'my delight is in her'. It has been used in England since the seventeenth century, another of the names popular with the Puritans.

The pianist Hephzibah Menuhin (1920–1981), renowned for her performances of Mozart concertoes, is well known.

HERMIA
From the Greek, meaning 'daughter of Hermes'. She is the daughter of Egeus of Athens in Shakespeare's *A Midsummer Night's Dream*. Hermia escapes to the woods with Lysander rather than marry her father's choice, Demetrius.

HERMIONE
In Greek mythology, the daughter of the beautiful Helen and King Menelaus, abandoned by her mother at the age of 9 when Helen eloped to Troy with Paris. Hermione later married her cousin, Orestes. She is the rival to Andromache in a tragedy of that name by the Greek playwright Euripides (c.480–c.405 BC).

Shakespeare's Hermione was Queen of Sicily in *The Winter's Tale*.

HESTER
A medieval variation of Esther (q.v.), once interchangeable but now quite independent. Hester Thrale (1741–1821) is remembered for her friendship with Dr Johnson and his break with her when she married the musician Gabriel Piozzi (a foreigner!). Her diaries are an invaluable source of biographical information.

Hester Prynne is the heroine of Nathaniel Hawthorne's masterpiece, *The Scarlet Letter* (1850).

HILARY
From the Latin, meaning 'cheerful'. Once bestowed on both boys and girls, it is now considered purely feminine.

St Hilary of Poitiers (315–367) was a French bishop who devoted his life to the fight against Arian heresy. His feast day (on January 13th in the Anglican Church) gives the name to Hilary Term, one of the four portions of the year in which the High Court sits. (The other terms are Michaelmas, Easter and Trinity.)

HILDA
From the Old German, meaning 'battle'. The greatly revered St Hilda (614–680), grand-niece of King Edwin of Northumbria, founded an abbey at Whitby. She ruled over both men and women religious, one of whom was the poet Caedmon.

The name was revived by the Tractarians of the nineteenth century, although it had never completely dropped from favour in the north of England.

HOLLY (Hollie)
From the plant, used as a first name since the late nineteenth century. Pagans believed that holly prickles would repel witches and evil spirits; being an evergreen, it also symbolised immortality and good fortune.

HONEY
The nectar of flowers, collected and converted into a delicious food by bees, has been adopted as a popular modern name.

Maria Edgeworth (1767–1849) has some appropriate advice in her novel *Ennui*. 'Have done being wild, honey-dear, and be a credit to your family.'

HONOR
The shortened form of Honoria, brought to England at the Norman Conquest. Puritans of the seventeenth century bestowed it on both males and females, but it is now used only for girls.

The actress Honor Blackman is a well-known bearer of the name.

HOPE
One of the three main Christian virtues (together with Faith and Charity), used as a first name by the Puritans and still popular today.

The English metaphysical poet Richard Crashaw (c.1612–1649) wrote *On Hope*, from which came the following lines:

> Dear Hope! Earth's dowry and Heaven's debt,
> The entity of things that are not yet.
> Subtlest but surest being!

HORTENSE
The feminine version of an ancient Roman family name. This has been used in Britain since the nineteenth century.

Hortense, French maid to Lady Dedlock, is the murderer of the lawyer Mr Tulkinghorn in Dickens' novel *Bleak House* (1852).

HYACINTH
In Greek mythology, the young boy Hyacinth was beloved by Apollo, who accidentally killed him while throwing the discus. The distraught god caused a flower to grow from Hyacinth's blood. Several early Christian martyrs have borne this name.

Considered exclusively female in Britain, it came into use in the late nineteenth century when flower names for girls were all the rage.

IANTHE
From the Greek, meaning 'violet flower'. The name of a sea nymph, daughter of the sea god Oceanus, it was the name given to the daughter of the poet Shelley and his wife, Harriet Westbrook.

Walter Savage Landor (1775–1864) wrote the poem *Ianthe* for his early love, Sophia Jane Swift.

ILONA
The Hungarian version of Helen (q.v.), now generally used.

IMELDA
The Italian form of Irmhilde, meaning 'universal battle', now generally used. A well-known modern bearer of the name is the actress Imelda Staunton.

IMOGEN
From the Latin, meaning 'image'. Imogen is the daughter of Cymbeline, King of Britain, in Shakespeare's play *Cymbeline*, the faithful wife of Posthumus Leonatus. (And, if you are an opera fan, you will know that Imogen is a character in Vincenzo Bellini's *Il Pirata*, first produced at La Scala in 1827.)
The name became popular in Britain in the twentieth century.

INANNA
A very modern name, with a venerable history. The Mesopotamian goddess of love and war was known as Inanna in Sumerian. The British Museum is the proud possessor of a terracotta relief of Inanna, known as *The Queen of the Night*, purchased for £1,500,000 in 2003.

INDIA
The country; from the Greek 'indos', meaning the river Indus. A name increasing in favour in modern times.

INGRID (Inge)
From the Old Norse, meaning 'Ing's ride'. The name was mentioned in the Domesday Book but soon vanished, to be revived in the twentieth century.
Ingrid Bergman (1915–1982), the beautiful Swedish film star best remembered for her part in the classic *Casablanca*, popularised the name.

IOLE
In Greek mythology, Iole was the daughter of King Eurytus. Heracles won her as a prize in an archery contest, but her father refused to give her up. She later married Hyllus, Heracles' son. The Victorians revived this name in the late nineteenth century.

IONA
From the small Hebridean island. St Columba founded a monastery on Iona and sent missionaries from there throughout Scotland in the sixth century. Considered a holy place, it became the burial ground for Scots, Irish and Norse kings.

A modern name and very popular.

IPHIGENIA
In Greek mythology, the eldest child of Agamemnon and Clytemnestra. She was sacrificed by her father to ensure favourable winds for the Greek fleet, heading for Troy. Many plays, paintings and operas have used her story.

IRENE (Irena)
From the Greek, meaning 'peace'. St Irene (d. 304) was martyred at Salonika with her two sisters for refusing to eat food offered to the gods and for reading Christian books. It appears to have been used in Britain since the late nineteenth century.

IRIS
From the Greek, meaning 'the rainbow'. In Greek mythology she was the messenger of the gods, who used the rainbow as a bridge between the heavens and the earth. She was married to Zephyrus, the West Wind, and mother of Eros.
  It came into vogue at the end of the nineteenth century, when plant names were very fashionable.

ISABELLA (Isabel, Isabelle, Isobel)
Variations of Elizabeth (q.v.), used regularly in England since the twelfth century. There have been three queens of England with this name: Isabella of Angoulême (d. 1246), second wife of King John; Isabella (1292–1358), daughter of King Philip IV of France, wife of Edward II; and Isabella (1389–1409), daughter of Charles VI of France, second wife of Richard II.
  The beautiful and virtuous Isabella is the heroine of Shakespeare's play *Measure for Measure*.

ISADORA (Izzy)
The feminine form of Isidore (q.v.). The American dancer Isadora Duncan (1878–1927) was acclaimed worldwide. She was strangled when her flowing scarf was caught in the wheel of her car.

ISLA
Taken from the Scottish river, a modern name.

ISMAY
Possibly a variation of Esme (q.v.), now used independently.

ISMENE (Ismena)
In Greek mythology, a daughter of Jocasta and Oedipus. She appears in *Antigone*, one of the earliest known tragedies of Sophocles (496–406 BC).

ISOLDE
The Latin version of Isolt, the beloved of Tristram (q.v.).

Fans of Wagner will think of his opera *Tristan and Isolde*, first performed in 1865.

JACOBA (Jacobina)
The Jacobites of the eighteenth century had no time for the upstart Hanoverians, clinging to the Stuarts as the true kings of Great Britain. Jacoba and Jacobina were the names given to their infant daughters to demonstrate their feelings. These are now enjoying a revival.

JACQUELINE (Jacalyn, Jackie, Jacqui)
The French feminine form of Jacques (James), used in England since the thirteenth century.

Samuel Rogers (1763–1855), poet and patron of men of letters, wrote the poem *Jacqueline*.

The cellist Jacqueline du Pré is best remembered for her filmed rendition of Elgar's *Cello Concerto in E Minor*.

JADE
From the precious stone, used as a first name since the 1970s. In Chinese Taoism, the Jade Emperor is Father of Heaven, usually

depicted seated on a throne wearing green robes decorated with dragons. Chinese emperors made yearly offerings of silk and jade to him in the Temple of Heaven in Beijing.

JAEL
From the Hebrew, meaning 'deer'. In the Old Testament Book of Judges, Jael killed Sisera, a Canaanite commander and enemy of the Israelites, who had taken refuge in her tent.

This was another name used by the seventeenth century Puritans for their daughters.

JAIMIE
An extremely popular modern feminine form of James, q.v.

JAMILA
From the Arabic, meaning 'beautiful'.

JANE (Janice, Janie, Janine, Janis, Jayne)
A form of Johanna (see Joan), used regularly in England since the sixteenth century. Jane Seymour (1509–1537), Queen of England, the third wife of Henry VIII, was the mother of the frail Edward VI and died a few days after his birth. She is buried with her husband in St George's Chapel, Windsor Castle.

Jane Austen (1775–1817), who left only six completed novels, was one of our greatest writers. Her home in Chawton, Hampshire is now a museum. And Jane Welsh Carlyle (1801–1866), long-suffering wife of the dyspeptic Thomas Carlyle, is vividly alive in her many fascinating and acerbic letters. Leigh Hunt wrote the poem *Jenny Kissed Me* in her honour.

JANET (Jan)
A diminutive of Jane, once exclusively Scottish but now generally used.

JANNA
A modern variant of Joan (q.v.), now independently used.

JASMINE (Yasmin)
From the sweet-scented flower, first used at the end of the nineteenth century.

JEAN
A medieval variation of the French name Jehanne. The prolific 'Jean Plaidy' (1906–1993), writer of some 200 books, mostly fictionalised history, is well-known. (Her *real* name was Mrs Eleanor Hibbert.)

JEANETTE
An old Scottish diminutive of Jane, now generally used.

Jeanette MacDonald (d. 1965) trilled her way happily through such musical films as *Rose Marie* (1936) and *Sweethearts* (1938), aided and abetted by Nelson Eddy.

JEMIMA (Mima)
From the Hebrew, meaning 'dove'. The Old Testament Jemima was one of the three beautiful daughters of the later, prosperous Job.

The eponymous hero of *The Tale of Jemima Puddleduck* by Beatrix Potter is nearly killed by the fox in her attempt to find somewhere to lay her eggs.

JENNIFER (Jenna, Jennie, Jenny)
This was originally an exclusively Cornish form of Guinevere, wife of King Arthur, but has been used generally since the beginning of the twentieth century.

'The Swedish Nightingale', the soprano Jenny Lind (1820–1887), later a British subject, sang worldwide for over forty years.

At the other end of the spectrum, Jenny Diver (1705–1740), the most noted pickpocket of her time, was twice transported before being executed at Tyburn. She is mentioned by Macheath in *The Beggar's Opera*.

JESSAMY
A variation of Jasmine, used since the 1920s.

JESSICA
From the Hebrew, meaning 'he beholds'. The name given to Shylock's rebellious daughter who eloped with Lorenzo in *The Merchant of Venice* by Shakespeare; this seems to have begun the use of the name.

Jessica Landseer (1807–1880), devoted companion to her famous brother Edwin, painted miniatures and landscapes and had ten pictures hung at the Royal Academy.

Hesba Stretton (really Sarah Smith) was responsible for the phenomenally successful children's story of slum life, *Jessica's First Prayer* (1867), which was translated into every European language and many Asiatic and African ones as well.

JESSIE (Jessye)
Either a Scottish pet-name for Janet or a shortened form of Jessica, but sturdily independent.

JILL
A pet-form of Gillian, used since the Middle Ages. Its age is shown by the nursery rhyme *Jack and Jill*, who were both so unfortunate in their excursion to fetch water.

And Puck, as he squeezes juice on the eyes of Lysander in Shakespeare's *A Midsummer Night's Dream*, includes

> Jack shall have Jill;
> Nought shall go ill

in his spell.

JOAN (Joanna, Joanne, Johanna)
The medieval feminine form of John (q.v.). It was revived at the end of the nineteenth century. The 'bad' King John appears to have liked the name. He had two daughters on which this was bestowed: the first (d. 1237) married the Welsh ruler Llywelyn the Great; the second (d. 1238) married the Scottish King Alexander II.

And the 'Fair Maid of Kent', so called on account of her great beauty, was Joan, daughter of Edmund, Earl or Kent, who married the Black Prince and became the mother of Richard II.

JOCASTA
In Greek legend, the mother and unwitting wife of Oedipus. She is the tragic heroine of many dramas, from Sophocles' *Oedipus Rex* to Stravinsky's opera of the same name (1927). It seems to have been used first by the late Victorians.

JOCELYN (Joseline, Joslyn)
Brought to England at the Norman Conquest and originally a masculine name, it is now bestowed on both girls and boys.

The French writer Alphonse de Lamartine (1790–1869) wrote a long narrative poem entitled *Jocelyn*.

JODIE
A modern name derived from Judy; made popular by the actress Jodie Foster, who made her début in the exuberant children's musical *Bugsy Malone*.

JONQUIL
From the flower name, its use begun in the early twentieth century. The poet Anne Finch, Lady Winchilsea (d. 1720), held strong views of the plant, writing:

> Now the Jonquil o'ercomes the feeble brain;
> We faint beneath the aromatic pain.

JORDAN (Jordyn)
Crusaders of the twelfth century brought back bottles of water from the River Jordan to be used in the baptism of their children. (The royal family continues the tradition today.) It has always been a name given to both girls and boys.

JOSEPHINE (Jo, Josette, Josie)
The French female form of Joseph, q.v. The lady responsible for its popularity, the Empress Josephine (1763–1814), first wife of Napoleon, was actually named Marie Josèphe Rose Tascher de la Pagerie. (She preferred her pet-name.)

Josephine Butler (1828–1906), the fierce campaigner against the exploitation and degradation of women, is a well-known bearer of the name. And Jo is the best-loved of the four March sisters, heroine of Louisa May Alcott's classic novel *Little Women* (1868) and its three sequels.

JOY
From the Latin, meaning 'merry'. Used in the Middle Ages, it was revived by the Victorians. Two lines by the mystic poet, William Blake (1757–1827), are appropriate:

> I happy am,
> Joy is my name.

JOYCE
From the Latin, meaning 'merry'. A French hermit saint of the seventh century made the name a favourite for both men and women until the Middle Ages. It was revived in the late nineteenth century.

Joyce Grenfell, the actress and writer, is best remembered for her nursery school monologues.

JUDITH (Judie, Judy)

From the Hebrew, meaning 'praise'. In the Old Testament, Judith was a Hittite woman who married Esau, to the dismay of his parents. The heroine of the apocryphal Book of Judith saved her people by beheading the Assyrian leader, Holofernes.

The name was introduced early into England when Judith, daughter of King Charles the Bald of the Franks, married King Ethelwulf (d. 858).

William Shakespeare gave the name to his second daughter (d. 1662), twin sister to Hamnet.

Judy Garland (1922–1969), whose real name was Frances Gumm, is best remembered as Dorothy in *The Wizard of Oz* (1939).

JULIA (Julianne)

The feminine form of Julius, which became very popular in Britain in the eighteenth century. Robert Herrick (1591–1674), clergyman and poet, addressed many of his poems to Julia, notably *Upon Julia's Voice* and *Upon Julia's Clothes*.

Julia Cameron (1815–1879) was a brilliant and dedicated amateur photographer whose work now commands high prices. (And she did not begin until nearly 50 years of age!)

JULIET (Julie)

The English version of the Italian Giulietta, whose popularity began with Juliet Capulet, starcrossed lover of Romeo in the Shakespeare play.

Julie d'Étanges is the heroine of Rousseau's very successful *Julie or La Nouvelle Héloïse* (1761).

JULITA (Jullita)

The name of an obscure, male, Celtic saint. It is now bestowed on girls.

A chapel dedicated to St Jullitta was in use at Tintagel, Cornwall, in the eleventh century. The church was enlarged and extended when Tintagel Castle was built, standing outside the Inner Ward.

JUNE
From the sixth month, used as a first name since the early twentieth century. It was named after the Roman goddess Juno, wife of Jupiter, and was supposedly an auspicious month for marriages.

JUNIPER
From the plant name, one of the most widespread trees or shrubs in Europe. Leonhart Fuchs (1501–1566), physician and writer on plants, considered it extremely potent. He believed it could cure everything from upset stomach to tapeworm!

JUSTINE
The French feminine form of Justin (q.v.). *Justine* (1957) is the first of the four novels which made up the *Alexandria Quartet* by Lawrence Durrell.

JUTTA
A German version of Judith (q.v.), now generally used.

KARA
A popular version of Cara, from the Italian, meaning 'dear'. (The Kara Sea is one of the coldest seas in Russia, notorious for its dense fogs and frequent storms!)

KAREN
The Danish form of Catherine, now generally used. Baroness Karen Blixen (1885–1962), the Danish writer of *Out of Africa* and other books, used the pen-name Isak Dinesen.

KATE (Katie, Katy)

These diminutives of Catherine/Katherine have been used since the sixteenth century.

The illustrator Kate Greenaway (1846–1901), friend of John Ruskin, drew perfect children wearing immaculate frills, pinafores, bonnets and sashes in an arcadian setting: no wonder she has remained a favourite!

What Katy Did (1872), written by Susan Coolidge (real name Sarah Chauncey Woolsey), is a classic of children's literature.

KATHERINE

See Catherine.

KATHLEEN

The anglicised version of the Irish name Caitlin, used in Britain since the mid-nineteenth century.

Kathleen Ferrier (1912–1953), the Lancashire-born contralto, is a famous bearer of the name.

KATINKA

A Russian pet-form of Katya, increasingly popular.

KATYA

A Russian contracted version of Catherine (q.v.), now used in Britain.

KAY

A pet-form of Katherine or Karen, now used independently. Kay Kendall (1927–1959), the actress and film star, is best known for her part in *Genevieve*.

KAYLEIGH (Kylie)

A modern conjunction of Kyle and Kelly, perhaps. (Or one can even believe that Kylie is the Aborigine name for boomerang, as is often stated!)

KEIRA

The feminine version of Kieran (q.v.), made popular by the film star Keira Knightley.

KELLY (Keeley)

An Irish surname, meaning 'warlike one', now used as a first name for both boys and girls.

KEREN

The shortened form of Kerenhappuch, from the Hebrew, meaning 'horn of beauty'.

She was the youngest daughter of the Biblical Job, born after he had been restored to wealth and happiness.

KERRY

From the county situated in the south-west of the Republic of Ireland. Originally bestowed upon boys when the name was first used in the mid-twentieth century, it is now considered exclusively female.

County Kerry possesses the highest range of mountains in Ireland, called MacGillycuddy's Reeks, to the west of Killarney.

KESTREL

This has been used as a first name since the late twentieth century. The kestrel (*Falco tinnuculus*) is most noticeable as it hovers high in the sky, seeking its prey.

KEZIAH

From the Hebrew, meaning 'cassia'. The Old Testament Keziah was the second of three daughters born to Job when he had been restored to health and prosperity. (Her two sisters were Jemima and Keren-Happuch.) The seventeenth century Puritans began the use of the name.

Keziah Wesley (d. 1741) was the youngest of the seven sisters of the founder of Methodism, whose short life was made unhappy by poverty and illness.

KIMBERLEY (Kim)

A place name and a surname, used as a first name since the beginning of the twentieth century.

The South African diamond town of Kimberley was named after the English statesman, John Wodehouse, 1st Earl of Kimberley (1826–1902). During the Boer War it was besieged by the Boers from October 1899 until February 1900, when relieved by General Sir John French. It was this that began its use as a first name in Britain.

Rudyard Kipling wrote the novel *Kim* (1901), in which the hero, an Irish orphan named Kimball O'Hara, roams India with an old lama from Tibet and helps the English Secret Service!

KIMIKO (Kimi)
From the Japanese, meaning 'sovereign'.

KIRSTEN (Kirsteen)
The Danish form of Christine, popular in Scotland and now generally used.

Margaret Oliphant wrote *Kirsteen* (1890), the eponymous heroine of which supports her large and snobbish family by working with her hands – which enables them to despise her.

KIRSTY (Kirstie)
A Scottish pet-form of Christine, now generally popular.

KITTY
A medieval pet-form of Catherine (q.v.), regularly used since then. The Kitty of the nursery rhyme ('Lucy Locket lost her pocket, Kitty Fisher found it') was the mistress of several eminent men, and excellent horsewoman and a model for many artists. She died in 1767.

In Jane Austen's *Pride and Prejudice* (1813) Kitty Bennet is notable only for coughing!

KIZZY
A pet-form of Keziah (q.v.), now used independently.

KRISTIAN
The Danish form of Christian (q.v.), used in Britain for both girls and boys since the 1960s.

Oslo, the capital city of Norway, was named Kristiania until 1925. Destroyed by fire in 1624, the city was redesigned by the Danish king Kristian IV, hence the name.

KYLE
From the Gaelic, meaning 'channel between islands'. A place name and a surname, now used as a first name for both girls and boys.

(Should you be keen to travel 'over the sea to Skye', the Scottish village called Kyle of Lochalsh is your jumping-off point.)

KYRA
The Greek feminine version of Cyril, meaning 'lord'. St Cyril (c.827–869), apostle to the Slavs, is the reputed inventor of the Cyrillic alphabet used by the Russians and Bulgarians.

LACEY
A surname derived from Lassy, in France, brought to England by a Norman baron. Now used as a first name.

LALAGE (Lallie)
From the Greek, meaning 'babble'. A literary favourite since the Roman poet Horace (65–8 BC) used the name in one of his famous Odes.

Lalage is a character in *The French Lieutenant's Woman* by John Fowles.

LANA
A contracted form of Alana, brought to public attention by Lana Turner, the 1940s' Hollywood film star.

LARA
The pet-form of the Russian name Larissa. Lara, a nymph whose father was the River Tiber, refused to help Jupiter in his amours. He retaliated by pulling out her tongue and sent her down to the Underworld. She was the mother of the Lares, the household gods of the Romans.

Lara was the heroine of Boris Pasternak's *Doctor Zhivago* (1957), later filmed, which made the name a favourite.

LARGO
An unusual modern name, presumably bestowed by music-loving parents.

Largo is the tempo indication for a slow movement. It is also the popular name for the aria *Shade Never Was* from Handel's opera *Serse* (1738).

LARK
From the bird, used as a first name since the early twentieth century.

The haunting piece for violin and orchestra, *The Lark Ascending* by Vaughan Williams, was composed in 1914.

And to 'rise with the lark' is appropriate for new parents!

LAURA
From the Latin, meaning 'laurel'. The name has been used in England since the twelfth century.

Petrarch (1304–1374) wrote countless poems in honour of the beautiful and unattainable Laura, who died in the Great Plague of 1384. (And Thomas Campion (1567–1620) wrote of 'Rose-Cheeked Laura'.)

Dame Laura Knight (1877–1970), artist and Royal Academician, loved painting subjects connected with the circus, the theatre and the ballet.

LAUREL
From the trees and evergreen shrubs, used as a first name since the late nineteenth century, when the passion for plant names was at its height.

Universities had a custom of presenting a laurel wreath to graduates in rhetoric and poetry; Ben Jonson became the first Poet Laureate in England in 1619.

LAUREN
A modern feminine version of Laurence (q.v.), popularised by the actress Lauren Bacall (real name Betty Joan Perske). She first appeared in the film *To Have and Have Not* with her future husband Humphrey Bogart in 1944.

LAVENDER
From the sweet-smelling herb, brought to England by the Romans. (This, planted in your garden, will attract butterflies and repel ants.)

LAVINIA
In Roman mythology, the wife of Aeneas, from whom were descended Romulus and Remus, the founders of Rome. Lavinium, the ancient town to the south of Rome, was named after her.

The name became popular in England at the Renaissance. 'Gracious Lavinia, Rome's rich ornament', the daughter of Titus in Shakespeare's *Titus Andronicus*, comes to a gruesome end.

LEAH
From the Hebrew, meaning 'gazelle'. The Old Testament Leah, whose eyes were weak, became the first wife of Jacob by a ruse. The Puritans of the seventeenth century began the use of the name in England.

LEANDER
Originally considered an entirely male name, it is now bestowed on both boys and girls.

The prestigious Leander Rowing Club, founded in 1818, has pink as the club colour, a traditional favourite for small girls.

LEANNE (Lianne)
A modern name, perhaps taken from Julianne, first used in the 1960s.

LEDA
From Greek mythology, a queen of Sparta. She was mother to Castor and Pollux, and Helen and Clytemnestra. Their father, Zeus, came to her in the shape of a swan. The subject of *Leda and the Swan* has inspired many artists, including Michelangelo.

LEIGH
From the Old English place name, meaning 'field' or 'pasture', the feminine version of Lee.

LEILA (Layla)
From the Persian, meaning 'night'. Leila, beautiful concubine to the Caliph Hassan, is the heroine of Lord Byron's lengthy poem *The Giaour* (1813), which brought the name to public attention. Leila is also the heroine of a book of the same name by Edward Bulwer-Lytton (1803–1873).

LENA
A shortened form of Helena, used independently since the nineteenth century. The singer Lena Horne is a modern bearer of the name. (It is also the name of one of the largest rivers in Russia!)

LEONIE (Leoni)
The French feminine form of Leon, used in Britain since the early years of the twentieth century.

LEONORA
This became popular in Britain in the nineteenth century, perhaps chosen by parents who were music lovers.

Three operas – *Leonora or Wedded Love* by Gaveaux, first produced in 1798; *Leonora* by Ferdinando Paer; and the heroine of Beethoven's *Fidelio* (1814) – make the name unforgettable. (She is also a character in operas by Donizetti and Verdi!)

LESLEY
A Scottish place name, meaning 'garden by a pool', and aristocratic surname, used as a first name since the nineteenth century.

LETITIA (Lettice, Letty)
From the Latin, meaning 'gladness'. Lettice was the medieval version of the name, going out of favour in the eighteenth century to be replaced by Letitia. Both are now enjoying a revival.

Letitia Elizabeth Landon (1802–1838), English poet and novelist, is best remembered for her mysterious death in Africa. She accidentally overdosed on the prussic acid which she used to treat her spasms!

LEVI
From the Hebrew, meaning 'joined'. The use of this as a female name is very modern.

Levi, third son of the patriarch Jacob, was involved in the selling of his brother Joseph into slavery in Egypt.

LIBBY
A pet-form of Elizabeth (q.v.), now used as an independent name.

LIBERTY

From the Latin, meaning 'freedom'. A modern first name. The poet Edmund Spenser (1552–1599) puts it well:

What more felicity can fall to creature,
Than to enjoy delight with Liberty

(And should you wish to see the American Liberty Bell, made in England in 1752, it is placed in a glass pavilion in Philadelphia.)

LILAC

From the name of the sweet-smelling plant. This was brought to Europe in 1562, a rarity from the court of Suleiman the Magnificent in Constantinople. The first picture of a lilac was published in 1565.

LILIAN (Lillian)

From the Latin name Liliana, meaning 'lily', used in Britain since the late nineteenth century.

Lilian Baylis (1874–1937) was the manager of the Old Vic in London, turning it into the home of Shakespeare's plays. She was also responsible for reopening the Sadler's Wells Theatre in 1931.

LILITH

From the Hebrew, meaning 'night-monster'. In Babylonian mythology, it is the name of a female demon who goes abroad on stormy nights and is particularly dangerous to children. (Naughty ones, presumably!)

She is also mentioned as a night devil in Isaiah 34: 14, and included in Goethe's play *Faust* (1808).

LILY (Lilly)

From the name of the flower, used since the mid-nineteenth century. In tradition, the lily sprang from the tears of Eve as she was driven out of paradise. Christian art uses it as a symbol of purity.

Emilie Charlotte Langtry (1853–1929), British actress and society beauty, was always known as 'the Jersey Lily'.

LINDA (Lindy, Lyn, Lynda, Lynn, Lynne)

From the Old German, meaning 'serpent'. This is no insult: serpents performed wisdom and were venerated by many ancient peoples, including the pre-Hindu dwellers in India and the worshippers of a crowned snake goddess in Lower Egypt. (It is also the Spanish for 'pretty'.) The name has been used in Britain from the late nineteenth century.

LINDEN
A variation of Lyndon (q.v.), bestowed on girls. Ralph Vaughan Williams composed the song *Linden Lea* (1900), with lines by the Dorset poet, William Barnes.

And the Unter den Linden is a famous avenue of trees in Berlin.

LINDSEY (Lindsay, Lynsey)
From the Old English, meaning 'Lelli's island'. A place name and aristocratic surname, now used as a first name for both girls and boys.

LIZA (Lisa)
A shortened form of Elizabeth (q.v.), popular since the 1960s. *Liza of Lambeth* (1897) was the first novel of William Somerset Maugham, inspired by his experiences as a medical student in the London slums.

LOIS
From the Greek, meaning 'good'. The New Testament Lois was the Greek grandmother of St Timothy, friend and helper of St Paul. The Puritans of the seventeenth century began its use as they rejected all names not included in the Bible.

LORETTA
A pet-form of Laura (q.v.), in use since the late nineteenth century. The beautiful film star Loretta Young, who won an Academy Award for her part in *The Farmer's Daughter* (1947), popularised the name.

LORI (Lory)
A pet-form of Lorraine (q.v.), used independently. (A lory is also a brightly coloured Australian parrot which dines on the nectar and pollen of flowers!)

LORNA
A name invented by Richard Doddridge Blackmore (1825–1900) for the heroine of his best-known novel, *Lorna Doone*. The

Doones are outlaws on Exmoor, but Lorna turns out to be the kidnapped daughter of the Earl of Dugal. (Yes reader, the hero then marries her . . .).

LORRAINE
From the region in north-east France and a surname, used as a first name since the late nineteenth century.

The Cross of Lorraine, a red cross with two horizontal crosspieces, was adopted by the French as an emblem of resistance to German occupation in the Second World War.

LOTTIE
A pet-form of Charlotte, used independently since the nineteenth century.

Lottie Dod (1871–1960) won her first tennis singles title at Wimbledon in 1887 when she was not yet 16. (Her opponent was a Miss Bingley.) She also won the Women's Golf Championship in 1904.

LOUISE (Louisa, Lulu)
The feminine form of Louis (q.v.), fashionable in Britain since the eighteenth century.

St Louise de Marillac (1591–1660) was the French co-founder of the Daughters of Charity, who care for the sick poor all over the world.

Louisa May Alcott (1832–1888), the American novelist and poet, was a prolific writer but remains famous for the children's classic *Little Women*.

And Dame Louisa Aldrich Blake (1865–1925), who devoted her life to medicine, was the first woman to obtain the degree of Master of Surgery.

LOURDES
A name taken from the shrine in the Pyrenees, established as a place of pilgrimage for the sick in 1858.

LUCASTA
A version of Lucy (q.v.), used since the seventeenth century. Richard Lovelace (1618–1658) addressed several poems to his fiancée. The most famous, *To Lucasta, Going to the Wars*, contains the lines:

    I could not love thee, Dear, so much,
    Lov'd I not honour more.

LUCILLA (Lucille)
From the Latin, meaning 'light', the feminine version of Lucius. St Lucius was an African Christian martyr, executed at Carthage in 254. It has been used in Britain since the eighteenth century, when the passion for classical names was at its height.

LUCINDA
This was a literary variation of Lucia. The name was given to a character in *Don Quixote* (1605) by Miguel de Cervantes; it was later adopted by English poets of the eighteenth century.

James Thomson includes, 'thy lov'd Lucinda . . . with soul to thine attuned', in his best-known work, *The Seasons* (1726–1730). It has been used regularly since then.

LUCY (Lucie)
From the Latin, meaning 'light'. The virgin martyr St Lucy (d. 304), executed at Syracuse in Sicily, is the patron saint of those suffering with diseases of the eyes. She was greatly revered in the Middle Ages, which made the name a favourite. Lucie Manette was the heroine of Dickens' *A Tale of Two Cities* (1859). It was for her sake that the dissolute barrister Sydney Carton died on the guillotine.

LYDIA
From the Greek, meaning 'a woman of Lydia', a district of Asia Minor. The Biblical Lydia was a purple-dye seller, converted by St Paul together with her household. The seventeenth century Puritans began the use of the name in England.

The feather-brained Lydia Languish is the heroine of Richard Brinsley Sheridan's comedy *The Rivals* (1775). Another Lydia in the same mould elopes with George Wickham in Jane Austen's *Pride and Prejudice* (1813).

LYNETTE (Linnet)
This was popularised by Alfred, Lord Tennyson's poem *Gareth and Lynette* (1872), part of his epic *Idylls of the King*. Linnet was the medieval version of the name, still in use today. (The bird received its name from its passion for flax seeds, the botanical name 'linum'.)

LYS
A name inspired by the French 'fleur de lys' or lily, emblem of France.

A hermit had a vision of an angel, holding a beautiful shield emblazoned with three golden lilies. King Clovis adopted this as his coat of arms, being everywhere victorious.

MABEL
A shortened form of Amabel (q.v.), used as an independent name since the seventeenth century.

MABLI
A variant of Amabel (q.v.), now independently used.

MADDISON (Madison)
From the surname, meaning 'son of Maud', a modern first name for girls.

James Madison (1751–1836), fourth President of the United States of America, was in office when British troops captured Washington and burnt the White House in 1814. He is commemorated in Madison Avenue and Madison Square in New York.

MADELINE (Madeleine)
A medieval variation of Magdalen, used regularly since then. The beautiful Madeline is the beloved of Porphyro in John Keats' lengthy poem *The Eve of St Agnes*, a favourite subject for Pre-Raphaelite painters.

And the little girl who lived in an old house in Paris with eleven schoolmates and Miss Clavel is the heroine of the children's book *Madeline* (1939) and its sequels by Ludwig Bemelmans.

MAGDALENA (Magdalene)

From the Hebrew, meaning 'woman of Magdala', a town on the Sea of Galilee.

The Biblical St Mary Magdalene was the first to whom the risen Christ appeared; there was a great devotion to her in the Middle Ages.

Magdalene College, Cambridge possesses the manuscript of the diary of its most famous graduate, Samuel Pepys. Magdalene College, Oxford has a beautiful tower, from the top of which a Latin hymn is sung at sunrise on May Day.

MAHALA (Mahalia)

From the Hebrew, meaning 'tenderness'. In the Old Testament, one of five daughters, who asked help of Moses as they had no brothers.

The singer of spirituals, Mahalia Jackson, is well known.

MAIA (Maya)

From the Greek, meaning 'nurse'. In Greek mythology, the daughter of Atlas and Pleione. She was the eldest and most beautiful of the Pleiades, mother of Hermes by Zeus.

The Romans also honoured an ancient divinity of Spring with this name. They offered sacrifices to her on the first day of May, naming the month after her.

MAIKO

An unusual and modern first name. The maiko is an apprentice geisha, to be found in the four geisha enclaves of Kyoto. She wears a distinctive hairstyle, costume and embroidered collar. On becoming a fully fledged geisha, the collar is exchanged for a white one.

MAISIE

The Scottish pet-form of Margaret (q.v.), now generally used and gaining in popularity.

What Maisie Knew (1897), a novel by Henry James, deals with the problems of the young Maisie Farange whose parents are divorced. (She finally decides to live with her governess.)

MALIKA

From the Arabic, meaning 'queen'.

MANDY
A pet-form of Amanda (q.v.), used in Britain since the mid-twentieth century.

MANON
A French diminutive of Mary (q.v.), best known as the eponymous heroine of the operas *Manon Lescaut* (1893) by Puccini and *Manon* (1884) by Massenet. The beautiful Manon Lescaut becomes a beautiful 'kept woman' and toast of the demi-monde; her life the usual wine, parties, rich men and, of course, a tragic death.

MARA
A variation of Mary, now used independently. Westminster Abbey held the Handel Commemoration Concerts in 1784. Madame Mara, the soloist, sang so beautifully that 'it was extremely difficult to avoid bursting into tears'.

MARCELLA
The feminine version of Marcus (q.v.), used in Britain since the nineteenth century.
   St Marcella (325–410) organised a religious sisterhood at her mansion on the Aventine Hill in Rome. She was a friend to the bad-tempered St Jerome, and was not afraid to stand up to him. Suffering violence when Alaric the Goth sacked Rome, she died from the effects of this.

MARCIA
The feminine version of Marcus, ultimately derived from Mars, the god of war.

MARGARET (Madge, Maggie, Margot, Meg, Peggy)
From the Greek, meaning 'pearl'. The name of at least five saints, one of whom, St Margaret of Scotland (1045–1093), was married to Malcolm III and noted for her care of orphans and the poor. There have been several royal Margarets, both in Britain and in Europe, the latest being Princess Margaret Rose (1930–2002), the sister of Elizabeth II.
   Dame Margaret Rutherford (1892–1972), actress and film star, is well remembered for her portrayal of the delightfully dotty Madame Arcati in *Blithe Spirit*.
   Margaret Damer Dawson (1875–1920) was the founder of the Women's Police Service in 1914.

MARGUERITE
The French form of Margaret and a flower name, popular since the nineteenth century.

Marguerite of Navarre (1492–1549) was the sister of Francis I of France and the Queen of Navarre. A poet and a writer, she produced the first collection of French stories and the poetic *Les Marguerites de la Marguerite des Princesses* (1547).

Marguerite Gardiner (1789–1849) became the notorious Countess of Blessington, leading hostess of the day. Her *Conversations with Lord Byron* is still read.

MARIA/MARIE
See under Mary.

MARIANNE
A French conjunction of Marie and Anne, used since the eighteenth century. The work of the painter and explorer Marianne North (1830–1890) can be seen in the Marianne North Gallery in Kew Gardens. Over 800 of her vivid botanical paintings cover the walls. Her interesting autobiography is called *Recollections of a Happy Life*.

MARIELLE (Mariella)
The first is the French, the second the Italian diminutive of Marie, now generally used.

MARIETTA
A French diminutive of Marie, used in Britain since the nineteenth century.

Marietta is a character in Erich Korngold's opera *Die Tote Stadt* or *The Dead City* (1920).

MARIGOLD
Another of the flower names which first became popular in the late nineteenth century.

William Turner's *Herbal* of 1568 states that hair could be coloured yellow by using marigolds. (Quite how is not explained.)

MARILYN
A twentieth-century combination of Mary and the suffix 'lyn'.

Norma Jean Mortenson (1926–1962), far better known as the film star Marilyn Monroe, starred in many films, notably *Gentlemen Prefer Blondes* (1953) and *Some Like It Hot* (1959).

MARINA
From the Latin, meaning 'of the sea'. In Shakespeare's *Pericles*, Marina is the daughter of Thaisa and Pericles, called so 'for I was born at sea'.

The Greek Princess Marina, Duchess of Kent (1906–1968), gave her name to a shade of blue.

MARION
A medieval diminutive of Mary, brought to England at the Norman Conquest. Marion was the famous legendary girlfriend of Robin Hood. In 1332 a puppet play, *Robin et Marion*, was performed by students at Angers; the origin of marionettes, puppets worked by strings.

MARITA
The Spanish pet-form of Maria, now generally used.

MARJORIE (Margery)
The medieval English version of Marguerite. Marjorie (d. 1316) was the daughter of Scotland's national hero Robert the Bruce and his wife Isabella. (But the Marjorie Daw of children's nursery rhyme fame always springs to mind.)

MARNIE
A Swedish pet-form of Marina (q.v.), now generally used. Tippi Hedren starred in the Alfred Hitchcock thriller *Marnie* (1964).

MARTHA (Marta)
From the Aramaic, meaning 'lady'. The New Testament Martha was the sister of Lazarus and Mary, all three the close friends of Christ. She is the patroness of housekeepers and all who care for the needy. It has been used in England since the Reformation. Martha is always associated in the USA with the name of the wife of the first President, George Washington (1732–1799).

MARTINA (Marti)
The feminine form of Martin, q.v. Martina was a Christian martyr of the third century; but the name was brought to

prominence by the Czech-born tennis player Martina Navratilova (b. 1956), winner of the Wimbledon tennis singles title an amazing nine times.

MARY (Maria, Marie)

The English version of Miriam, from the Hebrew meaning 'bitterness'. There are seven women of this name in the New Testament, pre-eminent among them being the Virgin Mary, mother of Jesus. Considered too holy for common use, the name was not used in England until the thirteenth century.

Maria became fashionable in the eighteenth century and Marie in the nineteenth.

The tragic Mary I of England (1516–1558), daughter of Henry VIII and Catherine of Aragon, was the second wife of King Philip II of Spain who was responsible for the Spanish Armada.

Maria Montessori (1870–1952), Italian educationalist, developed the theory of non-interference with the freedom and individuality of children so popular today.

Mary Beale (b. 1633), a protégée of Sir Peter Lely, was the first woman in England to earn her living as an artist.

(But the famous bearers of this ever-popular name are innumerable.)

MATILDA (Matilde, Tilly)

From the Old German, meaning 'strength in battle'. The name was brought to England at the Norman Conquest by the wife of William the Conqueror. Matilda of Flanders was crowned Queen of England at Westminster Abbey in 1068.

The poet and painter Matilda Betham (1776–1852) was admired by Coleridge, who wrote a poem in her honour.

MAUD (Maude)

The French medieval version of Matilda, revived in the nineteenth century. Tennyson's lengthy poem *Maud* (1855), with such lines as 'Maud with her exquisite face', was probably responsible. And Whittier's poem *Maud Muller* (1854) contains the memorable lines:

> For of all sad words of tongue or pen,
> The saddest are these: 'It might have been.'

MAUREEN

An anglicised version of the Irish name Mairin, meaning 'little Mary'. It became popular in Britain from the early twentieth century.

The Californian tennis player Maureen Connolly (1934–1969), better known as 'Little Mo', was the first woman to win the world's four major singles championships or 'Grand Slam' in 1953 – France, Australia, United States of America and Wimbledon.

MAVIS

From the Old French, meaning 'song thrush'.

Mavis Clare was the heroine of Marie Corelli's bestseller *The Sorrows of Satan* (1895), reputedly an idealised portrait of the writer; this made the name a favourite with the Victorians.

MAXINE

A modern feminine version of Maximilian (q.v.).

MAY (Mae)

A pet-form of Mary or Margaret used in the nineteenth century, but now associated with the fifth month. The Romans honoured an ancient divinity of the Spring named Maia. They offered sacrifices to her on the first day of May, having named the month after her.

MEDEA

In Greek mythology, a sorceress and priestess of Hecate who helped Jason steal the Golden Fleece.

The enigmatic artist Frederick Sandys (1829–1904) painted the magnificent *Medea*, now to be admired in the Birmingham City Museum and Art Gallery.

MEGAN

The Welsh pet-form of Margaret, now generally used. Lady Megan Lloyd George (1902–1966), daughter of the Liberal Prime Minister, was also keen on politics. She became first a Liberal, then a Labour, Member of Parliament.

MELANIE

From the Greek, meaning 'black'. There are two Roman saints of the fifth century bearing this name, grandmother and granddaughter, friends of St Jerome. The name has been used in England since the seventeenth century.

The gentle Melanie Wilkes is the only truly admirable character in Margaret Mitchell's bestselling novel *Gone with the Wind* (1936).

MELINDA
A name coined in the eighteenth century and used regularly since then.

MELISSA
From the Greek, meaning 'a bee'; in Greek mythology, a nymph who introduced us to the pleasures of eating honey.

Melissa is a prophetess, living in Merlin's cave, in Ariosto's epic poem *Orlando Furioso*. The name came into favour in Britain in the nineteenth century.

MELITA
From the Latin, meaning 'sweet as honey'. It can also be derived from the Greek name for the island of Malta.

Always important, the island was occupied by the Phoenicians, followed by the Greeks, Carthaginians and Romans. St Paul was shipwrecked there in AD 58.

The name has been used in Britain since the nineteenth century.

MELODY
From the Greek, meaning 'singing of songs'. A modern name, although noted once or twice in the nineteenth century. And if we have to deal with sleepless, shrieking babies, the lines from John Keats' *Ode on a Grecian Urn* must spring to mind:

Heard melodies are sweet, but those unheard
Are sweeter . . .

MERCY
The virtue, used as a first name since the seventeenth century. Mercy, a neighbour, accompanies Christiana and her children to the Celestial City in the second part of *The Pilgrim's Progress* (1684) by John Bunyan.

MEREDITH
From the Welsh, meaning 'great lord'. A surname and male name, first used as a name for girls in the twentieth century.

MERIEL
From the Celtic, meaning 'sea bright'. This is a medieval version of Muriel, brought to England by the Normans. It was revived in the nineteenth century.

MERIOTH
From the Hebrew, meaning 'rebellious'. The father of Zadok the priest in the Old Testament, Merioth seems to be used as a female name in Britain.

MERLYN
Taken as a feminine version of Merlin (q.v.); or bestowed by admirers of the small falcon (*Falco columbarius*), who lays her purplish-brown eggs in May.

MIA
The Danish pet-form of Mary, made popular by the American actress Mia Farrow, best remembered for her part in *Rosemary's Baby* (1968).

MICHAELA (Micaela)
The feminine form of Michael, meaning 'Who is like God?', popular since the 1950s.
Micaela is a character in Bizet's last opera, *Carmen* (1875).

MICHELLE
The French feminine form of Michael (q.v.), now generally used. A ballad of the same name by the Beatles brought the name to public attention in the 1960s.

MILLICENT (Millie, Milly)
From the German, meaning 'strong worker'. The name was brought to England by the Normans, being revived in the nineteenth century.
Dame Millicent Fawcett (1847–1929) was a leading figure in the women's suffrage movement for fifty years. At the age of 81 she attained success, when the House of Lords passed the Bill allowing women the same voting rights as men.
The singer Millicent Martin is a well-known modern bearer of the name. (And the ageless Milly-Molly-Mandy, heroine of so many children's stories by Joyce Lankester Brisley, is another.)

MIMI

A French pet-form of Mary. The use of the name is generally linked to the heroine of Giacomo Puccini's opera *La Bohème* (1896). The Parisian seamstress Mimi (whose tiny hand is frozen) loves the penniless poet of the Latin Quartier, Rodolfo, and expires beautifully.

(This is also the name given by the aborigines of Australia to an earlier culture, which appears to have died out. Its only legacy is numerous cave paintings of mysterious running figures.)

MINNA (Mina)

From the Old German, meaning 'small', or a pet-form of Wilhelmina. This may have been introduced to Britain by the eponymous heroine of *Minna von Barnhelm* (1767), a comic play by Gotthold Lessing, or by Minna Troil, a character in *The Pirate* (1822) by Sir Walter Scott.

MIRABEL (Mirabella)

From the Latin, meaning 'glorious'. A medieval name, revived in the early nineteenth century. Now a girl's name, it was given to the hero of William Congreve's masterpiece *The Way of the World* (1700). Mirabell wishes to marry the beautiful Millamant, despite the opposition of Lady Wishfort, her aunt.

MIRANDA

From the Latin, meaning 'worthy of admiration'. Shakespeare seems to have invented the name for Prospero's daughter in his last play, *The Tempest*. Raised without human companionship on an enchanted island, Miranda marries Ferdinand, the son of the King of Naples.

A popular name in the twentieth century.

MIRELLA

A variant of Mirabel (q.v.), independently used.

MIRIAM

From the Hebrew, meaning 'bitterness'. The Old Testament Miriam watched over her infant brother Moses when he was hidden in the bulrushes. She led the music and dancing after the Israelites crossed the Red Sea in safety. The name came into use in England after the Reformation.

Miriam is Paul Morel's first love in D. H. Lawrence's autobiographical novel *Sons and Lovers* (1913).

MOIRA
The anglicised version of the Irish name Maire, or Mary, used generally since the early twentieth century.

The French novelist Julien Green wrote *Moira* (1950).

MOLLY (Mollie)
A pet-form of Mary, now independently used. Molly Mog (1699–1766) was an innkeeper's daughter and celebrated London beauty. The poet and playwright John Gay (1685–1732) wrote a ballad in her honour entitled *Fair Maid of the Inn*.

MONA
From the Irish, meaning 'noble'. The name has been used in Britain since the late nineteenth century, when Irish names became fashionable. (This is also the ancient name for the Isle of Man.)

MONICA (Monique)
St Monica (331–387) was the mother of St Augustine of Hippo, whose early dissolute life caused her much distress.

Monica Dickens (1915–1992), great-granddaughter of Charles, wrote many popular books. Her very first, giving a servant's eye view of society and called *One Pair of Hands* (1937), made her a household name.

Monique is the French version, now generally used.

MORAG
From the Gaelic, meaning 'great'. It is considered an exclusively Scottish name.

MORGAN
From the Welsh, meaning 'sea bright'. A surname, now used as a first name for both girls and boys.

The mysterious sorceress Morgan-le-Fay was sister to the legendary King Arthur. A fine picture entitled *Morgan-le-Fay*, painted by the Pre-Raphaelite artist Frederick Sandys (1829–1904), can be admired in the Birmingham City Museum and Art Gallery.

MORVEN
From the Gaelic, meaning 'mountain peak'. A modern first name.

Morven is a mountain in the Caithness district of Scotland. It rises to 2,316 feet.

MORWENNA
From the Welsh, meaning 'maiden'. An obscure saint, patron of Morwenstow in Cornwall, bears the name. This has been increasing in popularity since the mid-twentieth century.

MOYA
A modern variation of Maria, taken from the Irish name Maire.

MURIEL
From the Celtic, meaning 'sea bright'. The name was brought to England at the Norman Conquest and remained popular throughout the Middle Ages. It was revived in the latter half of the nineteenth century.

Muriel Spark was the author of *The Prime of Miss Jean Brodie* (1961), among other distinguished novels.

MYFANWY
From the Welsh, meaning 'my treasure'. Myfanwy Thomas, third child of the poet Edward Thomas (1878–1917), wrote about her father in *One of These Fine Days* (1982).

MYRA
This seems to have been invented by Sir Fulke Greville (1554–1628), English courtier, diplomat and Chancellor of the Exchequer as well as poet. He addressed many love poems to a lady of this name.

MYRTLE
From the plant name, used in Britain since the late nineteenth century. In Greek mythology the myrtle symbolised love, being sacred to Aphrodite.

NADIA (Nadine)
From the Russian, meaning 'hope', used in Britain since the early twentieth century. The wife of Vladimir Ilyich Ulyanov, better known as the Russian Communist leader Lenin, was a bearer of the name.

NANCY (Nan)
An eighteenth century pet-form of Ann, now considered an independent name.

The forthright American Nancy Astor (1879–1964) was the first woman to take her seat in the House of Commons in 1919. A blue plaque commemorating her has been placed on her home at 4 St James's Square in London.

NANETTE
A pet-form of Nan, itself an early diminutive of Ann. It has been used in Britain since the early twentieth century.

No! No! Nanette! (1925), an operetta by Vincent Youman, was fabulously successful in England and Europe. The actress Nanette Newman is the best-known modern bearer of the name.

NAOMI
From the Hebrew, meaning 'pleasure'. The Old Testament Naomi was the beloved mother-in-law of Ruth, whose story is told in the Book of Ruth. This became a favourite with the Puritans of the seventeenth century and has been used since then.

The prolific novelist Naomi Jacob (1884–1964) is well-known.

NATALIE (Natalia)
From the Latin, meaning 'birthday of the Lord'. It was often bestowed on girls born on Christmas Day.

St Natalia, a saint of the fourth century, instructed her husband St Adrian in the faith and had to see him martyred for professing it. Her feast day is 1st December.

The South African province of Natal was named by the Portuguese explorer Vasco de Gama, who landed at what is now the city of Durban on Christmas Day 1497, and dubbed it Terra Natalis.

NATASHA (Tasha)
The Russian pet-form of Natalia, now generally used. Natasha Rostova is the heroine of Count Leo Tolstoy's greatest novel, *War and Peace* (1863–1869). After an unhappy love affair with Prince Andrei she makes a *happy* marriage with Pierre Bezukhov. (A literary rarity!)

NELLIE (Nelly)
A pet-form of Eleanor (q.v.), now used as an independent name. The last words of Charles II (1630–1685) to his brother James, 'Let not poor Nelly starve,' are well known.

And James *did* help Charles's mistress, Nell Gwyn. He allowed her £1,500 a year, and paid off all her debts, saving her from debtors' prison.

NERISSA
From the Greek, meaning 'sea nymph'. Shakespeare seems to have invented the name he gave to Portia's astute waiting-woman and confidante in *The Merchant of Venice* (1595).

NERYS
A modern Welsh name, meaning 'lady'. The actress Nerys Hughes (b. 1941) brought the name to public attention.

NESTA
The Welsh form of Agnes (q.v.), used since the eleventh century. Nesta, a Welsh princess, was mother to Giraldus Cambrensis (1146–1220), writer and historian.

NETTIE
A pet-form of Jeanette, now independently used.

NIAMH

From the Gaelic, meaning 'beauty'. In Irish mythology, the daughter of the sea god, who fell in love with Oisin.

Niamh carried him over the sea, keeping him with her for 300 years. He was then allowed to return home, riding a magic steed, but forbidden to set foot on the ground. He disregarded this, of course, instantly becoming a very old, blind man.

W. B. Yeats wrote a narrative poem, *The Wanderings of Oisin* (1889), telling of his love for Niamh.

NICOLA (Nicole, Nicolette, Nikki)

The feminine forms of Nicholas (q.v.), now generally popular. Nicola has been used in England since the twelfth century.

Aucassin and Nicolette is one of the best-known of all medieval romances. Nicolette, a king's daughter enslaved by the Saracens, falls in love with Aucassin, son of the Count of Beaucaire. After imprisonment, shipwreck and various disguises, all ends happily.

NIGELLA

The feminine version of Nigel (q.v.). The Latin name for the beautiful flower Love-in-a-mist is *Nigella damascena*.

NIKITA

From the Greek, meaning 'unconquered'. A popular Russian male name, bestowed upon girls in Britain.

The Russian politician Nikita Krushchev, President of the USSR from 1958 to 1964, is best remembered for losing his temper and beating upon the table with his shoe!

NINA

A Russian pet-form of Anne, used in England since the nineteenth century. (It can also be derived from the Spanish, meaning 'little girl'.)

In Babylonian myth Nina was a marine goddess prone to uttering dire predictions.

Anton Chekhov's play *The Seagull* (1896) has a tragic heroine named Nina who compares herself to the dead bird of the title, destroyed by man's whim. (And the hero – you *knew* he would – commits suicide.)

NISSA
From the Hebrew, meaning 'sign'. A modern name.

NITA
A pet-form of the Spanish name Juanita, now generally used.

NOËLLE (Noeleen)
The French feminine form of Noël, meaning 'Christmas', an appropriate choice for girls born on that day.

NOLA
A feminine version of Nolan (q.v.), used in Britain since the 1940s.

NORAH (Nora)
The pet-form of Leonora (q.v.), now independently used. Nora Helmer is the heroine of *A Doll's House* (1879) by Henrik Ibsen.
  Considered a fool by her father and husband, she commits forgery in order to obtain the money needed to save the life of her spouse. The end of the play sees Nora leaving him to gain her independence.

NORMA
From the Latin, meaning 'precept'. *Norma* (1831), an opera by Vincenzo Bellini, appears to have brought the name to public attention. The eponymous heroine, a Druid priestess, is secretly married to a Roman pro-Consul. Naturally, it all ends in tears.
  (Norma is also the name of a constellation in the southern Milky Way.)

NUALA
From the Irish name Fionnghuala, meaning 'white-shouldered'. The beautiful Fionnghuala of legend was transformed into a swan by her evil stepmother and wandered the lakes and rivers endlessly. She could not be released from the spell until Christianity came to Ireland.

OCEAN

A modern name, with a venerable history. This was especially bestowed on a child born at sea.

Oceanus Hopkins was born on the *Mayflower*, which set sail on its memorable voyage from Plymouth on 6th September 1620. The passengers landed at what is now Plymouth, Massachusetts on 21st December.

And Lord Byron's epic poem, *Childe Harold's Pilgrimage* (1812), includes the appropriate line:

And I have loved thee, Ocean.

OCTAVIA

From the Latin, meaning 'eighth'. In Roman history, two unhappy ladies with this name are memorable. The first was sister to the Emperor Augustus and married Mark Antony, who promptly abandoned her on meeting Cleopatra.

The second (40–62) was a daughter of the Emperor Claudius and married to Nero. He divorced her in order to marry another (whom he later kicked to death), then had Octavia executed. Despite this, the name has been used in Britain since the eighteenth century.

A happier lady, who deserves our gratitude, was Octavia Hill (1838–1912), one of the three founders of the National Trust.

ODETTE

The French female diminutive of Odo, a medieval name meaning 'prosperity'. Its use in Britain began early in the twentieth century.

Odette de Crecy is an important character in Marcel Proust's epic novel, first published in sixteen volumes, *Remembrance of Things Past* (1913–1927).

Odette Sansom (later Hallowes) was the first woman to be awarded the George Cross for her bravery during the Second World War.

OENONE
In Greek mythology, a nymph from Mount Ida with the gifts of prophecy and healing. She was Paris's first wife. After he deserted her for Helen and was wounded, she refused to help him despite her promise to do so. On his death she committed suicide.

Alfred, Lord Tennyson's poems *Oenone* and *The Death of Oenone* made the name well-known to the Victorians. The name appears to be enjoying a revival.

OLGA
The Russian version of an Old Norse name, meaning 'holy'. St Olga (879–969) was the wife of Igor, Prince of Kiev, and baptised at the age of 80. Her grandson, St Vladimir, introduced Christianity to Russia. The name has been used in Britain since the nineteenth century.

Grand Duchess Olga (1895–1918) was the first daughter of Tsar Nicholas II, murdered with all her family by the Bolsheviks in the cellar at Ekaterinburg.

OLIMPIA
In Greek mythology Mount Olympus was the home of the gods, presided over by Zeus.

Olimpia leads an exciting life in the *Orlando Furioso* (1516) of Ariosto. The poor girl commits murder, is trapped by brigands and exposed to a sea monster. Finally she marries a king of Ireland.

OLIVE (Olivia)
The olive tree was sacred to the goddess Pallas Athene in Greek mythology. It signified peace and, when carried by new brides, fecundity. The name has been used in England since the thirteenth century.

Olivia is the Italian version of the name, popularised by the rich countess in Shakespeare's play *Twelfth Night*. It is also a 'romantic' name, bestowed upon a daughter of Dr Primrose in Oliver Goldsmith's novel *The Vicar of Wakefield* (1766).

OLWEN (Olwin)

From the Welsh, meaning 'white footprint'. Olwen was a giant's daughter in Welsh mythology; as she walked, white flowers sprang up beneath her feet.

OONAGH

See under Una.

OPHELIA

From the Greek, meaning 'help'. Ophelia is the daughter of Polonius in Shakespeare's *Hamlet*. She becomes mad and drowns herself because her heart is broken. It was a favourite subject with the Pre-Raphaelite painters; the most famous example was painted by John Everett Millais in 1852. His *Ophelia* can be seen in the Tate Gallery, London.

OPHIRA

From the Hebrew, meaning 'gold'. Mentioned in the Old Testament, Ophir was renowned for its precious stones, silver and ivory. It was believed to be the source of King Solomon's treasure. (Sadly, its location is unknown.)

ORCHID

Another of the flower names, first used in the 1920s. First popular with the ancient Greeks, the orchid has always been considered a thing of beauty.

Nature provided 35,000 species of this flower. Man, seeking ever to improve, has produced no fewer than 50,000 named hybrids. Enough to drive a botanist mad!

ORIEL

Now a probable variation of Auriel, meaning 'golden'; but the Normans *did* bring Oriel to England at the Conquest and it may be a revival.

Oriel College was founded by Edward II in 1326 and is the oldest royal foundation in Oxford. Sir Walter Raleigh was one of its famous members.

ORINDA

Katherine Philips (1631–1664) was a poet much admired in her day, dubbed the 'Matchless Orinda'. She died of smallpox, her collected poems published in 1667. The name was invented by her in her correspondence with Sir Charles Cotterell.

ORLAITH (Orla)
From the Gaelic, meaning 'gold princess'.

ORYNTHIA
In Greek mythology, a nymph beloved by the North Wind. She bore him three sons, who accompanied Jason and the Argonauts on their quest for the Golden Fleece.

OTTILIE
From the Old German, meaning 'fatherland', a feminine version of Otto.

St Ottilia (d. 720), who was reputedly born blind and regained her sight, is the patroness of Alsace and invoked by those afflicted with diseases of the eyes.

PAIGE
An occupational surname, meaning 'page'; now a modern first name for girls. In the Middle Ages, a boy who wished to become a knight had to serve an apprenticeship as a page in a royal household or nobleman's castle, waiting upon the family.

PAMELA (Pam)
Supposedly coined by Sir Philip Sidney (1554–1586) in his pastoral romance *Arcadia*, the name became a favourite after the

publication of *Pamela* (1740) by Samuel Richardson. The unsophisticated heroine, Pamela Andrews, convinces the son of her wealthy employer to marry her after rejecting his dishonourable attentions.

PANDORA
From the Greek, meaning 'all gifts'. In Greek mythology Pandora was the first woman, created by Zeus. Out of curiosity, she opened the box containing diseases and sorrow and all the woes now rife in the world. Only hope, slower than the rest, remained to give comfort.

PANSY
A flower name, first used in the late nineteenth century. The pansy signified 'think of me' in the Victorian language of flowers.

PARIS
The name of the man who abducted Helen, causing the Siege of Troy; and often found as a surname in English medieval records. It is now a popular first name for girls.

Mozart's *Paris Symphony*, K297, was written and performed in the city in 1778.

PASCALE
The French feminine form of Pascal (q.v.), used in Britain since the 1960s.

PATIENCE
One of the Christian virtues, made a favourite by the Puritans of the seventeenth century. Sir Thomas Crewe, Speaker of the House of Commons from 1624 to 1625, had four daughters named Patience, Temperance, Silence and Prudence. Patience is the hero of the comic opera by Gilbert and Sullivan in which Oscar Wilde is caricatured, entitled *Patience or Bunthorne's Bride* (1881).

PATRICIA
The feminine form of Patrick, meaning 'noble'. Victoria Patricia Helena Elizabeth of Connaught (1886–1974), known as Princess Patricia, granddaughter of Queen Victoria and a painter, made the name a favourite.

PATSY
A pet-form of Patricia (q.v.), now used independently. (It is also American slang for someone who has been tricked!)

PAULA
The German feminine form of Paul (q.v.), used in Britain since the early twentieth century. The Roman St Paula (347–404) was noted for her tact; as a friend and helper of the bad-tempered St Jerome it was much needed. She built a hospice for pilgrims in Bethlehem.

Paula is the eponymous heroine of Arthur Wing Pinero's best-known play, *The Second Mrs Tanquerary* (1893). She has a lurid past and an unhappy present, becoming yet another literary suicide.

PAULINE
The French feminine form of Paul (q.v.), now generally used. Pauline Bonaparte (1780–1825) was the second and favourite sister of Napoleon I; she married Prince Camillo Borghese and lived a rather flamboyant life!

PEARL
A jewel name, which came into use in the late nineteenth century along with many others. Pearls have always been a royal favourite and remain so today. Queen Alexandra (1844–1925) once delayed the State Opening of Parliament because her string of pearls snapped. Everything came to a halt while they were being retrieved.

The American writer Pearl Buck (1892–1973) received a Pulitzer Prize for her novel *The Good Earth* (1931) and the Nobel Prize for Literature in 1938.

PENELOPE (Penny)
From the Greek, meaning 'weaver'. In Greek mythology, Penelope was the wife of Odysseus. While he was wandering the globe she was besieged by suitors. Penelope promised to choose one to replace her vanished husband when her incessant weaving was done. As she unpicked the day's work every night, this was impossible. (Odysseus returned in time to slay all the suitors, who were becoming a trifle angry.) The name has been used in England since the sixteenth century.

PEONY

From the flower, first used in the late nineteenth century. According to Greek mythology, the peony was named by the god Apollo. Sir Joseph Banks brought the tree peony to Kew Gardens from China in 1789. (And a particularly beautiful variety of the flower is the aptly named 'Bowl of Beauty'.)

PERDITA (Purdie)

From the Latin, meaning 'lost'. Perdita, the heroine of Shakespeare's play *The Winter's Tale*, is abandoned on a deserted shore and raised by a shepherd. As she is *really* a princess, everything ends happily. Shakespeare appears to have invented the name.

PERSEPHONE

From the Greek, meaning 'dazzlingly bright'. In Greek mythology, she was the daughter of Zeus and Demeter. While picking flowers in Sicily, she was kidnapped by Hades, god of the Underworld. Her mother rescued her, on the understanding that she had eaten nothing while abducted. Unfortunately, Persephone had devoured six pomegranate seeds and so had to remain in the Underworld for six months of each year. And that is why we have winter!

PETRA

From the Latin, meaning 'rock'. A modern feminine version of Peter. Petra, the ruined Jordanian city immortalised by the well-known line, 'a rose-red city half as old as time', was rediscovered by the Swiss explorer Johann Burckhardt in 1812. (It is now in peril from too many tourists.)

PETRONELLA

The name of an early Christian martyr, it has been used in England since the twelfth century. Medieval legend decided that Petronella was the daughter of the apostle Peter and she was invoked by those suffering from fever.

PHILIPPA

The feminine version of Philip, meaning 'fond of horses'. Queen Philippa of Hainault (1314–1369), wife of Edward III, was responsible for introducing the herb rosemary into England. She later led the English army against the invading Scots. It was also the name of Geoffrey Chaucer's wife.

Philippa Garrett Fawcett (1868–1948) made history in 1890 when she was classed 'above Senior Wrangler' in the Mathematical Tripos at Cambridge. Being a woman, she was denied the title, but her college celebrated with fireworks and singing all the same. This prompted a *Punch* cartoon, showing her sitting alone in a railway carriage, with the title 'First Class. Ladies Only'.

PHOEBE
From the Greek, meaning 'bright'. In Greek mythology, Phoebe was a Titaness, one of the many children of Uranus and Gaia. The New Testament Phoebe carried St Paul's letter to the Church in Rome from her home in Corinth. The name became popular in England after the Reformation.

Phoebe Tozer is the ebullient heroine of Mrs Oliphant's nineteenth century novel *Phoebe Junior*.

PHYLLIDA
From the Greek, meaning 'leafy'. The Phyllida of Greek mythology hanged herself because her lover did not return to marry her as he had promised. The poor girl was transformed into an almond tree.

An anonymous Elizabethan poet wrote *Phillada Flouts Me*. The name appears to have been used in England since the seventeenth century.

PHYLLIS
From the Greek, meaning 'leafy'. The name of a Thracian princess in Greek mythology, classical poets considered it a suitable name for beautiful country maidens. John Milton included 'neat-handed Phyllis' in his poem *L'Allegro*.

It was particularly popular in England in the eighteenth century.

PIA
From the Latin, meaning 'dutiful, godly'. This pretty Italian name is a modern favourite in Britain.

PIPER
An occupational surname, now used as a first name. Its popularity seems to have begun in America.

PIPPA

A pet-form of Philippa (q.v.), now used independently. Robert Browning made the name a favourite with his long poetic drama *Pippa Passes* (1841). Pippa works at the silk mills in Asolo in Italy; her songs affect the lives of all who hear her. She it is who sings the well-known lines:

> The lark's on the wing;
> The snail's on the thorn;
> God's in his heaven –
> All's right with the world!

PLEASANCE

From the Old French, meaning 'to please'. This was brought to England by the Normans.

POLLY

A venerable pet-form of Mary, via Molly; its age is demonstrated by various nursery rhyme characters.

The lovely Polly Peachum marries Captain Macheath in *The Beggar's Opera* by John Gay, first performed in 1728. A sequel to this, called *Polly*, was not popular with the government of the day who took umbrage at Gay's satire.

POLLYANNA

This name was made a favourite by the American writer Eleanor Hodgman Porter (1868–1920), who bestowed it upon the cheerful eponymous heroine of her best-known novel *Pollyanna* (1913).

POPPY

Another of the flower names which first became popular in the late nineteenth century.

The flower was established in England by the Bronze Age. It is most famously associated with the Royal British Legion and its November Poppy Appeal, which assists ex-service men and women and their families.

The Canadian soldier-poet John McCrae (d. 1918) inspired the use of the flower when his poem *In Flanders Fields* was published in *Punch* in 1915.

> We shall not sleep, though poppies grow
> In Flanders fields.

PORTIA

From the Latin, meaning 'hog'. The name of an ancient Roman family, it was given by Shakespeare to the heroine of his play *The Merchant of Venice*. Portia, disguised as a lawyer, prevents Shylock from claiming his pound of flesh from Antonio. It is she who speaks the famous lines:

> The quality of mercy is not strained,
> It droppeth as the gentle rain from heaven.

POSY

This seems to have become popular in the 1920s, perhaps a logical progression from the Victorian love for flower names.

Posy is the ballet-obsessed youngest of the three Fossil sisters in the classic children's story *Ballet Shoes* (1936) by Noel Streatfeild.

PRIMROSE

A flower name, popular since the late nineteenth century. It is also a surname, most notably of the Earls of Rosebery. The Primrose League was founded in 1883 to promote the principles of the Conservative Party.

PRIMULA

A botanical name, used as a first name since the late nineteenth century. Cowslip, oxlip and polyanthus are just three of the flowers which belong to the primula family.

PRISCILLA (Cilla, Scilla)

From the Latin, meaning 'ancient'. The New Testament Priscilla and her husband, Aquila, were close friends with St Paul and involved in the tent-making business of Corinth, as he was. The name became popular with the Puritans of the seventeenth century.

PRUDENCE

From the Latin, meaning 'discretion'. Although used in the Middle Ages, the Puritans of the seventeenth century took up the name and make it a favourite.

PRUNELLA

From the Latin, meaning 'little plum'. This is another of the botanical names favoured by the Victorians. (It is also a smooth, woollen fabric much used in the eighteenth century for clerical and academic garb.)

The actress Prunella Scales, always remembered as the long-suffering Sybil Fawlty in the manic television series *Fawlty Towers*, is the best-known modern bearer of the name.

PSYCHE

From the Greek, meaning 'soul'. In Greek mythology a beautiful maiden, beloved by Eros. After many trials they were married and she became immortal.

The Bath of Psyche, painted by Lord Leighton in 1889, can be viewed at Tate Britain. And Psyche is the name given to a crater on the Eros asteroid; number 433 should you wish to track it.

QUINTA (Quitana)

From the Latin, meaning 'fifth'. The feminine form of Quintin and much used in ancient Rome. Quintana is a modern variation.

(And if you didn't already know, the 'via quintana' was the place for exercise in a Roman soldiers' camp and Quintana Roo is a state in Mexico!)

RACHEL (Rae, Raquel)

From the Hebrew, meaning 'ewe'. The Old Testament Rachel was the beautiful second wife of Jacob. Her tomb, which stands just outside Bethlehem, is venerated by Christians, Jews and Moslems alike. The name came into general use in England after the Reformation.

Rachel was the stage name of Elizabeth Felix (1820–1858), the French tragic actress renowned worldwide.

REBECCA (Becky)

From the Hebrew, meaning 'heifer'. The Old Testament Rebecca, a Syrian, was the wife of Isaac and mother of Jacob and Esau. The name came into general use in England after the Reformation.

Ten-year-old Rebecca Randall, heroine of Kate Douglas Wiggin's bestseller *Rebecca of Sunnybrook Farm* (1903), made the name a favourite.

Becky Sharp is the interesting but far from pleasant main character in *Vanity Fair* (1848) by William Makepeace Thackeray.

REESE

A version of Rhys (q.v.), now considered a female name. This has been made popular by the film star Reese Witherspoon.

REGAN

From the Irish surname, meaning 'descendant of the little king'. Its use for girls is taken from Shakespeare's *King Lear*.

One of the king's three daughters, Regan was the wife of the Duke of Cornwall. Not a pleasant character, she is finally poisoned by her obnoxious sister Goneril.

REGINA
From the Latin, meaning 'queen'. This was originally bestowed
upon girls in the Middle Ages, referring to the Virgin Mary
under her title 'Queen of Heaven'. It was revived in the nineteenth century.
    Regina is the capital of the Canadian province of Saskatch-
ewan, named in honour of Queen Victoria.

REMI
The feminine version of the French name Remy, meaning 'oarsman'. This is now used in Britain.
    St Remy (438–533) became Bishop of Rheims at the early age
of 22. He baptised King Clovis of the Franks on Christmas Day
496, an important event in French history.

RENÉE
A French feminine name, meaning 'reborn', now generally used.
This was derived from the Latin Renatus, popular with the early
Christians. St René Goupil (d. 1642) was martyred by North
American Indians for making the sign of the cross.

RHEA
In Greek mythology, the wife and sister of Cronos, mother of
Zeus and other Olympians.
    Rhea Silvia was the mother of Romulus and Remus, the
founders of Rome.

RHIAN
From the Welsh, meaning 'maiden'. A modern name.

RHIANNON
From the Welsh, meaning 'nymph' or 'goddess'. In Celtic
mythology the wife of Prince Pwyll, falsely accused of murder-
ing her kidnapped baby son. After seven years her innocence
was proved when the boy returned.

RHODA
From the Greek, meaning 'rose'. In the New Testament, she was
the servant girl who was too excited to let St Peter into the house
after he had been miraculously released from prison in Jerusalem by an angel. The name came into use in England after the
Reformation.

Rhoda Fleming (1865), a novel by George Meredith, concerns the efforts of the eponymous heroine to help her sister Dahlia.

RHONA (Rona)
A Scottish place name, used as a first name since the late nineteenth century.

RHONDA
A twentieth-century name derived from two Welsh rivers, Rhondda Fawr and Rhondda Fach.

The American film star Rhonda Fleming (b. 1923) made the name known in the 1940s and 1950s.

RHONWEN
A Welsh traditional name, meaning 'slender fair', popular with medieval poets.

RIA
A pet-form of Maria, used independently since the eighteenth century.

RICHENDA
An eighteenth century feminine form of Richard, q.v.

RILLA
From the German, meaning 'brook'.

RIPLEY
A surname, meaning 'clearing of the people of Ripon', now used as a first name.

RITA
A pet-form of Margarita, used independently. St Rita of Cascia (1381–1457) married at the behest of her parents a man who was ill-tempered and profligate. After his violent death, she became an Augustinian nun and many miracles were attributed to her.

The film star Rita Hayworth, best remembered for her appearance in *Gilda* (1946), made the name a favourite.

ROBERTA (Bobbie)
The feminine form of Robert (q.v.), used since the mid-nineteenth century. Roberta (together with her sister Phyllis and her brother Peter) is one of the heroines of Edith Nesbit's *The Railway Children*, first published as a book in 1906.

ROBYN (Robina)
A feminine form of Robin, itself once considered a pet-form of
Robert, now used independently.

Robyn is a character in the Coventry Mystery Play of the
fifteenth century. (And Oliver Cromwell, Lord Protector of
England after the execution of Charles I, had a sister named
Robina.)

ROCHELLE
From a French place name, meaning 'little rock'. La Rochelle is
a French fishing port, situated on the Atlantic coast.

ROISIN (Rosheen)
An Irish version of Rose (q.v.), popular since the early twentieth
century.

ROMA
From the city, used as a first name in modern times. The goddess
Roma had a temple built to her honour in Rome by the Emperor
Hadrian (76–138), and her cult spread throughout Greece and
Asia Minor.

ROMAINE (Romayne)
A French feminine name, meaning 'Roman', now generally used.

ROMILLY
A surname, now used as a first name. Sir Samuel Romilly
(1757–1818), whose portrait can be seen in the National Portrait
Gallery, was Solicitor General and law reformer. Romilly Street,
near Shaftesbury Avenue in London, is named in his honour.

ROMOLA
The feminine form of Romulus, one of the legendary founders
of Rome.

Romola is the title of a novel, set in fifteenth century Florence,
by George Eliot. Published in 1863, it was illustrated by Lord
Leighton.

ROMY
The German pet-form of Rosemary (q.v.), now generally used.
The Austrian film star Romy Schneider (1938–1982) made it
known.

ROSALIE
The French feminine form of Rosalia, now generally used.
Rosalia was the name given to the yearly ceremony of hanging
garlands of roses on the tombs of the dead in ancient Rome. The
twelfth century St Rosalia is the patron saint of Palermo.

ROSALIND
Brought to England at the Norman Conquest, the name was
made popular by Shakespeare when he bestowed it upon the
courageous and witty heroine of his play *As You Like It*.

The English poet and physician Thomas Lodge (1558–1625)
wrote *Rosalind's Madrigal*.

ROSAMOND/ROSAMUND
The name was brought to England by the Normans and has
remained in use since then.

'Fair Rosamund' Clifford (d. 1176) was the mistress of Henry
II. She lived at Woodstock Palace, Oxfordshire; reputedly at the
heart of a maze to prevent discovery by the outraged wife,
Eleanor of Aquitaine. (The site is now enclosed in the grounds
of Blenheim Palace.)

Algernon Charles Swinburne wrote a play about her, *Rosa-
mond* (1860).

ROSANNA
A conjunction of Rose and Anna, first used in the eighteenth
century and now very popular.

ROSE (Rosie)
From the Old German, meaning 'horse', but now considered
purely a floral name. It was brought to England by the Normans, and has always been the most popular of all the flower
names. St Rose of Lima (1586–1617) was the first person in the
Americas to be canonised.

A mural containing a pink rose was painted before 1450 BC at
Knossos, in Crete; the Imperial Chinese had over 600 books
about them before 500 BC and the Romans loved them, encir-
cling the heads of newborn babies, statues, tombs and themselves with rose garlands.

Dame Rose Macaulay (1881–1958), the English novelist, is a
famous bearer of the name.

ROSEMARY

From the Latin, meaning 'sea dew'. Another of the botanical names which became popular at the end of the nineteenth century.

The plant has long been an emblem of remembrance, prompted by the following lines from Shakespeare's *Hamlet*:

> There's rosemary; that's for remembrance;
> Pray, love, remember . . .

ROSITA

A Spanish pet-form of Rose, now generally used. Rosita Forbes (1890–1967) was an explorer and author.

Her first great journey was to Libya in 1920 when she became the first non-Muslim woman, and only the second European, to enter the closed city of Kufara.

ROWENA

From the Celtic, meaning 'fair'. The name was made popular by Sir Walter Scott in his novel *Ivanhoe* (1819). Wilfred, knight of Ivanhoe, loves Rowena, his father's ward; he finally marries her after rejecting the far more interesting Rebecca.

ROXANA (Roxanne)

From the Persian, meaning 'dawn'. Roxana was the Persian wife of Alexander the Great, remembered for stabbing a rival in a fit of violent jealousy.

Roxane is the heroine of *Cyrano de Bergerac*, a play by Edmond Rostand (1868–1918).

RUBY

From the precious stone, first used by the Victorians in the late nineteenth century. Fine quality rubies are the costliest of all gems, found particularly in Burma.

One of the most renowned jewels owned by the Crown is the Timur ruby, once the property of Tamerlane, conqueror of Afghanistan, India and Persia. It was presented to Queen Victoria after being displayed at the Great Exhibition of 1851.

RUFINA

The feminine version of Rufus, q.v.

RUTH

From the Hebrew, meaning 'beloved'. The Old Testament Book of Ruth tells the story of its eponymous heroine, daughter-in-law to Naomi and great-grandmother to King David. The name came into use in England after the Reformation.

The Pre-Raphaelite painter Thomas Matthews Rooke (1842–1942) painted *The Story of Ruth* and this can be admired at the Tate Gallery in London.

SABINA (Sabine)

From the Latin, meaning 'a Sabine woman', used in England since the seventeenth century. Sabine is the French version.

The Sabines were an ancient Italian people, crushed by the Romans in 290 BC. Romulus, needing wives for his men, lured away the male population, telling his men to help themselves to the women remaining.

SABLE

A modern name, particularly appropriate for a child with black hair. (It is, of course, the heraldic term for black.)

The poet William Drummond (1585–1649) penned the lines:

Phoebus, arise,
And paint the sable skies . . .

SABRAH

Reputedly the daughter of a king of Egypt, Sabrah was rescued from the dragon by St George, later marrying him.

This name originated in *The Golden Legend*, one of the most popular books published by William Caxton in 1483.

SABRINA
The Latin name for the River Severn. In legend, the daughter of King Locrine and his mistress Estrildis, drowned by the jealous Queen Gwendolene.

Sabrina is the nymph who helps the heroine to escape the attentions of Comus in the masque of the same name by John Milton, first performed in Ludlow Castle in 1634.

SADIE
A pet-form of Sarah (q.v.), used as an independent name since the late nineteenth century.

Sadie Thompson is the eponymous flamboyant 'heroine' of a short story by William Somerset Maugham (1874–1965), later successfully dramatised as *Rain*.

SAFFRON
A modern name, taken from the flower or spice. Saffron is the most expensive spice in the world. It takes approximately 4,000 flowers to produce a mere 28 grams of it, and all have to be picked by hand.

The Essex town of Saffron Walden once specialised in the growing of saffron crocuses.

SAGE
From the Old French, meaning 'wise'. A modern first name. (Or perhaps it was prompted by the aromatic herb, of the genus *Salvia*, used in cooking.)

SAKURA
From the Japanese, meaning 'cherry-blossom'. The Japanese consider that Spring does not officially begin until the cherry trees bloom in early to mid-April: this is celebrated countrywide by cherry-blossom parties.

SALOME
From the Aramaic, meaning 'peace'. The Biblical Salome is remembered as the daughter of Herodias, who danced for Herod Antipas. She claimed the head of John the Baptist as a reward.

Salomé, the play written by Oscar Wilde and published in 1894 with illustrations by Aubrey Beardsley, was considered extremely daring.

SALLY (Sallie)

A pet-form of Sarah, used as an independent name since the eighteenth century. The English poet and composer Henry Carey (1687–1743) is remembered for his lengthy ballad *Sally in Our Alley*:

> Of all the girls that are so smart
> There's none like pretty Sally;
> She is the darling of my heart,
> And she lives in our alley.

SAMANTHA

A feminine version of Samuel, coined in America in the eighteenth century.

The American composer Cole Porter (1893–1964) had a hit with the song *I Love You, Samantha* in the 1950s; while the nose-wriggling witch in the television series *Bewitched* also bore the name. The English actress Samantha Eggar (b. 1939) is well-known.

SANDRA (Zandra)

A diminutive of the Italian Alessandra or Alexandra, now generally used. The British dress designer Zandra Rhodes (b. 1940), whose clothes and character are larger than life, keeps the name in the public eye.

SANDY/SANDI

A pet-form of Sandra, now used independently. The American actress Sandy Dennis (1937–1992) won an Oscar for Best Supporting Actress in the film *Who's Afraid of Virginia Woolf?*

SAPPHIRE

From the jewel, its colour a deep transparent blue. On Queen Victoria's wedding day, Prince Albert gave her a large sapphire brooch which remained a favourite.

Today the Queen wears 'Albert's brooch' on her Garter ribbon.

SARAH (Sara)

From the Hebrew, meaning 'princess'. In the Old Testament she was the wife of Abraham, who gave birth to her son Isaac at the age of 90 and lived to the ripe old age of 127. The Puritans of the seventeenth century made the name a favourite, but it has been used in England since the Middle Ages.

Mrs Sarah Siddons (1755–1831) was the greatest tragic actress of her generation, famous for playing Lady Macbeth and Zara in Congreve's *The Mourning Bride*.

Sara Teasdale (1884–1933), the American lyric poet, received the Pulitzer Prize for *Love Songs* (1917).

SARITA
A Spanish diminutive of Sarah, now generally used.

SASHA
A Russian pet-form of Alexander, used increasingly for girls in the last few years.

SASKIA
A Dutch name, popular in Britain recently. This was the name of the wife of the Dutch painter, Harmensz Rembrandt (1606–1669). Married in 1634 Saskia was his favourite model until her death in 1642: *Self-Portrait with Saskia* (1636), which can be seen in Dresden, is the finest example of this.

SAVANNAH
A popular modern name, adopting the term for a plain without trees.

The hero of Daniel Defoe's novel *Robinson Crusoe*, first published in 1719, thought them delightful. 'I found many pleasant Savannas, or meadows, plain, smooth and cover'd in grass.'

SCARLETT
From the vivid red colour, made popular by the heroine of Margaret Mitchell's bestselling (and only) novel *Gone with the Wind* (1936). Vivien Leigh played the beautiful and selfish Scarlett O'Hara in the equally famous film.

SELINA
From the Greek, meaning 'moon', or from the Latin, meaning 'heaven'. In Greek mythology, she was the goddess of the moon who bore two daughters by Zeus, Herse ('dew') and Pandia. Her brother was Helios, the god of the sun. The name has been used in England since the seventeenth century.

Selina, Countess of Huntingdon (1707–1791), devoted all her time and energy to religion and good works after being converted to Methodism in the 1730s.

SERENA
From the Latin, meaning 'calm'. Two early saints bore this name, and it has been used in England since the thirteenth century.

William Hayley (1745–1820), the English poet and biographer, chose Serena as the heroine of his lengthy poem *The Triumph of Temper*.

SHANNON
The name of an Irish river, the longest in the British Isles, now a popular choice for girls.

SHARON (Sharron)
A Hebrew place name, meaning 'a plain', which stretches from Jaffa to Caesarea Philippi on the coast of Israel. The Biblical 'Rose of Sharon' is now considered to have been a narcissus. It has been used as a first name in Britain since the mid-twentieth century.

SHEENA
The anglicised version of the Gaelic name Sine, the Scottish form of Jane, used generally since the 1950s.

The singer Sheena Easton is a well-known bearer of the name.

SHEILA (Shelagh)
The English version of the Irish name, Sile, itself a form of Cecilia. Shelagh Delaney (b. 1939), the English playwright, had a success with her very first play, *A Taste of Honey*, later made into a film.

SHELLEY
An Old English place name, meaning 'clearing on a plateau', and surname, now used as a first name.

Exclusively masculine in the nineteenth century, it is now bestowed on girls. Perhaps this was prompted by the American film star Shelley Winters who won an Oscar as the Best Supporting Actress in *The Diary of Anne Frank* (1959).

SHIRLEY

An Old English place name, meaning 'bright wood', and aristocratic surname, used as a first name since the nineteenth century. It is the surname of the earls Ferrers.

Shirley Keeldar is the heroine of Charlotte Brontë's novel *Shirley* (1849), set in Yorkshire at the end of the Napoleonic Wars.

Shirley Temple (b. 1928), the American child star, made the name very popular indeed after her début in the film *Red Haired Alibi* at the grand old age of 3.

SHONA

The anglicised version of the Gaelic name Seonaid, a form of Joan, used in England since the mid-twentieth century.

SIÂN

The Welsh form of Jane, now generally used. The actress Siân Phillips (b. 1934) has made the name known.

SIBYL (Sibella, Sybil)

From the Greek, meaning 'prophetess'. The ancient world had many sibyls, in Babylonia, Italy, Greece and Egypt. The Sibyl of Cumae sold three books of oracles to Tarquin Superbus, the last king of Rome, which were consulted by the Senate in times of danger. These were destroyed in the great fire which swept Rome during the reign of the tyrant Nero.

St Augustine included a sibyl in his great work *The City of God*, which made it acceptable as a Christian name.

Robert, Duke of Normandy, a son of William the Conqueror, married Sibylla and she introduced the name to England. Dame Sybil Thorndike (1882–1976), the English actress, remains the best-known modern bearer of the name.

SIDONY (Sidonie)

From the Latin, meaning 'person from Sidon'. This has been used in England since medieval times.

St Sidonius of Clermont (432–482) was made a bishop in 470, despite the fact that he was a layman at the time. His letters survive, giving a lively description of what it was like to live during the break-up of the Roman Empire.

The French novelist Sidonie Gabrielle Colette (1873–1954) used the pen name Colette.

SIENA (Sienna)
From the Italian city, used as a first name since the nineteenth century. The ancient, originally Etruscan, city is famous for its magnificent collection of art treasures and its famous 'Palio', held in August. The citizens parade in medieval costume and compete in a horse race through the narrow winding streets.

SIGRID
From the Scandinavian, meaning 'beautiful victory', now generally used.

Sigrid the Haughty was married to King Sweyn of Denmark, who usurped the throne of England in the autumn of 1013. (The reign was very brief. He died on 3rd February 1014 in Lincolnshire.)

SILVESTRA
The feminine version of Silvester, meaning 'of the woods'.

SIMONE
The French feminine form of Simon, meaning 'snub-nosed'. The French character actress Simone Signoret, who won an Oscar for Best Actress in the film *Room at the Top* (1958), made the name known worldwide.

SINÉAD
The Gaelic form of Janet, now increasing in popularity generally.

SIOBHAN (Shevaun)
A Gaelic name, an Irish version of Joan, widely favoured in recent years.

SKY (Skye)
A very modern name, its use originating in America. (I hope the baby will find the words from Sir Walter Scott's poem *Marmion* to be untrue: 'November's Sky is chill and drear.')

SONIA (Sonya)
The Russian pet-form of Sophia, used in Britain since the early twentieth century.

Sonya Marmeladova is the heroine of Dostoyevsky's masterpiece *Crime and Punishment* (1866). Forced into crime to support her father, stepmother and their small children, she urges

Raskolnikov to confess to the murder he has committed and accompanies him when he is sentenced to exile in Siberia.

SOPHIA (Sofia, Sophie)
From the Greek, meaning 'wisdom'. The name of a number of early Christian martyrs, the great church in Istanbul called St Sophia is dedicated to Holy Wisdom. The name has been used in England since the seventeenth century. There is a touching monument to Princess Sophia, who was born the youngest daughter of James I in 1606 and lived for only three days, in Westminster Abbey. The baby is sculpted asleep in her cradle.

Countess Sophie Chotek married Archduke Franz Ferdinand of Austria in 1900. Their assassination in 1914 precipitated the First World War.

SORCHA
From the Gaelic, meaning 'brightness'.

SORREL (Sorel)
From the plant, characterised by a sour taste. It has been used as a first name since the early twentieth century.

Sorel Bliss is a character in the Noël Coward play *Hay Fever* (1925).

STACEY
A modern pet-form of Anastasia (q.v.), used since the 1970s.

STAR
A modern first name. If one were to represent the distance between the earth and the sun by one inch, the nearest star would be four miles away!

On a lighter note, this verse is to be found in Byron's *Vision of Judgement*:

> The angels all were singing out of tune,
> And hoarse with having little else to do,
> Excepting to wind up the sun and moon,
> Or curb a runaway young star or two.

STELLA
From the Latin, meaning 'star'. Sir Philip Sidney loved Lady Penelope Devereux and celebrated her under the name of Stella in his sonnet series *Astrophel and Stella* (1591). The name has

been used in England since the Middle Ages, originally in
honour of the Virgin Mary under her title 'Stella Maris' (Star of
the Sea).

STEPHANIE (Steffi)
The French feminine form of Stephen (q.v.), used in Britain
since the early twentieth century.

STEVIE
A modern feminine version of Steven. The English poet Stevie
Smith (1902–1971), whose real name was Florence Margaret
Smith, is best remembered for her poem *Not Waving But Drowning*.

STORM
From the term for a wind force of 10 on the Beaufort scale, used
in the twentieth century as a first name.
    The novelist Storm Jameson (1891–1986), who often set her
stories in Yorkshire, is well-known.

SUMMER
A modern first name, bestowed on babies born at the appropriate time of year.
    The poet John Keats (1795–1821) includes the following in his
famous *Ode to a Nightingale*:

> In some melodious plot
> Of beechen green, and shadows numberless,
> Singest of Summer in full-throated ease.

SUSANNA (Sue, Susan, Susannah, Suzanne, Suzie)
From the Hebrew, meaning 'lily'. Mentioned in the New Testament as one of the women who gave assistance to the disciples, it
is best known through the apocryphal Susanna who was surprised by the Elders as she was bathing and falsely accused of
adultery. The name has been used in England since the thirteenth century. Shakespeare gave the name to his eldest daughter, born in 1583.

SVETLANA
A Russian name, meaning 'light', now generally used.
    Svetlana Alliluyeva (b. 1926), daughter of Joseph Stalin,
defected to America. Her memoirs, *Twenty Letters to a Friend*
(1967) and *Only One Year* (1969), are fascinating.

SYLVIA (Silvia, Sylvie)

From the Latin, meaning 'wood'. Rhea Silvia was the mother of Romulus and Remus, the founders of Rome in 753 BC.

In Shakespeare's play *Two Gentlemen of Verona* Silvia is the beautiful daughter of the Duke of Milan, who finally marries Valentine. The use of the name in Britain appears to have stemmed from this. (A picture entitled *Valentine Rescuing Sylvia from Proteus* (1851) by William Holman Hunt hangs in the Birmingham City Art Gallery.)

If you are a ballet fan, you will think of Delibes's *Sylvia* (1876), the heroine of which is beloved by Amynta.

SYRIE

A feminine form of Cyril, from the Greek meaning 'lord'. It is best remembered as the name of the wife of the writer William Somerset Maugham. She swept away the fussiness of décor in the 1920s and 1930s and began the craze for white paint and austere furnishings. The name is now enjoying a revival.

TABITHA

From the Aramaic, meaning 'gazelle'. In the New Testament, Tabitha was a woman full of good works who became ill and died. The Christians of Lydda sent for St Peter who, after prayer to God, raised her to life. (Dorcas is the Greek equivalent of the name.) The Puritans of the seventeenth century began its use in England.

On a less rarefied level, Beatrix Potter created Tabitha Twitchit, the long-suffering mother of the naughty Tom Kitten.

TALITHA

From the Aramaic, meaning 'little girl'. In the New Testament Gospel of St Mark, Christ raised a child from the dead, saying to her, 'Talitha cumi' or 'Little girl, I say to you arise.'

The name seems to have been used in Britain since the early nineteenth century.

TALLULAH

From the American Indian place name, meaning 'running water'. Tallulah Falls is a notable beauty spot in the American state of Georgia.

The name was brought to prominence by the actress Tallulah Bankhead (1903–1968), who was named after her grandmother.

TAMARA (Tammy)

The Russian version of an Old Testament name Tamar, meaning 'palm tree'; the granddaughter of King David, she was noted for her beauty. It has been used in Britain since the 1950s.

The Russian composer Mily Balakirev (1837–1910), inspired by Lermentov's poem, wrote a piece of music entitled *Tamara*. This dealt with a beautiful Caucasian princess who lured her victims to a violent death. It later became a ballet.

Tamara Karsavina (1885–1978), the legendary Russian ballerina and teacher, a member of Diaghilev's Ballet Russe, married an Englishman and settled in England. A commemorative blue plaque has been placed on her home at 108 Frognal, London NW3.

TAMSIN

The Cornish pet-form of the medieval Thomasin, a now obsolete feminine form of Thomas.

Tasmin is a modern variation. The violinist Tasmin Little has brought the name to public attention.

TANSY

From the flower, derived from the Greek 'athanasia', meaning 'immortality'. The pretty yellow, button-like flowers and aromatic leaves were used in the sixteenth century as a medicinal herb, or strewn upon the floor to scent the air. It became popular as a first name in the twentieth century.

TARA

An Irish place name, used as a first name since the late nineteenth century. The kings, princes and bards of Ireland met at a castle on the hill of Tara, in County Meath, to decide on matters of public importance. Thomas Moore (1779–1852) included the song *The Harp That Once Through Tara's Halls* in his *Irish Melodies*. (It is also the name of Scarlett O'Hara's home and estate in *Gone with the Wind*.)

TATIANA (Tania, Tanya)
A Russian name, used as a first name in Britain since the early twentieth century. St Tatiana was martyred in Rome in the third century AD.

Grand Duchess Tatiana (1897–1918), second daughter of Tsar Nicholas II, was murdered by Bolsheviks in the cellar at Ekaterinburg, together with all her family.

TAYLOR
An occupational surname, now used as a first name by both girls and boys. The English-born American novelist Taylor Caldwell is best remembered for *Dear and Glorious Physician* (1959).

TEAL (Teale)
Taken from the name of a small duck. Teal is also used to describe a shade of dark blue, similar to the patches sported on the head and wings of the fowl.

TERESA/THERESA (Teri, Terry, Tessa)
From the Greek, meaning 'to reap'. St Teresa of Avila (1515–1582), reformer of the Carmelites and mystic, and St Theresa of Lisieux (1873–1897), who became a saint by doing ordinary things extraordinarily well, made the name very popular. It has been used in England since the eighteenth century. Mother Teresa of Calcutta (1910–1997), the Albanian foundress of the Missionaries of Charity is a well-known example.

THALIA (Talia)
In Greek mythology one of the nine Muses, daughters of Zeus and Mnemosyne. Thalia is the muse of comedy, represented in art as holding a comic mask and a shepherd's crook.

THEA
A pet-form of Dorothea, now independently used. A distinguished bearer of the name is Dame Thea King, the English clarinettist.

THELMA
This was invented by the bestselling writer Marie Corelli (1855–1924), for the Norwegian heroine of *Thelma: a society novel* (1887).

THEODORA (Thea)
From the Greek, meaning 'divine gift', the feminine form of Theodore. Theodora (500–548 BC), the beautiful wife of the Byzantine Emperor Justinian I, was notorious before her marriage as an actress and dancer. She became empress in 527. The name came into use in England in the seventeenth century.

THOMASINA
The medieval feminine form of Thomas (q.v.), revived in the mid-nineteenth century.

THYRZA (Thirza)
From the Hebrew, meaning 'cypress tree'. *Thyrza* is the title of a novel written by the gloomy George Gissing, published in 1887. Thyrza Trent spurns her fiancé for the idealistic Walter Egremont. Egremont tires of her, so she promptly dies of a broken heart. One feels like shaking her!

TIA
A popular modern name, meaning 'aunt' in Spanish and 'princess' in Greek.

TIFFANY
From the Greek, meaning 'manifestation of God'. The name was originally given to girls born on the 6th January, the feast of the Epiphany, when the Three Kings brought their gifts to the Infant Jesus. The film *Breakfast at Tiffany's* (1961), starring Audrey Hepburn, made the name very popular and was a good advertisement for the eponymous New York jeweller's shop.

(It was also the name of a material. The first hot-air balloon, made by Monsieur Testu, rose up from Paris in 1786. It was made of glazed tiffany and sported wings.)

TINA
The modern pet-name of Christina, now used independently. The American singer Tina Turner (born Annie Mae Bullock) is well-known for the songs *River Deep Mountain High* and *What's Love Got To Do With It?*

TOPAZ
From the precious stone or, if one is a bird-lover, the beautiful topaz humming-birds of South America.

In 1822 the Emperor Alexander I of Russia fell madly in love with the Marchioness of Londonderry. He gave her precious stones to remember him by, including an immense pink topaz.

TOPSY
A literary name, taken from a character in *Uncle Tom's Cabin* (1852), written by Harriet Beecher Stowe. When questioned as to who made her, Topsy is remembered for stating, 'I 'spect I grow'd. Don't think nobody never made me.'

TORREN
A surname, meaning 'hill', now used as a first name.

TRACY/TRACEY
The French place name and surname, used as a first name since the beginning of the nineteenth century.

It was originally bestowed on boys, but is now considered exclusively feminine. The film *High Society* (1956), in which Grace Kelly starred as the heiress Tracy Samantha Lord, was responsible for its great popularity.

TRILBY
A literary name, taken from the title of the novel by George du Maurier, published in 1894.

Trilby O'Ferral becomes a great singer under the influence of the sinister Hungarian musician (and hypnotist) Svengali. When he suddenly dies, she is no longer able to sing at all, and expires soon after.

TRINITY
From the Italian, meaning 'three'. John Gerard's *Herbal* (1597) lists Herbe Trinity as an old name for the hearts-ease, or pansy, from the three colours of the flower.

TRIXIE
A pet-form of Beatrix (q.v.), now used independently.

TRUDY
A pet-form of Gertrude (q.v.), now used independently.

TYLER
An occupational surname for someone who tiled roofs, now bestowed as a first name on both girls and boys.

ULRIKE
The German feminine version of Ulrich, now generally used.

UNA
From the Latin, meaning 'one', or an anglicised version of the Irish name Oonagh. Una is the heroine of the first part of Edmund Spenser's allegorical epic poem *The Faerie Queene* (1596). After interminable misfortunes, including a rampaging dragon, she is married to the Red Cross Knight.

The actress and television personality Una Stubbs (b. 1937) is a well-known bearer of the name.

UNITY
From the Latin, meaning 'one'. It is another of the names liked by the Puritans of the seventeenth century.

URSULA
From the Latin, meaning 'she-bear'. This has been used in England since the Middle Ages, prompted by devotion to St Ursula. She was reputedly the daughter of a British king, martyred with her 11,000 companions by Huns at Cologne.

Ursula March is the heroine of Mrs Craik's classic novel *John Halifax, Gentleman* (1856).

VALENTINA
The feminine version of Valentine, q.v. The Russian cosmonaut Valentina Tereshkova was the first woman in space in June 1963.

VALERIE
The feminine form of Valerius, derived from the Latin 'strong', the name of an ancient Roman family. It came to Britain from France in the late nineteenth century.

VANESSA
This was invented by the clergyman, satirist and poet Jonathan Swift (1667–1745), being a partial anagram of the name of his friend, Esther Vanhomrigh. She is the heroine of his poem *Cadenus and Vanessa* (1713).

The actress Vanessa Redgrave is a well-known bearer of the name.

VENETIA
The Latin form of the city of Venice, used as a first name since the sixteenth century. The noted beauty Venetia Stanley married Sir Kenelm Digby in 1625. She was reputed to drink viper wine to preserve her looks; perhaps that is why she died at the early age of 33. Her husband never shaved again, which is an unusual way to express grief, while Ben Jonson and many other poets mourned her in verse.

VERA
From the Russian, meaning 'faith'. The name was popularised by its use in several novels published in the nineteenth century, notably *Moths* (1880) by the sensational English novelist Ouida (Marie Louise de la Ramée).

Dame Vera Lynn, the singer notable as 'The Forces' Sweet-
heart' in the Second World War, must always spring to mind.

VERITY
From the abstract noun, meaning 'truth', first used by the
Puritans of the seventeenth century.

VERONICA
From the Latin, meaning 'true image'. St Veronica was reputed
to have wiped the face of Christ with a cloth as he suffered on
the way to crucifixion. An image of his features remained on the
material.

The name has been popular in Scotland since the seventeenth
century, but was not used in England until the nineteenth.

VICTORIA (Vickie, Vicky, Vikky)
From the Latin, meaning 'victory'. Queen Victoria (1819–1901),
christened Alexandrina Victoria, was solely responsible for
bringing the name into favour. Her influence was incalculable;
she gave her name among other things to cities, railway stations,
fruit and a military medal, while her outlook characterised most
of the nineteenth century. She was survived by six of her nine
children, forty grandchildren and thirty great-grandchildren.
Her statue in Kensington Gardens was the work of her daughter, Princess Louise.

VIDA
The pet-form of Davida, used independently since the mid-
nineteenth century. (It is also the Spanish for 'life'.)

VIOLA
From the Latin, meaning 'violet'. Shakespeare bestowed the
name on the heroine of his play *Twelfth Night*. She disguises
herself as a boy and becomes a page to Duke Orsino, whom she
later marries. This character made the name a favourite.

Viola is the title of the last, unfinished opera of the Czech
composer Bedrich Smetana (1824–1884).

VIOLET (Violette)
From the flower name, used in England since the Middle Ages.
The French form – Violette – is also used.

The Londoner Violette Szabo (née Bushell) (1921–1945)
worked as a secret agent in France during the Second World

War. Captured, tortured and executed, she was posthumously awarded the George Cross for bravery. Virginia McKenna portrayed her in the film *Carve Her Name With Pride* (1958).

VIRGINIA (Ginnie)

From the Latin feminine form of Virginius, the name of an ancient Roman family. The French novel by Bernardin de Saint-Pierre, entitled *Paul et Virginie* (1787), made the name a favourite.

The first English child born in America in August 1587 was named Virginia Dare but she vanished mysteriously, together with the remainder of her colony. The reason has never been established.

VITA

From the Latin, meaning 'life'. Vita Sackville-West (1892–1962), novelist, poet and critic, will always be linked to Sissinghurst Castle, Kent. She and her husband, Harold Nicholson, created the famous garden there in the 1930s.

VIVIEN(NE)

The feminine form of Vivian, made popular by Alfred, Lord Tennyson in his poem *Vivien and Merlin* (1859). The magician Merlin fell in love with the beautiful Vivien, Lady of the Lake. She turned his magic against him and imprisoned him in a castle of air, from which he could not escape.

WANDA (Vanda)

From the Old German, meaning 'a young shoot'. A novel entitled *Wanda* (1883) by Ouida brought the name to public attention.

WENDY

The name was invented by the writer J. M. Barrie. He had a young friend named Margaret Henley, who called him 'friendy' and then 'friendy-wendy'. Margaret died very young, and Barrie called the heroine of *Peter Pan* (1904), his most famous play, 'Wendy' in her memory.

(Incidentally, Margaret's one-legged father was the model for Long John Silver in *Treasure Island* by R. L. Stevenson. Surely a unique literary father and daughter!)

WHITNEY

From the Old English, meaning 'white island'. A place name and surname, now used as a first name.

The American singer Whitney Houston (b. 1963) is well-known. Mount Whitney, in Southern California, is the highest mountain in the contiguous USA.

WILLA

A pet-form of the German name Wilhelmina, now used independently. Willa Cather (1873–1947), the American writer, is best remembered for *Youth and the Bright Medusa* and *Death Comes For the Archbishop*.

WILLOW

A modern first name, taken from the beautiful tree found throughout Europe.

Charles-François Daubigny painted *Willows* (1874), to be seen in the National Gallery. And a church dedicated to St Wyllow is hidden away at Lanteglos-by-Fowey in Cornwall.

WINIFRED

From the Welsh, meaning 'blessed reconciliation'. The seventh century St Winifred was beheaded by Prince Caradoc for refusing to marry him. Restored to life by St Beuno, a spring of water appeared where her head had fallen. She lived the rest of her life as a nun in Denbighshire. Pilgrimages to St Winifred's Well, Clwyd, still take place today.

Winifred Ashton was the real name of the English playwright and novelist Clemence Dane (1888–1965).

WYNN

From the Welsh, meaning 'fair'. Used as a first name since the mid-twentieth century.

XANTHE
From the Greek, meaning 'yellow', so it is particularly suitable for a child with fair hair.

XENIA
From the Greek, meaning 'hospitality' or 'stranger'. In Greek mythology a Sicilian cowherd named Daphnis, son of a nymph and the inventor of pastoral poetry, wasted away with unrequited love for a princess named Xenia.

YASMIN
See Jasmine.

YOLANDE
A medieval French name, from the Greek, meaning 'violet flower', used in Britain since the early twentieth century.

YVETTE
The French feminine form of Ivo (q.v.), brought to England at the Norman Conquest.

YVONNE (Evonne)
Another French feminine form of Ivo (q.v.), meaning 'yew wood'. This has been used in Britain since the twentieth century; perhaps prompted by the Canadian actress Yvonne de Carlo (born Peggy Middleton), who is best-remembered as Lily in *The Munsters*.

ZANNA
A modern name, presumably a shortened form of Susannah, meaning 'lily'.

ZARA
From the Arabic, meaning 'brightness of the dawn'. The Yorkshire-born dramatist William Congreve (1670–1729) included an African queen with this name in his tragedy *The Mourning Bride* (1697).

The Princess Royal helped to make this a modern favourite when she bestowed it on her daughter, born in 1981.

ZELDA
A modern pet-form of Griselda, now independently used. Zelda Fitzgerald (1900–1948), wife of the American writer F. Scott Fitzgerald, whose tragic life reads like one of his novels, is well-known.

ZELIE
A French name, meaning 'ardent', now generally used.

ZENA
A variation of Xenia (q.v.), used regularly in Britain. Zena Dare (1887–1975) was a notable British beauty and actress.

ZENOBIA
From the Greek, meaning 'force of Zeus'. The third century Queen Zenobia briefly ruled the eastern part of the Roman Empire, her armies defeated in 271.

The wealthy and exotic Zenobia is a character in Nathaniel Hawthorne's novel *The Blithedale Romance* (1852). The poor lady drowns herself after rejection by the hero.

ZETA
The sixth letter of the Greek alphabet, but probably a variation of Zita (q.v.). The Welsh actress Catherine Zeta Jones has brought the name to public notice.

ZILLAH
From the Hebrew, meaning 'shadow'. The Old Testament Zillah was married to Lamech, a descendant of Cain, and was the mother of Tubal-Cain. The name came into use in England after the Reformation, when non-Biblical names were abandoned.

ZILPAH (Zilpha)
From the Hebrew, meaning 'sprinkling'. The Old Testament Zilpah was Leah's maid. When Leah believed herself to be past childbearing age, she gave Zilpah to her husband, Jacob, as a concubine. Two sons, Gad and Asher, were born of their union. The name came into use after the Reformation.

ZINOVIA
The Russian version of Zenobia (q.v.), attractive to parents who seek a more unusual name.

ZITA
From the Greek, meaning 'to seek'. St Zita (1218–1278) was a servant in one household from the age of 12. Her lavish gifts of food to the poor and punctiliousness in her work did not endear her to her fellow workers, but she is the patron saint of domestic servants. The name has been used in Britain since the late nineteenth century.

Zita (d. 1989) is remembered as the last Hapsburg Empress. She and her husband, Emperor Charles, abdicated on 11th November 1918.

ZOË
A Greek translation of Eve, meaning 'life'. It was popular with the early Christians and the name of a martyr of the third century. Not used in Britain until the nineteenth century, it has become a favourite.

ZOFIA
The Polish version of Sophia (q.v.), now used in Britain.

In the same series

THE EXPECTANT FATHER

Betty P., as thousands of mums and dads who have attended her ante-natal classes affectionately know her, is a legend. Her outstanding authority stems from over 30 years showing mothers-to-be and their partners how to share the magic of childbirth through *understanding*.

Whether or not you plan to be beside your partner at the birth, as prospective father you are the best placed person on earth to give her the growing comfort and confidence she is going to need. This deliberately dad-centred book prepares you to maximise that support.

As Betty masterminds your joint progress, any private worries, and the daily crop of questions which besieges every couple, will be resolved. Betty P. will instill the conviction – so precious when the birth day arrives – that, come what may, you will *both* cope admirably.

Uniform with this book

RIGHT WAY
PUBLISHING POLICY

HOW WE SELECT TITLES

RIGHT WAY consider carefully every deserving manuscript. Where an author is an authority on his subject but an inexperienced writer, we provide first-class editorial help. The standards we set make sure that every RIGHT WAY book is practical, easy to understand, concise, informative and delightful to read. Our specialist artists are skilled at creating simple illustrations which augment the text wherever necessary.

CONSISTENT QUALITY

At every reprint our books are updated where appropriate, giving our authors the opportunity to include new information.

FAST DELIVERY

We sell RIGHT WAY books to the best bookshops throughout the world. It may be that your bookseller has run out of stock of a particular title. If so, he can order more from us at any time – we have a fine reputation for "same day" despatch, and we supply any order, however small (even a single copy), to any bookseller who has an account with us. We prefer you to buy from your bookseller, as this reminds him of the strong underlying public demand for **RIGHT WAY** books. However, you can order direct from us by post or by phone with a credit card.

FREE

If you would like an up-to-date list of all RIGHT WAY titles currently available, please send a stamped self-addressed envelope to ELLIOT RIGHT WAY BOOKS, BRIGHTON ROAD, LOWER KINGSWOOD, TADWORTH, SURREY, KT20 6TD, U.K. or visit our website at www.right-way.co.uk